Privatization in the Transition to a Market Economy

Privatization in the Transition to a Market Economy

Studies of Preconditions and Policies in Eastern Europe

Edited by
John S. Earle, Roman Frydman and Andrzej Rapaczynski

St. Martin's Press
New York

C E U

Published in Association with the Central European University

First published in the United States of America in 1993

Printed in Great Britain

ISBN 0-312-09462-0

TP

Library of Congress Cataloging-in-Publication Data

Privatization in the transition to a market economy: studies of preconditions and policies in Eastern Europe/edited by John S. Earle, Roman Frydman, Andrzej Rapaczynski.
p. cm.
Includes index.
ISBN 0-312-09462-0
1. Privatization – Europe, Eastern – Case studies. 2. Europe, Eastern – Economic policy – 1989– – Case studies. 3. Post-communism – Europe, Eastern – Case studies. I. Earle, John S. II. Frydman, Roman, 1948–
III. Rapaczynski, Andrzej, 1947–
HD4140.7.P754 1993
338.947–dc20 92-36049
CIP

Contents

Acknowledgements

The editors are grateful to George Soros for his generous support and unfailing belief in the goals of the Privatization Project. They would also like to thank Frances Pinter for her enthusiasm and help in expediting the production of this volume, and Tatiana Nemeth for valuable editorial assistance.

INTRODUCTION

Privatization policies in Eastern Europe: diverse routes to a market economy

John S. Earle, Roman Frydman
and Andrzej Rapaczynski

After decades of experience with malfunctioning command economies and unsuccessful attempts to improve their performance through moderate 'market socialist' reforms, the countries of Eastern Europe and the former Soviet Union are struggling to radically transform their economic systems. Although the common avowed aim of the transformation is a market economy based on private property, the routes to this goal, as manifested in the policies undertaken by East European governments, are quite diverse. This book explores the hypothesis that the diversity in the formulation and implementation of privatization policies stems from differences in the histories of these countries under socialism.

The establishment of command economies in Eastern Europe involved wholesale nationalization of private companies and their reorganization into administrative units of the state. The capitalist economic system based on property-related arrangements and market mechanisms was superseded by an administrative structure striving to control the behavior of each agent directly. In this sense, not only was the economic, political and social organization of the communist countries consciously constructed so as not to allow a role for private property, but the socialist economies of Eastern Europe arguably had *no* system of stable legal entitlements corresponding to the usual notions of property (state or private) governing their productive activities.

Thoroughly centralized governance of enterprises, however, quickly proved to be infeasible, and as early as the 1950s the communist governments began to undertake various reforms in the attempt to improve economic performance. These reforms typically reorganized the administrative control structure and, to degrees varying across countries, involved a partial devolution of control from central planning offices to enterprise insiders (managers and workers). Although these decentralizing measures did not formally grant complete property rights to insiders, the partial and informal arrangements were often viewed, for instance in Hungary and Poland in the 1980s, as *de facto* creating property-like entitlements. After the fall of communism, the entrenched special interests coalesced around these entitlements have often attempted to convert them into formal ownership rights. The cross-country variation in these configurations of interests has proved to be a major determinant of the differences in the privatization policies pursued by the countries in the region.[1]

Part I of this volume contains discussions of some of the historical preconditions of the privatization process in Hungary, Czechoslovakia, and Poland. These chapters provide insights into the relative positions of central authorities and enterprise insiders, as well as the distribution of power among various groups of insiders, at the time of the fall of the Communist regimes.

The chapter by Laszlo Szakadat traces the evolution of the structure of control in the Hungarian economy since its nationalization in the late 1940s, and analyzes the periodic changes in legal rules governing relationships between various layers of state administration. Although legal rules mostly played a secondary role in communist economies, as compared to direct commands and various *ad hoc* arrangements, Szakadat claims that the cumulative changes in the legal rules provide an informative picture of the evolution of the communist economic bureaucracy and the peculiar concatenation of special interests competing for power and resources under the conditions of the 'shortage economy'.

Michal Mejstrik and Jiri Hlavacek's chapter analyzes the pervasive bargaining between the center and various types of enterprises in the Czechoslovak command economy. They argue that the metaphor of the 'planned economy', in which information flows upward and commands flow downward, has partial validity only as a description of the relationship between the state and smaller enterprises. In the case of large units, the actual process involved negotiation over the plan between middle-level bureaucrats in the central administration, whose objective was plan fulfilment, and enterprise managers, who attempted to hide their true productive capacities and extract the most advantageous production quotas for the next plan period.

The final chapter in this part, by Jan Szomburg, provides a transition to the next part of the volume by explicitly relating the choice of privatization policies in Poland to the role of workers in the governance structure of socialized enterprises in the 1980s. The chapter argues that the growth of the influence of labor during the Solidarity period gave it effective veto power over subsequent privatization proposals, and presents data showing the prevalence of insider arrangements in 'privatization through liquidation'.

Part II consists of chapters describing and analyzing various aspects of the privatization process in Poland, Hungary, Czechoslovakia, and Romania. Eva Voszka investigates the roles of insiders and the state in Hungarian 'spontaneous privatization', maintaining that by the time the post-communist government took control, much of the course of Hungarian privatization had been fixed by the success of managers in creating a maze of new entitlements with the help of a series of laws enacted in the late 1980s.

The chapter by Laszlo Urban examines the role of the legislature in Hungarian privatization, contending that the rules set by Parliament function only as a framework within which outcomes are determined by bargaining. The revenue from privatization, expected at the beginning of the process to be large enough to retire some of the country's foreign debt, is likely to be consumed by politically motivated grants to enterprise insiders, local governments, previous owners, and the social security fund.

The next two chapters analyze privatization policies implemented under much more centralized conditions. Jan Mladek presents a panoramic view of the process in Czechoslovakia, particularly emphasizing the evolution of ideas and political debates that resulted in the unusually important role given to reprivatization, the prevalent use of competitive mechanisms, and the openness and lack of special preferences for insiders in both small and large privatization programs.

John S. Earle and Dana Sapatoru focus on Romania's large privatization program, which they argue must be understood in the context of the hypercentralization of the Romanian economy under communism. This hypercentralization could have been a potential advantage in the transition to a market economy, because the problems associated with a lack of clarity of property rights, which were prevalent in Hungary and Poland, were not posed in Romania. The privatization program is therefore also highly centralized and grants no initiative and little power to insiders and branch ministries. According to Earle and Sapatoru, however, the successful completion of the program is threatened by an excessive entanglement of the state with the new institutions implementing privatization, and the prevalence of administrative allocation over market-type methods seems inconsistent with the goal of a market economy.

The chapter by Piotr Tamowicz, which closes Part II, examines privatization of municipal property in Poland. It also focuses on the relationship between insiders and the state, and complements Szomburg's analysis, which addresses this relationship for the case of assets under the jurisdiction of the central government. Tamowicz shows that special treatment of insiders is a pervasive feature of small privatization in Poland, despite a number of attempts to open the process to wider public participation.

Many of the privatization routes in Eastern Europe use unconventional techniques designed for the special conditions of post-communist developments. Yet Hungary has relied, far more than any other country in the region, on its own adaptations of standard Western privatization techniques. The two chapters in Part III of the book provide some preliminary evidence on the course of the two most conventional routes to privatization in Hungary. The chapter by Kalman Meszaros discusses the initial public offerings and the Budapest stock exchange, while Tivadar Faur describes the pattern of foreign investment in Hungary, including privatization sales.

1. Preconditions

The industrial base of the classical command economy consisted of so-called 'socialized enterprises' (SEs). Many SEs were created through nationalization of formerly autonomous industrial companies and reorganized as units of the state administration. Each SE became subordinate to one of the newly-created branch ministries, with the minister exercising primary control over the enterprise. Although each enterprise was supervised by a general manager, the latter was appointed by the minister and received detailed orders from the respective branch ministry. Finally, the lowest level of the state administration hierarchy was occupied by the non-managerial employees of SEs.

Despite the enormous size and vertical and horizontal integration of enterprises, there were still too many units for ministries to be able to exercise effective direct control over them. Therefore, intermediate layers of state administration were also created. However, both the intermediate bodies and the enterprises were originally subordinate to the ministries. As described in Szakadat's chapter, which depicts this process in Hungary, the various reorganizations of the Hungarian state administrative structure before 1968 represented fruitless attempts to improve the efficacy of central control.

The 'New Economic Mechanism' (NEM), introduced in Hungary in 1968, represented a significant break from the classical command system of the communist economies. The NEM replaced the system of compulsory plans and direct administrative control over enterprises with indirect controls based on financial indicators and incentives. Although the center retained control over some key aspects of economic activities of socialized enterprises, NEM was based on the principle of limited enterprise autonomy. Hungarian socialized enterprises ceased to be mere units of state administration.

However, despite its commitment to a certain measure of market-governed economic relations, the NEM only attempted to introduce a *socialist* market system, and thus stopped short of replacing the administrative control structure with property-based relations characteristic of capitalist market economies. As a result, the primary effect of the new arrangements was simply to strengthen the position of managers of the socialized enterprises relative to the higher levels of the state administration.

A further strengthening of the position of Hungarian managers took place in 1984, when so-called 'Enterprise Councils' were created and a large group of enterprises were given the right of 'self-management'. As pointed out by Voszka, the managers of most 'self-managing' SE's exercised a great deal of influence over the key decisions of their Enterprise Councils. As the Communist authorities found themselves unable to cope with mounting economic difficulties, they granted progressively more power to enterprise managers.[2]

The next important milestone in the evolution of Hungarian property relations involved the permission to create subsidiaries with assets of socialized enterprises, granted to the Enterprise Councils in the 1988 Company Law.[3] This law was the first opening for a conversion of property-like entitlements, acquired by enterprise managers and other insiders during the post-1968 reform period, into formal ownership rights. Consequently, when the first post-Communist government assumed power in 1990, so-called 'spontaneous' privatization, which was mostly initiated by enterprise managers, was already widespread. These initial conditions have strongly affected the subsequent choice and outcome of Hungarian privatization policies.

By contrast, the balance of power in highly centralized Czechoslovakia remained much more favorable to the state. To be sure, as argued by Mejstrik and Hlavacek, the late 1960s also witnessed a shift of power from the central state administration toward the managers of SEs. But the character and strength of this shift was greatly affected by Czechoslovakia's particular history: the Soviet-led invasion of 1968 terminated the formulation of large-scale Hungarian-style reforms. After the invasion, the structure of the classical command economy was again imposed in Czechoslovakia.

As the Czechoslovak economy gradually degenerated in the 1980s, the Party and the government recognized the need for some reform of the system, but only very limited measures were actually carried out. Czechoslovak managers, even those of the largest enterprises, were therefore unable to convert their influence within the state administrative structure into more formal entitlements, much less the nearly full property rights enjoyed by many of their Hungarian counterparts. Consequently, when the first post-Communist government in Czechoslovakia announced its determination to carry out a large scale privatization program, which could result in a diminution of the power of insiders, the latter were in no position to hamper the program seriously, or to assure for themselves a preferential outcome.[4]

The situation was quite different in Poland in 1990, when the government and parliament were deciding on a privatization strategy. As pointed out by Szomburg, 'the problems and particularities of

Polish privatization can only be understood within the dual context of the self-management system of enterprise control . . ., and the weakness of the political structures that accompanied systemic change. . . In fact, the only organized group capable of articulating a position on privatization was the self-management movement and the political lobby that grew out of the Employee Council system of enterprise management'.

The decision-making powers of employee councils and assemblies were based on the legal guarantees of worker participation in the management of SEs, which Solidarity forced upon the Communist authorities in September 1981. Despite the imposition of martial law in December 1981 and the subsequent military rule, during the 1980s the control over Polish SEs shifted further from the state administration to enterprise insiders, especially workers. The decline of Communism reduced the state's power over the enterprises still more, and left employee councils and general assemblies as dominant supervisors of enterprise activities. The rights of these bodies ultimately resembled those bestowed upon the Board of Directors and the general shareholders' meeting in a Western-style corporation.

2. Privatization policies

Its name notwithstanding, the process of 'spontaneous privatization' in Hungary has transferred only a small proportion of state assets to genuinely private ownership.[5] We have seen that the Hungarian Company Law of 1988 allowed SEs to create subsidiaries with part of their assets.[6] Further erosion of state control resulted from the 1989 Transformation Law, which gave enterprise councils the right to transform their socialized enterprises – in whole, rather than in part – into corporate form.[7] Under both processes, Hungarian 'privatization' has involved the legal transformation of an SE (or its parts) into a new legal entity, the new owners of which, however, are typically other state institutions. The owners of the new entity include state banks, other SEs, and other state-owned, similarly transformed units.[8]

Nevertheless, Hungarian-style privatization represents real change, because the resulting opacity of property relations implied a substantial loss of control by the state administration over SE property (moreover, presumably the best portion of SE assets). By the time the first post-Communist government came to power in 1990, most property-like entitlements to 'socialized' assets had therefore already devolved to enterprise and company management. This inheritance from the previous regime has had a lasting influence on Hungarian privatization policies.

The ambivalence and inability of the government to reassert the state's property rights over socialized assets has been evident in the operations of the State Property Agency (SPA), established in the

Spring of 1990 in response to the public outcry against the abuses of enterprise-controlled corporatizations. The SPA has indeed exercised some control over the transformation process and succeeded in curbing the gross improprieties which were previously widespread, but it has largely limited its activities to passive supervision, rather than reorienting the ongoing spontaneous privatization process. In Voszka's words, 'in autumn 1990, the SPA considered the most important result of its activities that it had not upset the speed of enterprise-initiated transformations'.

One of the consequences of the dominance of managers over the Hungarian privatization process is that Hungary, until recently, never seriously considered a mass privatization program similar to those elaborated in other East European countries.[9] This political decision may have been related to a number of other factors as well. But such mass programs are usually characterized by free distribution of shares to the general public and by the creation of a new governance structure that shifts control of enterprise property from insiders to new intermediary institutions. This fact could not but significantly affect existing institutional arrangements, and it thus seems likely that the implementation of this privatization route would have encountered serious opposition.

Despite shying away from any giveaway to the public at large, the Hungarian legislature has resorted to using free or preferential transfers of assets to solve specific political and social problems. These programs, briefly surveyed in Urban's chapter, include discounts on purchases by insiders, the use of vouchers to compensate previous owners of now nationalized property, and the planned transfer of a significant part of the assets held by the SPA to the Social Security Fund(s).[10] As Urban emphasizes, although the free or discounted transfers of property to particular groups may have sometimes sped up the privatization process in Hungary, they have usually been motivated by narrow political interests.

In sharp contrast, the Czechoslovak government is in the process of implementing a mass privatization program, briefly described in Mladek's chapter.[11] Most SE property is obligatorily included in the Czechoslovak program, with the exception of small businesses and shops falling within the scope of 'small privatization' and enterprises intended to remain in the state sector. Due to the paucity of domestic savings, a nearly free distribution of privatization vouchers constitutes the core of the program.[12] Participating citizens may choose between using their vouchers to bid directly for shares in corporatized enterprises or exchanging them for shares in newly established intermediary institutions.[13] This created an interesting possibility that the intermediaries would become large (possibly dominant) shareholders in newly privatized companies – a possibility that does not seem to have been clearly appreciated by many of the participants in the process. In particular, many managers have proposed privatization projects for their enterprises involving large voucher components, presumably in the hope that the resulting share ownership will be dispersed among individual citizens[14] rather than concentrated in large stakes held by the financial intermediaries.[15]

One of the most striking features of the Czechoslovak privatization process is the absence of any formal preferences for insiders, either workers or managers. Although managers had a considerable informational advantage when creating their privatization projects (proposals about the method of privatization) for their own enterprises, their projects faced competition from projects submitted by other interested parties: participation was unrestricted.[16]

The small privatization policy also reflects the weak position of enterprise insiders in Czechoslovakia. Despite considerable pressure to restrict outside participation and to grant employee preferences, the government chose to privatize shops and other assets through open auctions in which all Czechoslovak citizens could participate. The parliament even refused to grant special credits to insiders, giving everyone an equal chance to become a new owner. The combination of the strength exhibited by the Czechoslovak state *vis-à-vis* insiders, together with the authorities' determination to base both large and small privatization programs on open market-like mechanisms, is the unique feature of the Czechoslovak privatization route, distinguishing it from those pursued by the other countries in the region.

The impact of special historical circumstances, traceable to the governance system of the late communist period, is also visible in Poland, which provides a model of a labor-dominated privatization process. As explained by Szomburg, the political power of the employees' representatives found its expression in the formulation of the Privatization Law enacted in the summer of 1990. The Law specifies two 'paths' to privatization. On one path, an SE is transformed into a joint-stock or limited liability corporation. The newly created corporation can subsequently be privatized through an initial public offering, by direct sale to domestic or foreign investors, or under the aegis of the mass privatization program. In almost all cases, however, corporatization requires the consent of a majority of employee representatives, thus giving them effective veto power over the decision. The provision of the Law that allows the Prime Minister to force an enterprise to corporatize without obtaining the consent of the employees has remained essentially unexercised, and the pace of corporatization has been very slow.

The other path involves 'liquidation' of an SE, the enterprise's assets being simultaneously leased or sold by the state to a newly created corporation. The employee councils and enterprise management, not the state administration, typically initiate this type of privatization, and the new corporation is nearly always dominated by insiders, sometimes supported by an outside financial broker. Although a series of state approvals is required, the Law prescribes an expeditious procedure which makes it difficult for state organs to oppose a liquidation proposal, especially when it involves the participation of a significant proportion of the employees. The prices at which the property is conveyed are usually very advantageous to the buyers. Not surprisingly then, privatization through liquidation, mostly in the form of long-term leasing with an option to purchase, has been the most common method of ownership transformation in Poland.

Insiders in Poland have been able to assure for themselves still more preferential treatment in small privatization, the privatization of assets under the jurisdiction of municipal governments. Most municipal property in Poland consists of shops and small service establishments, and demand by the rapidly emerging private sector for municipally owned space is potentially quite large. Yet, as shown by Tamowicz, local governments have found it difficult to resist demands from insiders that the establishments in which they have been employed be rented to them, rather than sold or rented through open auctions involving outside participants. As a result, only a small proportion of retail establishments were allocated through competitive auctions, despite the fact that the competitive auction price was sometimes several times higher than the administratively determined rent for a comparable unit. The predominance of insider privatization may have led to a scarcity of suitable commercial real estate and therefore restricted opportunities for new entrepreneurs, who might have been more qualified to establish small private businesses than insiders. On the other hand, Tamowicz also argues the possibility that the insider-dominated process was responsible for a lack of opposition to this form of privatization, and therefore contributed to the very high pace of growth in the private retail sector.

While a situation in which the state is weak relative to special interests seems to lead inevitably to insider-dominated, decentralized privatization, the Romanian approach to mass privatization provides an example that a strong, centralized state administration cannot always be counted on to push through programs based on competitive market-like mechanisms, as shown by Earle and Sapatoru. The Romanian version of Communism was even more centralized and totalitarian than in Czechoslovakia. Furthermore, until they were overthrown in December 1989, Romania's rulers violently suppressed all expressions of popular or group interests. Thus, when the first post-Communist government came to power, it did not face the entanglement of property-like entitlements that the governments in Hungary and Poland encountered.

Nevertheless, although the Romanian mass privatization program is highly centralized and includes most of the country's SEs, like the Czechoslovak program, there exist significant differences between them. Following corporatization, 70 percent of the shares in Romanian SEs are transferred to the State Ownership Fund (SOF), while the remaining 30 percent of the shares of state companies are administratively allocated to five 'Private Ownership Funds' (POFs), which are established by the state but owned by all adult Romanian citizens through their 'Certificates of Ownership'. The Romanian Privatization Law (August 1991) stipulates that the SOF will sell one-seventh of its holdings every year, thereby liquidating the state's holding by the end of the seventh year. However, there are no guarantees that such a sales policy will succeed. Aside from the experience of Eastern Germany, sales programs have been spectacularly slow in all of the transition economies, which is of course a primary motivation for adopting a mass privatization program. Moreover, subsequent revisions of the policy have assigned partial privatization responsibilities to the POFs and the National Agency for Privatization as well as the SOF, clouding the clarity of institutional responsibilities articulated in the original program.

The retention by the state of a majority stake in every Romanian company (even if only temporary) combined with the close relationship between the state and the nominally private intermediaries together pose numerous dangers for the institutional development of the Romanian economy.[17] These dangers include the impossibility of credible precommitment by the state not to subsidize companies undergoing a badly needed restructuring or suffering from serious financial difficulties in a new economic environment. Furthermore, such a strong state presence in the major new economic institutions increases the likelihood that excessive bureaucratization of the economy will seriously undermine the Romanian transition, especially in light of the difficulties of selling so much state property within the prescribed seven year period.

3. The stock market and foreign capital: some evidence from Hungary

Unconvinced of the merits of the rapid ownership changes which can be carried out through a mass privatization program, privatization officials in a number of East European countries have often opted for more conventional approaches. These methods involve sales of individual enterprises through initial public offerings or direct trade sales, as well as contributions in-kind to newly formed joint-ventures with domestic and foreign companies. Although the more conventional approaches have resulted in a much slower progress of privatization, they have often been seen as leading to a more 'genuinely private' ownership structure. This view has been particularly prevalent in Hungary, which has relied on its own adaptations of Western-style privatization techniques, far more than any other country in the region. Interesting evidence on the actual implementation of these procedures in Hungary and the resulting ownership structure of the privatized enterprises is only now beginning to emerge; this evidence is the subject of the last part of this volume.

The re-creation of the Budapest Stock Exchange is described by Meszaros, who presents some evidence on the pricing of new issues and the resulting ownership structure. The most striking characteristic of the initial public offerings on the Budapest stock exchange is that they are primarily used to augment the share capital of mixed state-private companies. Thus, in most cases, stock exchange sales have not resulted in a new ownership structure, in which private owners could exert control over management. Even foreign investors have largely remained minority stakeholders in the Hungarian companies traded on the Budapest exchange.[18]

A similar ownership pattern has resulted from most foreign investment in Hungary, which typically takes the form of joint-ventures with domestic state or private companies or with SEs. Perhaps the most remarkable feature of foreign investment in Hungary, as described by Faur, is that foreign investors seem quite willing to acquire minority stakes in Hungarian companies. In particular, the average foreign ownership share in joint ventures of companies established under the 1988 Company Law (which are the least strictly supervised by the SPA) has been under 50 percent.

One explanation for this could be that Hungarian managers are viewed as significantly superior to their counterparts elsewhere in the region, so that external control by the foreign investor (for which ownership may be required[19]) is unnecessary. Other reasons, however, may actually be decisive. The most disturbing among them is the possibility that the foreign investor is offered a particularly attractive 'deal' by the insiders of the domestic parent company, who may be underpricing state assets in exchange for an assurance of maintaining their managerial control. Some additional evidence for this contention may be the fact that, according to recent estimates by the SPA, only $350 mln out of the total of $1.9 bln foreign investment in 1991 was spent by foreign investors on trade sales processed by the SPA. These observations have led some local observers to conclude that among the most important factors contributing to the Hungarian success in attracting foreign investment is the ability of Hungarian insiders to evade SPA supervision and conclude separate transactions with foreign investors.

We would like to close with a caveat. In this introduction, we have tried to trace the basic structure and hypothesis around which the chapters in this volume were conceived. Naturally, our guide to the specific topics considered by individual authors was reduced to essentials. The analysis in each chapter is rooted in a much richer texture of local conditions, which could not be conveyed in our introduction.

Notes

1. A comprehensive analysis of the relationship between decentralizing reforms of the Eastern European command economies and the post-Communist privatization process is outside the scope of this volume and our introductory essay. For a related discussion of these issues see Frydman and Rapaczynski (1992a) and Stark (1992). A more extensive analysis is attempted in Frydman and Rapaczynski (forthcoming 1993).
2. The fact that many managers had come from the ranks of the *nomenklatura* was probably another important cause of this devolution of power to the enterprises.
3. Hankiss (1990) interpreted this and other related legal acts as permissions to appropriate legal ownership rights granted by the *nomenklatura* to itself.
4. Although the Federal Parliament refused to grant any preferences to insiders, the specific mode of implementation of the Czechoslovak program does in fact give certain advantages to them. See the chapter by Mladek in the second part of this volume for a description and analysis of the Czechoslovak approach, and our discussion below for further remarks.
5. A glimpse of the public's understanding of the word 'privatization' can be obtained from some recent public opinion polls. It has been reported that over 40 percent of the Hungarian public believes that corporatization is essentially synonymous with privatization, while less than 20 percent is aware of the distinction between the two processes.
6. Urban reports that about 30 percent of the socialized assets have been affected by the 'spontaneous privatization' process.
7. This transformation procedure was made particularly attractive to insiders, who were granted the option of buying up to 20 percent of enterprise assets at a discount of up to 90 percent.
8. Some state assets have, of course, been transferred to private ownership. As Stark (1990) points out, managers of an SE have sometimes acquired shares of the self-created subsidiary with bonuses granted to them by the Enterprise Council. The primary form of privatization (in the narrow sense), however, is sales to foreigners.
9. These types of plans are discussed in the chapters in the rest of Part 2.
10. Urban also estimates the value of the assets that have been or are planned to be transferred free of charge.
11. An extensive analysis of the Czechoslovak program may be found in Earle, Frydman, and Rapaczynski (forthcoming, 1993) and Frydman, Rapaczynski, Earle, et al. (forthcoming, 1993).
12. Every citizen had the right to participate in the program by acquiring a book of vouchers for a fee of 1,030 Crowns (about 30 $US), approximately 25 percent of an average monthly salary.
13. According to some recent reports, two-thirds of all voucher holders invested 100 percent of their vouchers in the intermediaries. Since many other citizens invested a fraction of their vouchers with the new financial institutions, about 72 percent of the voucher capital was deposited with the intermediaries.
14. This would presumably reduce the effective control by the new owners over the managers. One may wonder whether this hoped-for outcome of

the Czechoslovak program lessened managerial opposition to the program.

15. Although the regulatory framework of the program limits the absolute size of the stake held by an intermediary in any particular privatized company, these stakes may still be large relative to those held by other new shareholders.
16. On the other hand, the minimal level of regulation of intermediaries and persistent legal ambiguities (for instance, concerning tradability of vouchers) are weaknesses of the Czechoslovak program.
17. For an extensive analysis of the perils of state involvement in mass privatization programs involving newly created intermediary institutions, see Frydman and Rapaczynski (1992a, 1992b).
18. Only one company, Novotrade, traded on the Budapest stock exchange since 1984, has a foreign majority stakeholder.
19. To be sure, a foreign investor may maintain a strong managerial presence, without owning a majority of the shares. See Csaki (1992) for some evidence on this point.

References

Csaki, G. (1992), 'East–West Corporate Joint Ventures: Promises and Disappointments', mimeo.

Earle, J.S., Frydman, R. and A. Rapaczynski (forthcoming 1993), 'Notes on Voucher Privatization in Eastern Europe', in *The New Europe: Evolving Economic and Financial Systems in East and West*, Kluwer Academic Publishers.

Frydman, R. and A. Rapaczynski (1992a), 'Privatization and Corporate Governance in Eastern Europe. Can Markets be Designed?', in G. Winkler (ed.) *Central and Eastern Europe: Roads to Growth*, International Monetary Fund, pp. 255–85.

Frydman, R. and A. Rapaczynski (1992b), 'Evolution and Design in the East European Transition', forthcoming in L. Paganetto and E.S. Phelps (eds), *Privatization Processes in Eastern Europe: Theoretical Foundations and Empirical Results*, Macmillan Publishing Co.

Frydman, R. and A. Rapaczynski (forthcoming 1993), *Markets by Design*, Basic Books.

Frydman, R., Rapaczynski, A., Earle, J.S., *et al*. (1992), *CEU Privatization Reports*, Vol. 1, No. 1 and 2, Central European University Press.

Hankiss, E. (1990), *East European Alternatives*, Oxford University Press.

Stark, D. (1992), 'Path Dependence and Privatization Strategies in East Central Europe', mimeo.

PART I

Preconditions

1

Property rights in a socialist economy: the case of Hungary

László Szakadát

This chapter[1] is concerned with the legal foundations of property rights for 'enterprises' in the socialist period in Hungary, 1948–89. I first describe the process of nationalization by which a market economy was transformed into a command economy. I then review the evolving legal context in which property rights for 'enterprises' were set.[2] I identify important actors among whom ownership rights were distributed: managers, leaders of intermediary directing organs, and ministers; and I distinguish three different bundles of ownership rights: possession, use, and disposal. I depict the changing legal rules determining the shifting distribution among the actors of these ownership rights with direct quotes from selected legal texts.

These legal concepts of ownership rights are commonly used in Hungary. However, they do not correspond perfectly to those used in the property rights literature, which, on the one hand, relies on the concepts of exclusivity and transferability, and, on the other hand, distinguishes a somewhat different group of rights of ownership:

> (a) the right to use the asset (usus), (b) the right to appropriate returns from the asset (usus fructus), and (c) the right to change the asset's form and/or substance (abusus).

In a market economy

> this last element, the right to bear the consequences from changes in the value of an asset, is the fundamental component of the right of ownership. It implies that the owner has the legal freedom to transfer all rights . . . or some rights . . . in the asset to others at a mutually agreed upon price.[3]

Nonetheless, in other economies possession which is defined as 'the acquisition of . . . physical control over a physical thing'[4] as another element of ownership rights plays a more or less important role compared to the right of disposal.

The entire socialist period in Hungary saw a trend from initially strong centralization of ownership rights to gradual decentralization. Nationalization and detailed mandatory plan targets at the beginning of the period essentially left enterprises with only the right of physical *possession* of assets. State enterprises in the command economy could not decide about the use of assets they possessed, for this was prescribed by mandatory targets. The gradual loosening of the plan and eventual abolition of mandatory targets gave enterprises increasing discretion in *use* of assets. In the Hungarian context, the right of use incorporates both usus and usus fructus. The right of *disposal* also gradually devolved to enterprises and accelerated in 1984 with the founding of Enterprise Councils; this right is still a battleground in the struggle between decentralizing and recentralizing trends.

Of course, other aspects of legal regulation and economic policy – taxation, restriction of profit, subsidies, monetary policy, administrative stipulations, etc. – also influence the behavior of owners. This chapter is unable to devote space to these problems, as further research would be needed.

One important problem in the analysis of legal rules is the connection between laws and reality. To what extent can we take the rules seriously? How did the legal framework affect actual economic processes? For instance, it is generally recognized that the center exercised informal and sometimes 'manual' (direct but non-formal) control even after the abolition of mandatory plans; it also launched campaigns and instructed economic agents, for example over the telephone. The prevalence of agents finding loopholes in or evading laws and of the non-enforcement of legal provisions are also inherent features of a socialist economy.[5]

Nonetheless, it is my conviction that we can use these rules if we interpret them cautiously. Although the laws and the decrees do not reflect the real world completely, they nevertheless tell us a lot. First, they indicate the policy that the center intended to be followed.[6] Second, they set, by and large, limits restricting alternatives available to economic agents in the sense of making large violations risky and thus potentially costly. Since the restrictions were serious, we can formulate statements not only on the trends (that is, whether these measures were tightening or easing the restrictions), but also on their extent. Finally, if the rules and the reality did not coincide with each other, it is worth asking why this happened. Did the principal not want to or could he not enforce what he wanted? What was the reason?

Nationalization[7]

We should start the analysis with the foundation of the socialist economy, that is, with the description of the process of nationalization. The result of the expropriation of private property coupled with strong centralization had far-reaching consequences; they determined some basic characteristics of the Hungarian economy for the whole socialist period. Moreover, these basic features (lack of private property in industry and services, a small number of state-owned enterprises with a never solved control problem, lack of small- and medium-size firms, monopoly positions, etc.) remained intact in spite of reform processes.

In Hungary nationalization was carried out gradually. Table 1.1 shows the increasing share of state-owned enterprises in different branches of the Hungarian economy during the first three-year plan.

Table 1.1 Process of nationalization during the first three-year plan (state ownership in percent)

Branches	July 1947	July 1948	Dec 1948	Dec 1949
Mining	91	91	91	100
Industry	37.5	80	87	100
Transportation	98	98	98	100
Banking		95	95	95
Wholesale trade		16	75	100
Retail trade			20	30

Source: Ránki, 1963, p. 204

Hungarian industry comprised 4,499 firms in 1943. Divided according to their forms of ownership rights, they were as follows: 1,636 proprietorships, 853 limited and unlimited partnerships, 237 limited liability companies, 1,337 corporations, 97 cooperatives, 77 state-owned enterprises, 189 municipal firms, 76 other legal entities. Forty-six years later, in 1989, 1,037 state-owned enterprises, 1,295 limited liability companies, 125 corporations, and 1,568 cooperatives operated in industry.[8] But the picture was completely different during the period between 1943 and 1990, the period known as the socialist economic system.

What does this phrase 'socialist economic system' mean in terms of property rights? Statistically it means nothing else than that, for example, there were only 37 private firms, and that there were 1,595 collectively owned enterprises – including state, municipal, and Soviet, or Soviet-Hungarian joint-stock companies – in Hungarian industry in 1950. Thirty years later the number of state enterprises was less than a thousand and there were only eleven corporations in all of industry, which in fact also operated as state enterprises.

In Hungary the most extreme form of the planned economy was reached by the end of 1952. Seven sectoral ministries were set up to direct the operation of 1,500 state enterprises in industry. By contrast, between 1945 and 1949 there was and since 1982 there has again been only one ministry to govern Hungarian industry. Under the socialist economic system, private property and activities were largely restricted. This is reflected in the enormous decline in the number of craftsmen and their employees, shown in Table 1.2.

Table 1.2 Number of craftsmen and their employees (thousands)

Year	Craftsmen	Employees
1948	168,4	170,8
1951	125,8	37,5
1952	83,4	14,1
1953	50,1	2,8
1954	106,8	10,7
1955	96,6	16,0

Source: Schweitzer, 1982, p. 34

What major steps in the course of nationalization led to a structure described as an 'overcentralized' economic management system?[9]

In Hungary, the Communist Party employed two different methods to transform the economy. One was the so-called 'dry way', and the other was through legal action. The former meant a gradual restriction and imposition of burden on private activities through price controls, credit rationing, and taxation until the only choice of private owners was to discontinue the activity.[10] More and more private firms accumulated huge debts to the state.[11] Private owners often offered to sell their property to the state, since they could then hope to receive at least some money for their assets. The other way, of course, was the nationalization of the means of production through administrative regulations and legislation. In what follows I will focus on the latter form of socialization of private property.

The first measure was the nationalization of coal-mines and their power stations on 1 January 1946. As a result of this, the employment share of the state in mining and industry increased to 22.2 percent from 10.5 percent in 1945. (Before the war this share was 5 percent.) Further steps followed this in the same year: in May the government placed the Hungarian National Bank under state supervision, in the summer the government nationalized certain power stations and their long-distance transmission lines, and in November came the nationalization of the four largest industrial enterprises. The result was that, by the end of 1946, 43 percent of all workers in mining and industry were employed in the state sector.

In 1947 there was a change of direction of nationalization, with more emphasis placed on indirect measures. In particular nationalization was directed at banks, which played a very important role in the economy because they held significant shares in industrial or other corporations. In 1938, the biggest banks had 141 affiliates and the wealth of the companies in which they had considerable shares represented 60 percent of all the capital of Hungarian corporations. In May, only the largest banks were placed under state control, and a few months later, Act No. XXX of 1947 declared the nationalization of ten banks that in 1938 had had a share in the total capital of financial institutions of 72 percent. As a consequence of this legal measure, the state's share in mining and industry increased to 58 percent. But

the policy of restriction of capital linked with partial and gradual nationalization, however, was followed only until the end of 1947. After the crucially important meeting of the delegates of nine European Communist Parties in the Polish winter resort town of Szklarska Poreba in September 1947, where the Cominform was founded, the gradualist strategy changed. Instead of capitalistic control and partial nationalization, radical expropriation was introduced.[12]

In February 1948, parliament enacted a law on the nationalization of bauxite mines and the aluminum industry; in practice it had already been in effect in the previous year.

The division of national income by sectors at that time is shown in Table 1.3.

Table 1.3 National income by sectors in the spring of 1948

Branches	Total	Private	Share	Social	Share
	million Ft		(%)	million Ft	(%)
Agriculture	5,115	4,603	90	512	10
Mining	697	47	7	650	93
Industry	5,819	1,170	20	4,650	80
Small industry	2,509	2,509	100		
Trade	1,786	1,520	85	266	15
Transportation	609	12	2	597	98
Others	2,494	780	28	1,714	72
Total	19,029	10,641	56	8,389	44

Source: Ránki, 1963, p. 112

On 25 March 1948, a government decree was passed which effectively brought all private firms employing more than 100 workers under state control. Managers of the firms were replaced with people selected by the Communist Party and appointed by the government. Many of the new managers appointed overnight were workers, and many of them had no skill or experience in management. Of the newly appointed directors 67 percent were workers by origin. Of

1,150 new top managers (including chiefs of industrial directorates and centers) 96 had not finished elementary school and 610 of them had only a high-school education. This measure covered 594 enterprises with 160,000 employees.[13] Table 1.4 shows the share of the social sector in large industry, 81.7 percent after this step.

Table 1.4 Employment in industry (24 April 1948)

Sector	Employees	%
State sector	278,076	72.5
Others in public sector	16,595	4.3
Soviet–Hungarian joint-venture	13,886	3.7
Cooperative sector	4,291	1.2
Total social sector	312,848	81.7
Foreign companies employing more than 100 people	21,023	5.6
Private companies employing less than 100 people	48,552	12.7
Total private sector	69,575	18.3
Total industry	382,423	100.0

Source: Ránki, 1963, p. 110

But in some branches of the Hungarian economy, shown in Table 1.5, the share of state enterprises was even higher: 100 percent in mining and metallurgy, 91 percent in engineering, 92 percent in building materials and printing; in others it was smaller: 77 percent in textiles, 55 percent in food processing and 54 percent in paper mills, etc. Small private enterprises played dominant roles in the latter fields.

Table 1.5 Ownership structure in industry (24 April 1948)

Branches	Employees		Share of
	Total	State and public sector	State and public sector
Metallurgy and engineering	162,974	149,247	91.6
Leather and rubber	10,256	9,025	88.0
Timber	9,834	6,959	70.8
Printing and film	8,530	903	92.6
Paper-making	5,967	255	54.6
Textile	74,593	57,743	77.4
Food processing	41,818	23,099	55.0
Chemical	25,570	13,782	54.0
Quarry, ground and glass	25,555	23,586	92.2
Energetics	13,174	13,000	98.7
Total	378,271	307,599	81.3

Source: Ránki, 1963, p. 111

But the process of nationalization was not finished yet. On 28 December 1949, the communist government expropriated all firms employing more than ten workers. In certain branches the limit was set even lower. In power stations, printing and pharmaceutical, every unit was nationalized. This measure indicated that the purpose of nationalization was to eliminate not only the large-scale but also small-scale private industry. In order to achieve this aim, the government took not only legal measures but also employed administrative, moral, or political pressures. One has to remember that small-scale industry played a very significant role in Hungary until the mid-twentieth century. One-quarter of industrial output was produced by this sector which employed more than 40 percent of all industrial workers.

This stage of nationalization realized at the end of 1949 involved – approximately – 1,400 private industrial firms, with 20,000 workers; 400 constructing firms, with 8,000 workers; 600 small printers, with 3,000 workers; 220 transport companies, with 2,000 workers; and 80 catering units, with 1,400 workers.

Figures of employment in construction, shown in Table 1.6, also reflect the trend of centralization. Employment in the state sector reached the highest level in 1952, and similarly, the number of employees in the private sector was the lowest in the same year.

Table 1.6 Employment in construction (thousands)

Year	State	Cooperatives	Home-made[a]	Private
1949	51	–	43	33
1950	121	–	23	20
1951	153	–	34	15
1952	170	6	39	8
1953	164	7	50	8
1954	118	8	60	25
1955	98	8	76	26
1956	109	9	76	24

a: estimation

Source: *Adatok es adalékok a népgazdaság fejlôdésének tanulmányozásához 1949–1955*, 1957, p. 138

Achieving the aims of the economic strategy and the creation of an extended public sector demanded a new institutional system for the national economy. The first steps in adopting the Soviet model were made in line with the nationalization in 1948. A new, Soviet-type banking system and a new organization for industry were created almost simultaneously.

Under the new banking system, the Hungarian National Bank was given the monopoly of short-term lending in addition to its former monopoly on issuing bank notes. The so-called single account system provided for all enterprises' payments and receipts to go through the National Bank. Around the central bank, the former big banks were organized into a system of specialized banks[14] [Investment Bank, Foreign Trade Bank, and National Savings Bank].

In the summer of 1948, 197 private financial institutions still maintained their operations, and 115 sub-offices were run in the country. They had, however, little importance: in November of 1948 the total value of assets in balance-sheets of Hungarian financial institutions was 3,616 million forints, of which 3,133 million forints were in the hands of the large nationalized banks. The number of these private institutions was only 14 a year later, and in that same year they were attached to the network of the National Bank and National Savings Bank.

In the fall of 1949, the government decided to finish the nationalization of wholesale trade by the beginning of the first five-year plan which started on 1 January 1950. In foreign trade, the purpose of this measure was to replace the existing domestic system with a specialized foreign trade network. In the summer of 1949, 1,820 merchants had wholesale licences. In fact, however, many of them had already ceased trading. In the fall, 318 of the 750–800 merchants who had still kept their licences played a significant role in trade. In spite of the 'dry way', the relatively high profit ratio and quick return on capital had made it more difficult to suppress the private sector in commerce. Here the communist government employed administrative means to realize its goals: directors were appointed to manage these ventures. By the end of 1949 the share of the state sector had become dominant.[15]

Table 1.7 Employment in trade (thousands)

Year	Workers and staff State	Farmer's cooperative	Socialist	Private	Total
1949	56	25	81	112	193
1950	93	42	135	79	214
1951	129	50	179	52	231
1952	161	55	216	21	237
1953	191	50	241	3	244
1954	212	51	263	7	270
1955	203	61	264	10	274
1956	204	68	272	10	282

Source: *Statistical Yearbook 1956*, 1958, p. 61

Just as in industry, retail trade was nationalized mainly by a combination of the 'dry way' with political pressure. But this was carried out later (see Tables 1.7 and 1.8). By the end of 1948 the share of state sector in retail trade was still only 10 percent of all turnover.

Table 1.8 Number of shops

Year	State-owned	Cooperative	Private	Total
1948	1,166	3,201	60,104	64,471
1950	7,820	5,750	40,490	54,060
1951	10,770	6,850	27,680	45,300
1952	14,186	7,164	2,714	24,064
1953	14,500	7,490	4,220	26,250
1954	14,310	8,820	9,010	32,140
1955	14,180	10,210	8,980	33,370

Source: *Statistical Yearbook 1953*, 1954, p. 153 and *Statistical Yearbook 1957*, 1959, p. 215

As can be seen from these data (Table 1.8), the state sector had become dominant in the Hungarian economy. The various forms of private property were transformed into fewer but both larger and more specialized state enterprises.[16] Table 1.9 shows the structural change in Hungarian industry between 1938 and 1954.

Table 1.9 Size of industrial firms according to number of employees

Year	Number of firms employing						Total
	0–20	21–50	51–100	101–500 people	501–1000	1000–	
1938	2,089	897	419	397	109[a]	–	3,910
1949	527	282	217	433	173[a]	–	1,632
1954	–	479[b]	–	835[c]	–	120	1,434

a: These figures include all firms employing more than 500 people
b: Figure includes the number of firms employing less than a hundred people
c: Number of enterprises employing more than a hundred, but less than a thousand people

Source: Schweitzer, 1982, p. 30

In 1954 the state sector produced 65.4 percent of the national income. Adding to this the 8.9 percent of cooperatives, the share of the socialist sector amounted to almost three-quarters of the national income. The capitalist sector provided 1 percent, and small-scale owners – operating especially in agriculture – produced 24.7 percent.

As shown in Table 1.10, these changes were also reflected in employment.

Table 1.10 Employment by sectors (thousands)

Year	Workers and staff State	Coop.	Private	Total	Collective farmers	Independents	Total
1949	1,164	26	274	1,464	48	30	1,818
1950	1,503	44	262	1,809	134	333	2,176
1951	1,815	53	164	2,030	286	169	2,487
1952	2,094	63	74	2,231	410	91	2,732
1953	2,295	58	46	2,399	461	59	2,919
1954	2,341	60	51	2,450	365	94	2,911
1955	2,279	70	49	2,398	384	118	2,900
1956	2,318	73	47	2,438	440	115	2,993

Source: *Statistical Yearbook 1956*, 1958, p. 59

The ratio of active earners between state and private sector reversed between 1949 and 1954. While 1,178,000 active earners (with a share of 30 percent of all active earners) worked in the socialist sector, and 2,748,000 (with a share of 70 percent) in the private sector in 1949, five years later 2,929,000 people were employed in the socialist sector (with a share of 66 percent) and 1,583,000 (with a share of 34 percent) in the private sector. The high share of the private sector in 1954 was due to the fact that the nationalization in agriculture was carried out in the late 1950s and early 1960s.

As a consequence of the expropriation of private property, the Hungarian government produced radical changes in the economy's structure over a short period. The communists had ambitious goals and thought that they could only be achieved on the basis of state ownership of property. But the economy based on state property did not work efficiently. Reformist efforts resulted in swings between decentralization and recentralization of ownership rights, with a gradual trend towards decentralization over the whole period. But before discussing the impacts of economic reforms on ownership structure, let us start with the investigation of the ownership structure of state enterprises in a directly planned economy.

Economic units in a command economy

By spring 1948, the basic elements of the socialist economy had been put in place. After the nationalization[17] on 25 March 1948, the major part of industry was taken in hand by the Hungarian government, and communists acquired legislative and executive authority.

The purpose of law No. XXXVII of 1948 was to adjust the legal position of state-owned enterprises to the new conditions. In accordance with this law:

A national enterprise is established with unlimited liability that is owned by the state. The *state is responsible for all the liabilities* of such an enterprise. . . . The founding of national enterprise *is ordered by the government*. . . . *Competent minister exercises primary control over the national enterprise*. On the basis of his authorization, the minister in charge *may take any measure* that is necessary to ensure the profitable operation of the enterprise within the limits of the deed of foundation and rules. The *instruction* of the minister in charge *is binding* for the enterprise and its organizations as well. . . .

Declaring *amalgamation* with another national enterprise, and ordering the *liquidation* of enterprise . . . *fall within the competence of the minister* in charge. . . .

The general *manager* (manager) *directs* the business of the *enterprise*. . . .

The general *manager's* (manager's) *instruction is binding* on all employees of the firm . . . .

The general manager (manager) is *appointed* on the basis of the competent *minister's proposal by the government*. . . . The *minister exercises the employer's rights*. . . .

The general manager (manager) is *responsible* for the business of the enterprise. . . . If the firm is permanently in debt, and in every case when it seems from an annual or interim balance-sheet that its liabilities surpassed its claims, or the firm ceases to meet its liabilities, the manager is obliged to report on this fact at once . . . to the supervisory organ or the minister in charge. . . .

The general manager (manager) . . . like other democratic minded workers, must be careful in handling public property to an increased degree. To such an extent they are responsible for loss they have caused deliberately or due to neglect of their duties. . . .

To declare *bankruptcy* against a national enterprise or to order a deed of arrangement without bankruptcy proceedings *is not permitted*.

If a national enterprise is dissolved . . . winding-up is acceptable. . . . Any surplus remaining after winding-up must be placed at the competent *minister's disposal*. (Translated and emphasis added by author)

Hardly a year after passing the Act on national enterprises, a new constitution was enacted in Hungary. It contained some paragraphs that were completely new:

In the Hungarian People's Republic, all power belongs to the working people. The working *people* of towns and villages *exercise power through their elected delegates* who are responsible to the people. . . .

In the Hungarian People's Republic the majority of the *means of production are the property of the state*, public institutions or cooperatives *as public property*. Means of production may also be in private ownership. . . .

The *economic life* of the Hungarian People's Republic *is determined by the state's national economic plans*. Relying on the enterprises, banks, and agricultural machine centers in social property the state directs and controls the national economy in order to develop the productive forces of the national economy, to extend social property, to improve systematically the material and cultural standards of citizens, and to strengthen the defensive forces of the country. . . .

Private property and private initiative must not be prejudicial to the interest of the community. . . .

Every citizen capable of work has the right and the duty to work according to his abilities. . . .

The *Council of Ministers a) directs the work of the ministries,* b) ensures the enforcement of laws and . . . law-decrees, c) *is responsible for the realization of national economic plans.*

These two laws include all the essential factors that determined the operation of economic units in the command economy. What were these factors?

State enterprises operating in a directly planned economy are not independent economic units: they are not enterprises in the usual sense but are part of public administration. They constitute the lowest level of the hierarchy of implementation: the bottom of the pyramid. In a command economy the state becomes a direct producer. 'Firms' only have rights to a limited extent that enable them to fulfil their tasks, namely to realize the plans that have been laid down. In the main, firms may make decisions on some operational questions and their rights are only extended to realize these targets. But the most important rights – that is, the rights to found, reorganize, liquidate a firm, or to utilize fixed and current assets, to use and dispose of the results or the income achieved – belong to the state. The government itself draws up plans for production. The national economic plan is further broken down by working places. These plans coordinate not only subordinative (vertical) connections between the owner (state) and its technical executive units, but the horizontal – exchange – connections among economic units as well.[18]

These inferences may be further buttressed by another rule enacted later than the other two. This government decree (No. 1077 of 1954) summarized the rights and duties of managers, who had 'material, disciplinary and criminal responsibility', in unified form for the first time. We know from an article published at that time that this government decree 'repeal[ed] many former restrictions and declare[d] some new rights', and the aim of this decree was to achieve 'that our managers really become managers, individually responsible leaders of firms'.[19]

The manager's payment and his premium payments are determined by the person who appointed him. . . .

The manager is *responsible* for: *fulfilling the plan* according to the specifications, retaining and handling the entrusted assets, maintaining and increasing wealth; . . . complete implementation of rules and instructions issued by directing organs; ensuring labor discipline within his firm. . . .

For fulfilling his tasks it *must be assured* for the manager: a) firm *plan* approved within the framework of the state plan, b) *fixed and current assets* necessary for successful realization of the plan, c) rights to choose his colleagues, to hire, fire, reward and discipline the workers. . . .

The most important task of the manager is that *the enterprise is to realize* its approved *plan as a whole and in quality and variety prescribed* in the plans, with adherence to prescriptions for lowering costs. . . .

Consent of the head of directing organ *is necessary to change the range of manufacture* of the enterprise. . . .

The manager may not refuse to produce goods or services listed in the range of manufacture approved when, concerning the goods in question, he was given a target figure, or there is a demand for goods (or services) produced by the firm and its productive capacity is not completely committed. . . .

On the basis of approved plan, the enterprise is obliged to make delivery contract for its products (services). . . . *Production of such goods* (or performance of services) *which are not included in any contract is only permitted on the basis of preliminary consent of the directing organ.*

The directing organ is obliged to place fixed and current assets at the firm's disposal for successful fulfilment of the firm's plan, or to ensure conditions that enable the firm to acquire them. [Manager] is obliged to offer and *return to the national economy's disposal* those fixed and current *assets* which cannot be utilized profitably in the firm. The manager may only alienate or scrap fixed assets entered in inventory with the permission of directing organ. However, he may scrap fixed assets if their book value is less than 25,000 forints.[20] . . .

The manager has the right to realize investments of minor value which serve to modernize production, or as an improvement of working conditions. For this purpose he may use 25 percent of the profit in excess of its planned amount, and 3 percent of the redemption fund in every year as well. In addition . . . he is allowed to borrow money . . . with an engagement to repay it in a year. . . .

He determines the wages of workers *within the framework* of the current wage-system.

Despite the existence of some small decision-making powers delegated to managers, I think it is unquestionable that the most important part of ownership rights was in the hands of the government. The *right to use* – rights to make decision on what the property in question can be used for – fell to the government. It had the right to make decisions on what could (or was to) be produced. The National Planning Office eventually decided on these questions. Some rights of use relating to operational (technical-technological) decisions were, however, not centralized. These elements of the ownership rights – connected to how firms could use resources entrusted to them – were in part left at the level of economic units. Although standards and norms were prescribed and firms were instructed to follow some technological directions, the government could not determine every action in advance.[21]

Concerning the *rights of disposal* we can state the same. The question of who (what firm) could use resources was also decided in the ministries.[22] This was true in cases of natural as well as financial plans. Sectoral ministries in cooperation with functional organs allocated materials and equipments. They had rights to reallocate resources from one plant to another. Financial organs determined the amount of money the firm could have. They could remove a firm's profit and place it at another firm's disposal. The insubstantial remaining rights fell to the enterprises.

The only right which was not given to the level of ministries was that of *possession*. These rights remained at the level of economic units. Firms possessed equipment and other resources. The state –

through its rights of disposal – entrusted its economic units (enterprises) to utilize these resources within the range depicted above.

However, the connection between the government and economic units was mostly indirect. The large number of firms – 750 enterprises at that time – prevented the industry ministry from managing economic policy and governing enterprises simultaneously in 1948.[23] Even before the law on national enterprises was passed, the government declared the setting up of twenty-nine industrial directorates in its decree No. 5380 of 1948. In addition to the rights to found directorates, the minister in charge had the right to reorganize and supervise their operation. These industrial directorates wielded administrative rights over firms. They took care of drawing up plans and ensured the realization of plans approved, and they wielded rights of control over materials and prices taken from the National Planning Office. Directorates might order their firms to provide data or to follow standards and norms. They might control the production, finance, and management of firms. Directorates were led by a director appointed by the government. The minister might usually decide on questions concerning management of directorates, but with respect to enterprises, directorates already had sweeping rights. They directed the production of different branches of the economy. They might control the production and investment plans, coordinate R&D activities, suggest the production of some goods in a given quantity and quality, or to finish the production of certain goods. They determined the connections in foreign and internal trade,[24] and controlled the finances of their firms. Organizing cooperation among firms, and suggesting that firms take the necessary measures to reduce costs fell within the scope of these medium-level organs too. They were obliged to see labor and social policy executed, to register inventories, to supply stocks, to supervise the observance of the resolutions on price and material control, etc. Despite all of these rights, government decree No. 5390 of 1948, issued at the same time as the decree on industrial directorates was promulgated, declared that eventually the management of the enterprises would be the duty of ministers. Ministers 'might take every measure which might be necessary for the efficient and profitable operation of the enterprise'. As far as the purpose of this analysis is concerned, the most important rights which fell within authority of the ministers were: appointment and relieving of managers, use of profits, approval of costs, transfer of assets and licenses from one enterprise to another, founding, closing, and winding up firms, making decisions on use of resources, etc.

But even in May, soon after the foundation of directorates, new medium-level, intermediary organs were created. They were the so-called industrial centers. Their role was almost the same as that which directorates had played. These intermediary organs coordinated the production of firms producing similar goods or services. However, directorates were not dissolved, but gradually amalgamated into the ministries. So they continued their operation as a new level within the government structure. This simply meant that economic management became multi-layered in a short period. The purpose of this change was to improve the efficiency of state control. Policy-makers thought that this restructuring gave the government a chance to separate the direct management of firms from the administration of the whole economy.

In principle, industrial centers received the tasks of directorates in the summer of 1948, but before the Act No. XXXVII of 1948 on national enterprises was enacted. Their foundation was declared on the basis of government decree No. 7210 of 1948. The rights of foundation of a center was in the hands of the government for a short time, and then the Commission on the National Economy exercised this right. Centers were led by general managers. A general manager was employed by the minister in charge. The minister supervised the operation of the center. The task of these centers was 'the direct management of enterprises subordinated to the center'. The center as well as subordinated enterprises held their legal personalities. Concerning the direct management of firms, a center 'might order everything within its scope that seemed to be necessary to ensure profitable and efficient production of state enterprises'. But the competent minister might also take every measure which was necessary for efficient and profitable operation of the center and firms subordinated to it.

Tasks coming within the scope of an industrial center especially are:

> *Obtaining raw materials*, semi-finished and finished *goods* necessary for the production of state enterprises . . . *making general agreements* in case when it is more beneficial from the firm's point of view, or *managing purchasing activities* of state enterprises . . . *determining the production* of state enterprises . . . *reallocation of assets* among subordinated firms . . . *introduction of inventions* and ordering research on this field . . . *making standards obligatory*, ordering to give patents up between subordinated firms . . . ordering to take measures to reduce costs . . . *realization of products* of the firms . . . or coordination of the realization activity of subordinated firms. (Decree No. 7210)

The rights of the minister supervising industrial centers were:

> To *create* new plants within the framework of state enterprises, to *merge* and *divide* these firms, or to *close* them for a long time, and to wind up . . . to make integrated management and administration obligatory . . . to approve the estimate of costs of firms . . . to *appoint* . . . the responsible manager of state enterprise . . . [minister] may draw himself the rights of decision previously delegated to an industrial center, or may give binding instruction. . . .
>
> In respect of direct management of industrial center, affairs for the competent minister to decide are as follows: a) proposal for the government to organize, wind up, or merge industrial centers, b) to move a state enterprise from one center to another one. (Decree No. 7210)

The costs of operation of these industrial centers were borne by subordinated firms in proportion to their turnover. (The costs of operation of directorates were covered from the state budget.)

Medium-level directing organs were reorganized again in the early 1950s. Instead of industrial centers, in case of smaller firms 'unions' and in case of larger enterprises 'trusts' were created in order to unify the operation of firms. They were also legal entities. Government decree No. 102 of 1950 on unions declared:

> The union is an economic organ with the task to manage state enterprises tightly . . . the state is responsible for its liabilities to an unlimited extent. . . .
> The minister in charge exercises control over the union . . . may take every measure which may be necessary for efficient operation of the union. . . . The competent *minister* has the right to *move* a firm from one union to another one . . . [but for doing so] the consent of Commission of the National Economy[25] is necessary. . . .
> A *manager* governs the activity of the union. . . . He is individually *responsible* for the operation of the union and its subordinated firms. His responsibility does not affect the responsibility of managers of affiliates. . . . The *employer's rights* [over the manager] *is exercised by the directing organ*. . . .
> Foundation of a union, amalgamation of it with another union, or winding-up is ordered by Commission of the National Economy. . . .
> The existence of the union does not cease the organizational, legal, or accounting autonomy of subordinated firms. . . .
> The *union breaks down* further its approved *plan* for subordinated firms. In a reasonable case it has right to modify plans of the affiliates, if this change does not affect the plan of the union. . . .
> A *union may enter into delivery contract in the interest of its affiliates*. . . . It has the right to make *available* resources of a subordinated firm for another one and to *utilize* temporarily . . . financial *assets of firms* that seem to be surplus and *transfer* them to another enterprise. . . . The union may order to obtain materials or other equipment, and to supply goods jointly. The union carries out these activities in exchange for reimbursement of costs. . . .
> Competent minister may order to place some enterprise under direct control of another one with the consent of Commission of National Economy.

Trusts also had a legal personality. Government decree No. 122 of 1951 on trusts stated:

> The trust is an economic organization ordered to manage centrally the operation of state enterprises . . . the state is responsible for its liabilities as simple guarantor . . . its operation . . . is under control of minister in charge. . . .
> A trust is directed by a manager . . . individually responsible for the operation of trust and its affiliates. . . . *Workers of the trust are employed by the manager*. . . .
> The foundation of trust, amalgamation of such a trust with another one or its liquidation is ordered by Commission of the National Economy. . . . Decision on foundation of an enterprise affiliated to trust under control of minister, the amalgamation of such a firm with another one, or liquidation of it is made by a) Commission of the National Economy in the case of every firm of which the operation is in accord with basic activity of the trust, or in

the case of other firms employing more than 250 people, b) minister in charge, on the basis of the proposal of the manager of the trust and in agreement with the minister of finance, and president of National Planning Office. . . . Subordination of certain firms to trust, and of enterprise under control of a trust to directing organ directly, or rearrangement of a firm from supervision by one trust to control by another one is the right of the competent minister in agreement with the minister of finance and president of National Planning Office.

Directing organ appoints and relieves . . . the manager of the firm affiliated to trust. Directing organ may delegate this right to the manager of the trust. . . .

The fact that a firm operates under control of a trust does not affect the organizatory, legal and settlement autonomy of the firm subordinated to a trust. Trust is responsible for the liabilities of its affiliates as simple guarantor.

A *trust has the right to modify plans of its subordinated firms* for good cause during the time of drawing up monthly plans if this change does not affect the targets of the quarterly plan of the trust. . . .

Trust may *reallocate* firm's *fixed assets* [within certain limits]. . . . Trust may *redistribute* firm's *current assets* without any restriction. . . .

All costs of operation of the trust accrue to affiliates. . . . Trust distributes these costs among firms quarterly.

Commission of the National Economy determines detailed rules about the operation of a trust, and, especially, the connections between the trust and its affiliated firms. . . .

Before summing up my inferences from these rules, it is worthwhile continuing the analysis of directing organs. In some cases, as the government decree cited shows, a minister might not decide without the consent or approval of the Commission of National Economy, or in other cases the Commission alone might make the decision. For instance, in many cases the Commission of National Economy had exclusive rights of foundation, merger and winding-up over government enterprises. In addition to the rights of foundation, certain rights of disposal were also in the hands of the government. But we can find these at different levels within the government: some of these ownership rights were in the hands of the competent minister, others in the hands of directorates, and those remaining fell to medium-level directing organs.

What conclusions can be drawn from these decrees and laws about the directly planned economy as far as the legal status of state enterprises is concerned? Economic policy-makers of the Communist Party organized the economy along a hierarchical government structure. Ownership rights of firms were delegated to different levels of this hierarchy. An economic unit could be founded only on the basis of a resolution issued by the highest level of government hierarchy (right of founding). This highest administrative level (the supreme economic committee of the government) held the rights of disposal – here I mean rights to wind up and amalgamate firms, or fire and hire managers, to use the profits of firms – for itself and ministries, or delegated them to intermediary organs such as industrial centers, trusts, and unions. Rights to use, eventually, were in the hands of ministers, that is, delegated to the government, too. In practice, the National Planning Office played a distinguished role in this field. The use of resources entrusted to economic units was determined through national plans broken down further to enterprises. To the lowest – executive – level, in addition to certain rights of use of less importance, only the rights of possession were left. These ownership rights could not be centralized to higher levels because production would have been stopped. To fulfil the commands on production (instruction for use), resources necessary for the realization of targets were left in the hands of the economic units. In this respect, government property means a kind of division of the ownership rights. But we know that the separation of different bundles of ownership rights leads to a principal-agent problem.[26] In addition, this was not a simple two-tier principal-agent problem, but a multilevel one. The public administrative system already had several layers: the supreme economic committee of the government, the ministries with their divisions (directorates) competing with each other for resources within the ministries, and the medium-level, intermediary directing organs. Obviously, an executive level was also attached to this hierarchy. In fact, it contained agency problems in itself too.

In what follows, I will show changes occurring after 1956. First, I will demonstrate 'the evolution' of ownership rights of state enterprises until 1968. Then I will continue the analysis from the introduction of the new economic management system up to 1989 when the Act on the Transformation of Economic Organizations and Associations was enacted.

Loosening of direct planned economy (1956–68)

In this period one remarkable change took place.[27] The government declared a reorganization of medium-level directing organs in decree No. 2 of 1963. The purpose of this decree on organizational problems of state enterprises and medium-level directing organs was 'the development of national economy and the improvement in efficiency of the management of industry' that necessitated 'centralization of the means of production and their more efficient utilization'. According to this decree, three types of state enterprises could operate in industry: enterprises under the control of a minister (head of an agency of nationwide competency) or council, and firm functioning under the control of minister and trust. This government resolution stated:

> Supervision, control over industrial firms, great industrial enterprises, and trusts operating under the control of minister, and, in addition . . . the direct relations . . . between these organizations and the departments of ministry are regulated by the minister in charge. . . . The minister . . . in general delegates tasks previously performed by industrial directorates gradually to

industrial firms and trusts operating under his control. But unified control and management of the industry and certain branches of the national economy must be retained in the future too. Therefore, decisions about the determination and realization of production targets of firms, or supervision of outcomes of firms are not transferable. These especially include: a) determination of the range of production (profile), and targets; b) approval of investment projects coming within the scope of minister . . . d) determination of the sphere of authority in relation to price control . . . and h) of financial incentive system.

This rule also dealt with the problem of various types of firms. As a result, great industrial enterprises were created by the merging of several industrial firms and other organizations (research institutes, design offices), or the minister had the right to give this status to some enterprises deemed as 'important from the point of view of the national economy'.[28]

As was the case earlier, a great industrial enterprise was directed by a general manager who was individually responsible. The minister in charge appointed him. As a new element, a Board of Managers had to be set up. This body was only a consultative organ to the general manager at that time. The manager's duty was 'the division of targets of the great industrial enterprise, and redistribution of resources ensured in plans to realize targets among economic units'. He had also the right within the great enterprise 'to reallocate means of production, or rearrange the profile, and tasks of production'. On the basis of this resolution, plants within great industrial enterprises must be organized as autonomous, self-accounting economic units. These units were headed by managers vested with the rights to command. A manager was responsible for the production of the plant – and especially, for its profitable operation.

The government resolution defined a trust as 'a state economic organization managing several state enterprises or other organizations (research institutes, design centers) engaged in similar production activity or cooperating with each other'. It was an important change that this rule explicitly declared trusts to be not only medium-level directing organs, but rather organizations performing economic activities as well. (The unions were dissolved after this government decree.) Both trusts and enterprises had kept their legal personalities.

The trust is headed by a general manager who is appointed by the minister in charge. He is responsible for the operation of the trust, and firms operating under control of the trust. . . . Managers of firms operating under control of the trust . . . are appointed by the general manager of the trust. . . . The Board of Managers as a consultative body must be organized to the trust general manager as an individually responsible manager. . . .

The plan of the trust is approved by the minister, and those of firms affiliated to the trust is approved . . . by general manager of the trust. . . . In the interest of realization of the plan, general manager of the trust may reallocate fixed and current assets of enterprises – including assets of renewing and development fund – in conformity with special rules relating to this.

General manager breaks down investment estimations on investors and investments in accordance with the rules dealing with this. The general manager disposes of technical development fund of affiliated firms, handled jointly, and directs the use of it. The general manager of trust . . . may order some economic activities to be performed centrally. . . .

The costs of operation of the trust accrue to trust and its affiliated firms. These costs are distributed among firms by the general manager. (Decree No. 2, 1963)

The dramatic change is that some elements of the ownership rights were delegated to the level of production, even if these rights were given to the trusts or great enterprises performing administrative tasks too. The manager of a trust and great enterprise – for instance – obtained the rights to reallocate resources within their organizations.

The reform of the economic mechanism (1968–89)

The first step on the road to reform was taken after 1953 and was the beginning of a slow process which was interrupted several times. The date of 1968 is considered as having outstanding importance because compulsory plan instructions were abolished at that time. Towards an economic reform, the government issued a new resolution on state enterprises at the end of 1967. The aim of this new rule was to re-adjust the legal status of state firms to the new conditions. In certain respects, the government widened the economic autonomy of firms – except for public utilities. Some significant changes were introduced, among which the most important one was the abolition of the system of mandatory plans.[29] Reallocation of the ownership rights was a corollary. Firms no longer operated as the lowest level of public administration, but as 'autonomous' economic units. Legal regulation of the operation of state enterprises was changed to a 'system of negative regulation': firms were permitted to do everything except what was prohibited by the rules. And the state was allowed to directly intervene in the operation of firms only in exceptional cases.[30]

A state enterprise can be established by a minister, head of an organ vested with nation-wide authority . . . and executive committee of council (hereinafter called founding organ). . . . Supervision of the firms is exercised by the founding organ. . . . Founding organ is obliged to provide . . . firm with property necessary for its operation. . . .

A firm has the right to *perform* those *complementary activities* that are necessary for profitable fulfilment of the range of activity. Founding organ may change . . . the range of activity of enterprise. . . .

State enterprises *may associate* . . . with each other and other socialist economic organizations, or the latter ones with each other too, and within these associations they may create . . . syndicates; they may establish . . . joint ventures in the form of corporations.

A state enterprise is led by a manager. Within the limits of the legal rules, the *manager makes decisions on* the affairs of the firm independently and with personal responsibility. Especially on a) drawing up the *plan* of firm, b) exercising the employer's rights, c) affairs of technical development, d) borrowing and making contracts . . . f) *determination of production and supply,* g) development (*investment*) carried out *on the basis of resources of the firm* . . . i) creating economic association with another economic organization. . . . The *manager* of the firm . . . is *appointed and relieved* by the *founding organ*. . . . A manager determines the internal management best suited for the firm to perform its tasks. He settles the rules of procedures (organizational and operational) of the enterprise. . . .

A *state enterprise based on the property entrusted to it is responsible for its liabilities* . . . it disposes of its wealth in compliance with current rules. *Assets* of the firm – except for reorganization . . . and firms affiliated to trust – *may not be withdrawn* from the firm. . . . Profit remaining after taxation may partly increase the wealth of the firm (development fund, reserve fund), and in part can be used to increase wages of workers, or for the purpose of social welfare and culture (sharing fund). . . .

The manager of a firm is obliged to report in written form to the founding organ if, as a consequence of losses, its reserve fund has been consumed. In this case, or if the firm's assets have decreased below their initial value, the founding organ may order a special auditing of the operation of the firm in order to reorganize its finances . . . provided profitable operation of the enterprise cannot be ensured otherwise. . . . If a profitable operation of the firm cannot be achieved [rehabilitation] committee makes a proposal to wind it up. . . .

A *founding organ may wind the firm up* in cases of a) the national economy does not require the activities of the enterprise; b) the profitable operation of the enterprise cannot be ensured; c) such activities could be ensured in a more efficient way within the framework of another enterprise. . . .

In case of liquidation . . . a founding organ decides on the use of residual net wealth in agreement with the *minister of finance*. . . .

In the interest of the national economy, the founding organ may order – in exceptional cases – the reorganization of the firm without liquidation . . . certain parts of the firm (workshop, section of a factory, plant, etc.) can be given up to other enterprises. . . .

The *founding organ* within its scope: a) evaluates the operation of the firm; b) on the basis of this evaluation *assesses the performance of the manager* and his deputies, and *decides on their remuneration and rewards*. . . . The *founding organ* has right to *supervise* the operation of the *enterprise*. . . . The founding organ *may instruct* a firm *in exceptional cases,* if the interest of the national economy (resolution of security interests, fulfilment of international obligation, etc.) cannot be guaranteed at all, or not in an efficient manner by normal economic means. . . . The founding organ which instructed the firm ensures that the implementation of the instruction does not cause any disadvantage in respect of efficient operation of the enterprise. . . .

The founding organ may order setting up of a Supervisory Board in important firms. The tasks of the supervisory board are to submit comprehensive reports on the business of the firm . . . and make proposals to the founding organ. . . . Supervisory board has no right to take measures in affairs of firm. (Resolution on State Enterprises, 1967)

This decree also dealt with the different forms of enterprises.[31] As mentioned, the abolition of the system of binding instructions brought about some changes in the ownership rights of state enterprises and this was also reflected in the legal position of trusts and their affiliates. Instead of rights to instruct, trusts were vested with rights of disposal, but the founding organ could restrict these rights. Besides this formal change, it was more noteworthy that the authorization of trusts to operate as medium-level directing organs disappeared. They became economic units without any public administrative authority. It seems to be worth citing one more sentence. 'The trust is responsible to the state for meeting the liabilities of its affiliated firms.' A Board of Managers might be vested with rights of decision-making, but the rule did not provide further details. The founding organ might delegate the employer's rights in relation to managers subordinated to the general manager.

This government decree was amended by a new law ten years later. Now state enterprises vested with a legal personality were seen as economic ventures of the state. The law stated that 'the property of firms are owned by the state: firms exercise their economic activity autonomously in order to perform their tasks'. As a new element, the preliminary consent of the minister of finance must be obtained for the foundation of a state enterprise. Act VI of 1977 on state-owned enterprises declared the tasks of a manager deciding on enterprise transactions autonomously and with individual responsibility as follows:

> His task is . . . to determine the plan of the enterprise; to utilize and increase material and intellectual resources of the enterprise efficiently; to determine and . . . rationally modernize the products and services pattern; to protect social property . . . to determine the business and price policy of the enterprise, and conclude contracts . . . to organize internal auditing, information and accounting system; to exercise the employer's rights . . . in accord with the Labor Code . . . to manage employment policy and activity of the firm.

The Board of Managers could only be set up again as a consultative body to the manager. Employer's rights over the manager were still exercised by the founding organ.

> The enterprise autonomously manages the property entrusted to it by the state as well as the manpower employed within the frame of legal rules and the activity sphere determined by the endowment. . . . All rights in connection with its management, within the administration of entrusted property, must be ensured unless these are curtailed by provisions of law. . . . The enterprise is obliged to *draw up a plan in line with targets of nationwide economic plans*. . . .
>
> The scope of activity of the enterprise is determined by the founding organ. The founding organ may stipulate . . . some activity as a fundamental task for the enterprise. A firm may limit or stop such an activity with the preliminary consent of the founding organ and of the sectoral minister. . . .

The assets of the enterprise cannot be withdrawn from the enterprise by the founding organ – except as laid down in paragraph (2) and (3). (2) In case of modification of the enterprise's scope of activity, and of regrouping of certain sections of the firm to other ones, the founding organ may withdraw some assets belonging to the scope of activity of the enterprise. In this case, the founding organ has the right to exercise the rights obtained, and is obliged to assign another economic organization to meet the obligations already undertaken. (3) The Council of Ministers may stipulate other cases of withdrawal of firm's assets. . . .

Enterprises . . . may establish economic associations and organizations. (Act VI, 1977)

State enterprises could only be instructed to perform certain economic tasks in exceptional cases, as was laid down in the government decree issued ten years before. Rules on liquidation were not changed either. A new element in this law was that it mentioned – even if to a limited extent – public utilities as a special form of economic organization. The public administrative character of control played a decisive, dominant role in public utilities. Finally, this rule also treated trusts separately. According to the law, trusts were 'economic organizations operating as an enterprise'. But, of course, some changes were introduced. For example, the general manager of a trust might appoint managers of affiliated firms.

Changes in regulation of state enterprises concerning their ownership rights have occurred more frequently since 1977. According to the law decree No. 20 of 1981, the Council of Ministers might delegate its right of foundation to other organs. This concretely meant that enterprises were allowed to create subsidiaries.[32] But further modifications were also introduced with this resolution. Enterprises obtained the authority to carry out complementary activities promoting their profitable operation, even if these did not belong to the scope of activities determined by the endowment.[33] This rule stated that 'Council of Ministers may transfer some of the tasks falling within the scope of supervision to other organs having no rights to found enterprise.'

Three years later the legal status of state enterprises was changed again. I should like to emphasize the importance of law decree No. 22 of 1984 which modified Act VI of 1977, on state-owned enterprises. The most important change introduced by this law was new forms of management of state enterprises. After passing this decree, state enterprises could be managed not only by managers, but also other bodies.

The general *management* of a state enterprise is performed by: a) *enterprise council*, or b) general assembly of workers or delegate meeting (hereinafter called: *general assembly*), or c) manager. General assembly of workers elects . . . a directorate. The Council of Ministers determines the affairs on which the rights to make decisions fall to the enterprise council, general assembly, directorate, or board of managers. The manager intervenes in questions falling within the scope of these bodies according to the resolutions of these bodies, and, on the other hand, he manages the firm autonomously, and with personal responsibility. . . . *If the firm is managed by an enterprise council or general assembly, the appointment and relieving of the manager is decided by these bodies,* and in the case of firms under public administration supervision[34] the manager is nominated and relieved by the founding organ.

On the basis of this rule firms were authorized not only to carry out complementary activities promoting their profitable operation, but were also permitted to change the scope of their activities. In the case of firms operating under public administrative supervision, the Council of Ministers might restrict these rights. Concerning Hungarian privatization slowly taking place at present, I should like to call attention to an important change still in force that was introduced with this resolution: 'Assets belonging to the enterprise cannot be withdrawn; in the case of firms under public administration control Council of Ministers may order differently'.

In 1989 the legal position of state enterprises was modified again in connection with the promulgation of the Act on Transformation of Economic Organizations and Associations. State enterprises were given further rights. We should already pay attention to the first change: 'The state enterprise . . . is an economic organization established by organs authorized by the state to found enterprises that manage the assets entrusted from state property to it autonomously within the frame of legal rules and with responsibility determined by the rules.' We can better understand the importance of this sentence if we read a passage from the implementation decree supplementing this rule.

Changes in the trustee's rights and experience of the management of firms necessitated the use of the phrase of 'property entrusted'. Firms operating under the general management of an enterprise council or general assembly (delegate meeting) dispose of the property entrusted to them as their own. These rights include *rights of possession, use,* collection of profits, and *disposal;* in spite of this fact, *firms are not owners* of these assets. This special situation is expressed in the particular formulation that the founding organ entrusted these assets to the enterprises.

The people who prepared this rule must be conscious of this contradiction, because they built a loophole into it. The former statement of 'property entrusted to firms cannot be withdrawn' remained in force, but with a short supplement: 'if the law does not make any exception'.

It is still worth mentioning that the range of exceptional cases for state intervention was restricted further and rules were laid down in respect of transformation of state enterprises into economic associations.

Some conclusions

How do we briefly summarize our findings on changes in legal status of state enterprises in the light of these rules?

Many elements of the ownership rights that previously fell to the government were gradually delegated to enterprises. Further, in the case of enterprises operating under management of Enterprise Council or General Assembly all the elements of ownership rights essentially devolved to these enterprises. But the law decree No. 22 of 1984 still stated that the Council of Ministers eventually may draw any firm under public administration supervision, and nowadays, when the government intends to privatize state enterprises, this provision has a growing importance.

As far as the consequences are concerned, the government gradually has given up its ownership rights, but, as a result of this decentralization, these rights were obtained by collectives or collective bodies rather than private owners. Certain restrictions were abolished, but new forces, delimitations providing for efficient operation of enterprises did not emerge in their place. In a modern economy, the most important discipline is private property. Now everyone acclaims the market in Hungary. But we know *'Markets without Property: A Grand Illusion'*.

Notes

1. I am indebted to John Earle for his encouragement and help.
2. I am only concerned with the changes in the legal position of state-owned industrial firms operating under the control of ministries. I do not deal with those that were founded by councils as local organs of the state or other organs and operated outside the goods-producing industry.
3. Eirik G. Furubotn and Svetozar Pejovich, 'Introduction', in: E.G. Furubotn and S. Pejovich, *The Economics of Property Rights*. Ballinger Publishing Company (Cambridge, Mass., 1974), p. 4.

   In another paper Pejovich defines usus as a form of ownership when 'the direct users of capital goods . . . have only the right to use an asset belonging to [someone else], but not appropriate its yields, nor to sell it, nor to change its quality', and usus fructus as another form when the 'user has the right to use an asset belonging to someone else (the state in socialist community) and to appropriate its yield, but not to sell it, nor to change its quality'. Svetozar Pejovich, 'Towards a General Theory of Property Rights', *Zeitschrift für Nationalökonomie*. 1971, 31, pp. 148 and 152.
4. *Encyclopedia Britannica*, Micropedia, Vol. VIII. Helen Hemingway Benton, Publisher (Chicago and London, 1976), p. 151.
5. See Károly A. Soós, *Terv, kampány, pénz* (Plan, Campaign, Money). KJK, Kossuth Kiadó (Budapest, 1986); and Károly Fazekas and János Köllô, *Munkaerôpiac tôkepiac nélkül* (Labor Market without Capital Market). Manuscript, Institute of Economics (Budapest, 1987).
6. Works dealing with Hungarian economic history after 1945 show that important laws, decrees, resolutions, etc. were submitted to the highest

organs of the Communist Party – to the Politburo or Secretariat. The proposals were, in general, debated and approved by one of these bodies.

7. In this section I will focus on nationalization of Hungarian industry. I will take into consideration some events that took place in other fields – for instance in commerce – but agriculture, in spite of its importance, will not be discussed.

8. In the economy as a whole, besides cooperatives and some other forms of ownership of less importance, 4,485 limited companies, 307 corporations, 2,399 state enterprises operated in 1989. The number of limited companies and corporations changed considerably in the last two years. In September 1991, these figures were 33,581 and 968, respectively. Sources: *Statistical Yearbook 1946*. KSH (Budapest, 1947) pp. 116 and 132; *Statisztikai Havi Közlemények 1991/10*. (Monthly Statistical Report) KSH (Budapest, 1991) p. 72; and *Statisztikai Zsebkönyv 1989*. (Statistical Pocket-Book 1989) KSH (Budapest, 1990) p. 109.

9. It may seem to be redundant that the command economy is described as overcentralized, but in fact there was more than one ministry (center) which managed the economy. For me, the notion of overcentralization means not one center to direct the whole economy, but an economic management system where decisions are made at a level higher than that where problems can be efficiently solved.

10. For example, in the summer of 1948, the long-term interest rates were 1 percent for state enterprises, 3–5 percent for cooperatives, 7–10 percent for private firms. (In fact, only state enterprises could borrow money from banks. Cooperatives and private firms could have borrowed at these rates, if the banks had lent money to these sectors.) Short-term interest rates were 7 percent for state enterprises, 12 percent for private industrial firms, and 18 percent for trade companies.

11. 'One of the country's most important electric firms . . . owed 4 million forints in unpaid taxes and 41 million forints in bank and state irrecoverable debt and was pushed to the brink of bankruptcy. The four largest iron, steel and engineering firms found themselves in the same situation. The iron and steel firm of Rimamurányi accumulated a debt of more than 53 million forints, the Manfred Weiss Co. 43 millions, Ganz Co. 30 millions and the engineering firm of Gyôr a debt of more than 18 million forints.' Iván T. Berend and György Ránki, *The Hungarian Economy in the Twentieth Century*. Croom Helm Ltd. (London and Sydney, 1985) p. 193.

12. Berend and Ránki, op. cit., p. 194. Ernô Gerô, the chief economic leader of the Communist Party, said at the meeting of the Politburo on March 3, 1948: 'As a result of domestic and international developments and contrary to our previous conceptions, a new and serious forward step is possible in the nationalization of industry and, in part, of commerce. As it is known, our original plan was to effect nationalization gradually. That time, however, we did not reckon with the events in Czechoslovakia [communists taking power], etc. In my view, it would be a mistake to adhere to the original schedule and not take advantage of the favorable circumstances.' Iván T. Berend, *Ujjáépités és a nagytôke elleni harc Magyarországon 1945–1948* (Reconstruction and Capital Expropriation in Hungary, 1945–1948). (Budapest, 1962) p. 373.

13. Firms in the hands of foreigners were not affected by this law. At that time these enterprises were still not nationalized. The communist

government could choose between two alternative ways to acquire all shares of these companies. The government might make use of the 'dry way' of nationalization, which was usually successful. For instance, Egyesült Izzó Co. had debts of 41 million forints owed to state banks and unpaid tax of 4 million and the government was willing to lend more money in exchange for newly issued stocks. After this and some similar transactions the state obtained 51 percent of the shares. Several foreign owners were willing to sell their shares to the Hungarian government after their ownership rights were restricted; in these cases the price was set at a very low level and in general the government paid certain goods instead of money as compensation. The alternative method was for the government to 'expose sabotages', as happened to some corporations owned in part by American or English investors, and then expropriate them. In the second part of 1949, eighty-six companies with foreign stake, employing about 20,000 workers (4.9 percent of all workers) operated in Hungary.

14. Berend and Ránki, op. cit. p. 208.
15. The nationalization of foreign trade companies was made easier by the fact that significant shares of these companies were in the hands of banks. After the nationalization of the banks, the state acquired their ownership rights as well. In the fall of 1948, the share of the state sector of imports was 58.6 percent and 70.5 percent of exports. By the end of the year, these figures increased to 93.4 percent and 96.2 percent, respectively. Economic leaders formed specialized trade companies in this sector too. So-called 'one-hand' foreign trade companies dealt with only particular goods which fell within their specialized scope. In this period their share increased from 61.5 percent to 75.5 percent of imports, and 43 percent to 85 percent of exports.
16. For example, in case of Hofherr Factory (an enterprise assigned to produce tractors for agriculture in Hungary) the specialization ('streamlining production') meant that although it produced 87 different types of product in 1947, after nationalization this firm intended to produce three kinds of machine only: 1,800 tractors, 1,200 motors, and 180 weaving looms a year. At the end of 1948, the Economic Committee of the Central Committee of the Communist Party suggested producing two of the five tractor types in the future. See Ránki, op. cit., p. 261.

    Or another example for shrinking of the variety of goods is that 'while before 1945, there were 80 kinds of men's shoes, in the 1950s, there were only 16 kinds'. Berend and Ránki, op. cit., p. 217.
17. In fact, managers were only appointed to the enterprises in March. The act on nationalization was enacted later. In essence this action, however, was no less than the elimination of private property rights and the introduction of state control.
18. These were the so-called 'plan contracts'.
19. Miklós Somogyi: 'Az iparvállalatok igazgatóinak jogairól' (On the Rights of Managers of Industrial Firms). *Statisztikai Szemle* 1955, February p. 147.
20. The manager had similar rights concerning the current assets.
21. 'In the shoe industry, factories have been made to specialize by sizes of shoes as well as by production processes and the chief varieties of products. For example, there are three factories engaged in making children's shoes: one makes sizes 19–22, another 23–28, etc.' János Kornai, *Overcentralization in Economic Administration*. Oxford University Press (London, 1959) p. 67.

22. Of course, the question of utilization or allocation of resources within the firm was decided on the spot.
23. This was a serious problem despite the expansion of the ministry from 200 employees in 1938 to 2,000 in 1949.
24. 'The fact that orders for the entire supply of woollen cloth for the whole country are placed by a single official of the Ministry of Domestic Commerce acting alone, after consulting two or three persons at the most, was mentioned sarcastically several times in the wool trade. This official decides upon the materials to be used in making the clothes of all of us. It is he who decides the range of cloths to be made even in such an enterprise as the Pomáz Budakalászi Factory, whose function is to produce 'exclusive' cloths in small quantities.' Kornai, op. cit., p. 154.
25. This commission of the government was the 'top' economic organ vested with a wide scope of authority. Its tasks were: determination of guidelines for the development of the national economy, planned direction of the economy, determination of main plan index numbers and control figures, determination of development plans of certain branches of the national economy, determination of tasks of state control and collection of statistical data, and the coordination of the work of economic ministries and national economic directing organs. The orders and instructions of this commission were binding for ministers and others.
26. See Michael C. Jensen and William H. Meckling 'Theory of the Firm: Managerial Behavior, Agency Costs and Ownership Structure', *Journal of Financial Economics* 3 (1976) pp. 305–60.
27. Again, I should like to strongly emphasize that in this chapter I deal with the changes of legal rules concerning the ownership rights of state enterprises directly. Many changes had happened in the economic environment in other respects. In Hungary various measures were introduced, like the reduction in the number of binding plan index numbers, or widening the choice between different wage forms, introduction of profit-sharing in 1954 and 1957, and others like these later.
28. The changes in the number of state enterprises show the extent of this centralization. In 1958 there were 1,479 state enterprises in industry. Three years later the figure was 1,309. In 1964 only 853 firms operated in this field of the Hungarian economy.
29. The system of mandatory plans was abolished, but the firms were obliged to draw up plans after 1968 too, and these enterprise plans had to 'be in harmony with' the targets included in national economic plans. The system of the approval of enterprise plans became known as 'plan-jury'.
30. I must note that in the former case the economic environment (that is, economic regulation by the state) left a narrow path for the enterprises, and in the latter case the 'wicket' left open for state intervention eventually provided sufficient room to take any measure that might be (or might have been) necessary 'in an emergency'.
31. The great enterprises continued their operations as simple state enterprises.
32. The wicket: 'Legal rules on subsidiaries are determined by the Council of Ministers'.
33. The wicket: 'The rules may tie the granting of permission to the pursuance of certain activities'.

34. The law considers the state enterprise as an enterprise under public administration control if it is directed by a manager, rather than an enterprise council or general assembly.

References

Adatok es adalékok a népgazdaság fejlôdésének tanulmányozásához 1949–1955 (Data and Contributions to Study the Development in the Economy). KSH (Budapest, 1957).

Berend, Iván T. (1962), *Ujjáépités és a nagytôke elleni harc Magyarországon 1945–1948* (Reconstruction and Capital Expropriation in Hungary, 1945-1948). KJK (Budapest).

Berend, Iván T. and Ránki, György (1985), *The Hungarian Economy in the Twentieth Century*. Croom Helm, (London and Sydney).

Encyclopedia Britannica, Micropedia, Vol. VIII. Helen Hemingway Benton, Publisher (Chicago and London, 1976) p. 151.

Fazekas, Károly and Köllô, János (1987), *Munkaerôpiac tôkepiac nélkül* (Labor Market without Capital Market). Manuscript, Institute of Economics (Budapest).

Furubotn, Eirik G. and Pejovich, Svetozar (1974), *The Economics of Property Rights*. Ballinger Publishing Company (Cambridge, Mass.).

Jensen, Michael C. and Meckling, William H. (1976), 'Theory of the Firm: Managerial Behavior, Agency Costs and Ownership Structure', *Journal of Financial Economics* 3, pp. 305–60.

Kornai, János (1959), *Overcentralization in Economic Administration*. Oxford University Press (London).

Pejovich, Svetozar (1971), 'Towards a General Theory of Property Rights', *Zeitschrift für Nationalökonomie*, 31, pp. 148 and 152.

Ránki, György (1963), *Magyarország gazdasága az elsô 3 éves terv idôszakában* (The Hungarian Economy in the Period of the First 3 Year Plan). KJK (Budapest).

Schweitzer, Iván (1982), *A vállalatnagyság* (The Size of Firms). KJK (Budapest).

Somogyi, Miklós (1955), 'Az iparvállalatok igazgatóinak jogairól' (On the Rights of Managers of Industrial Firms) *Statisztikai Szemle*, February, pp. 146–56.

Soós, Károly Attila (1986), *Terv, kampány, pénz* (Plan, Campaign, Money). KJK, Kossuth Kiadó (Budapest).

Statistical Yearbook 1946. KSH (Budapest, 1947).

Statistical Yearbook 1953. KSH (Budapest, 1954).

Statistical Yearbook 1956. KSH (Budapest, 1958).

Statistical Yearbook 1957. KSH (Budapest, 1959).

Statisztikai Zsebkönyv 1989 (Statistical Pocket-Book 1989). KSH (Budapest, 1990).

Statisztikai Havi Közlemények 1991/10 (Monthly Statistical Report). KSH (Budapest, 1991).

2

Preconditions for privatization in Czechoslovakia in 1990–92

Michal Mejstřik and Jiří Hlávaček

Introduction

This study argues that partial economic reform without privatization is not possible. Any such attempt would lead to a 'reform trap'. We explain conditions necessary for the privatization process, both those general to post-communist countries and those specific to Czechoslovakia, and analyze the initial results of this process in Czechoslovakia.

The first section depicts the historical roots of the nationalization of capital goods which occurred between 1945 and 1948, that is, before the communist takeover in February 1948. After 1948 the system of a centrally planned economy (CPE) imitating the Soviet pattern was imposed on Czechoslovakia. The CPE emphasized nationalization, collectivization, and industrial concentration, which had negative impacts on the structure and performance of the economy.

The biggest obstacles for the privatization process are firms' behavior and the distorted prices inherited from the CPE. Together they have created an anti-economic environment. Producers' behavior can be analyzed in two categories. Highly concentrated, monopolistic or oligopolistic firms used their informational monopoly to strengthen their power, which led to a 'reversed pyramid' of management. The central planning authority played a relatively minor role, while the managers of these firms, with the support of the local political elite, contributed to the gradual degeneration of the economic system. Simultaneously, in industries where the concentration was not as high (for technical reasons), the center kept its power and the goal of producers was a positive assessment by the center, which also led to inefficient behavior.

Besides reduced productive efficiency of enterprises, there was also a dramatic fall in the ability of the economy to allocate resources efficiently. The price system was strongly distorted and prices were mostly centrally controlled. We try to show that merely removing central price controls (that is, price liberalization) is not sufficient for a complete recovery of the price system: privatization cannot be avoided. Otherwise the economy will be forced into the reform trap.

It is impossible to escape from this trap without fulfilling many conditions. These include radical institutional changes, separation of the political and economic power of the state, separation of private and public law, redistribution of responsibilities of central agencies, and the liberalization of not only prices, but also foreign trade, foreign direct investment, and the labor market. In addition, the convertibility of the koruna and the development of small private firms cannot be avoided.

These conditions are necessary, but their fulfilment is insufficient to guarantee a smooth transition to a market economy. Above all, the external shocks and the supply responses to policy measures will pose the most challenging problems.

1. Initial conditions for the change of ownership

1.1 Nationalization and collectivization

Before considering the transition of Czechoslovakia to a market economy, we should assess the initial, inherited trends to arrive at a serious understanding of the point of departure. The pressure of inertial tendencies is sometimes very strong and cannot be easily reversed. To better understand the pitfalls of such a major transition, we should therefore first examine Czechoslovakia's previous transition to a CPE. In this respect, there are many differences among Eastern European countries.

Table 2.1 Relative positions of Czechoslovakia, Hungary and Poland in comparison with Austria (ratio of the estimated per capita dollar GNP to that of Austria (multiplied by 100))

	1937	1960	1970	1980
Czechoslovakia/Austria	90	91	78	70
Hungary/Austria	63	56	51	52
Poland/Austria	53	54	47	45

Source: Ehrlich, 1987

During the nineteenth century, the Czech lands were a highly industrially developed part of the Austro-Hungarian Empire, which broke down in 1918. (This fact is not in conflict with Table 2.1, which depicts the situation in 1937.) The market system developed in an independent Czechoslovakia (except under German occupation) until 1948. The end of the period 1945–48 was not typical because of Czechoslovak efforts towards nationalization.

From 1862 to 1948 there existed the legislative framework of a market economy. A refined Business Code, Corporation law, and other legislative components of a market economy had been adopted in Czechoslovakia and the Czech and Slovak people were very familiar with these concepts. Many Czechs and Slovaks have retained their understanding and knowledge of market principles throughout the communist era. The geographical location of Central Europe did not allow citizens to forget their capitalist neighbors: West Germany and Austria. Mass media (radio, TV) and contact with Western visitors (1 million per year in a country of 15 million Czech and Slovak citizens in the 1970s and 1980s). The Czech and Slovaks' long-term experience with Western market and business concepts is therefore quite distinct from the situation of the USSR and somewhat different from that of Poland and Hungary. This influenced the first attempt of Czechoslovakia among socialist countries (1968) to implement combined elements of plan and market policies.

However, the credibility of the West, and hence its market-oriented policies, were undermined in 1938 when Western allies sacrificed Czechoslovakia at Munich in favor of Hitler's demands. As a result, there was a backlash against implementing Western market-oriented policies. Hitler occupied the Czech lands (Bohemia and Moravia), and simultaneously separated the Slovak State. For the first time in their history, the less-developed Slovak lands (under the Austro-Hungarian Empire: Upper Hungary) were provided with an independent state, but at the cost of maintaining close ties with Nazi Germany. In 1945, Western allies interrupted the liberation of Europe near the Western border of Czechoslovakia and made it possible for Russia to liberate all of Czechoslovakia, Poland, Hungary, Bulgaria, and Romania and to gain popularity for a while.

Gradually since 1945 and decisively in 1948 under Russian influence, communists took power in Czechoslovakia, Poland, Hungary, and East Germany, liquidated political opponents and started to build 'socialism'. On behalf of the workers and the cause of the redistribution of income, they dismantled the market system and implemented a Soviet-type command economy.

In addition to the Soviet influence, there were strong political and economic sentiments within the Czech population for nationalizing their own economy; the communists were not alone in demanding the nationalization of the economy at this time. As described by V. Vrabec (1991), the criteria for decision-making on nationalization and widening of the public sector, included not only social and political, but chiefly economic and technological objectives. There was strong support for this reasoning by some non-communist parties, trade unions, and employees in plants. Also some economists, under the influence of Keynesian and Marxian economic theories, pointed out the importance of the public sector in expanding the economy. Some Czech entrepreneurs, who were not discredited during World War II, politically supported large-scale nationalization with the hope of gaining an advantage by weakening their stronger competitors, whose owners were mostly labelled as collaborators with the fascists.

A survey conducted by the Czechoslovak Institute of Public Opinion confirmed this wide support for nationalization in 1947. About 65 percent of respondents indicated their agreement with nationalization of mines, key industries, banks, and insurance companies. Only 15 percent did not agree and 20 percent had no opinion (see Vrabec (1991)). But the actual long-term development has proven the failure of both the economic and political rationale which supported the argument for nationalization.

Of course communists saw rapid redistribution of property rights as a basic prerequisite for the introduction of a CPE. They demanded rapid redistribution of property rights through the policies of *nationalization and collectivization* (for example, Czechoslovak agrarian reform created around 10,000 agricultural cooperatives and state farms as the predominant form of farm organization in the 1950s.) All mining, banking, and insurance firms and key industrial enterprises employing more than 500 persons had already been nationalized in 1945 (see Vrabec (1991)), and smaller enterprises with over 50 employees in 1948. In 1948, the private sector contributed only 33.4 percent to net material product (NMP) (see Table 2.2). The nationalization process had been completed by 1955, or 1959, when most of the small family businesses, private crafts, and service establishments were also either liquidated or nationalized and integrated into larger state-owned enterprises (SOEs), where the majority of them gradually lost their traditional character.

Table 2.2 The percentage share of the net material product produced by individual sectors, 1948–83 (current prices used)

	1948	1960	1970	1980	1983
Total NMP	100.0	100.0	100.0	100.0	100.0
Individual farms	1.1	5.0	3.5	2.1	2.6
Private sector	33.4	1.6	0.9	0.5	0.7
Socialist sector	65.5	93.4	95.6	97.4	95.7
state-owned enterprises	62.9	81.8	85.1	87.5	86.4
cooperatives	2.6	11.6	10.5	9.9	10.3

Source: *Historical Statistical Yearbook of ČSFR*, Federal Statistical Office, Prague, 1985

As can be seen in Table 2.2, by 1960, 93.4 percent of NMP was under state domination. The non-farming private sector share of NMP dropped from 33.4 to 1.6 percent in only the first twelve years since 1948. As the mid-1980s approached, Czechoslovakia's NMP was dominated by the state sector, accounting for 97 percent. Only 0.7 percent of the NMP was contributed by the non-farming private sector. As Table 2.3 shows, the situation was nearly identical in East Germany, but in Poland and Hungary, there was a much smaller percentage of state ownership. It is ironic because these two countries had a much shorter tradition of private industry and market economy.

Table 2.3 Shares of the state sector: output and employment (percentages)

Country	Output	Employment
Command economies		
Czechoslovakia (1986)	97.0	–
East Germany (1982)	96.5	94.2
Soviet Union (1985)	96.0	–
Poland (1985)	81.7	71.5
China (1984)	73.6	–
Hungary (1984)	65.2	69.9
Market economies		
France (1982)	16.5	14.6
Austria (1978–79)	14.5	13.0
Italy (1982)	14.0	15.0
Turkey (1985)	11.2	20.0
Sweden	–	10.6
Finland	–	10.0
United Kingdom (1978)	11.1	8.2
West Germany (1982)	10.7	7.8
Portugal (1976)	9.7	–
Denmark (1974)	6.3	5.0
Greece (1979)	6.1	–
Norway	–	6.0
Spain (1979)	4.1	–
Netherlands (1971/73)	3.6	8.0
United States (1983)	1.3	1.8

a: excludes government services, but includes state-owned enterprises engaged in commercial activities

Source: Milanovic, 1989

Personal ownership of residential property was, however, permitted. The same formally applied to agricultural land which belonged to private owners, but only on paper. *De facto*, the land was used free of charge by cooperatives and the landowners had no ownership rights.

Many of the systematic changes as the ČSFR moved from a

market economy to a centrally planned economy were supported by *the reorientation of foreign trade* from Western towards Eastern European markets. Further, pressure to develop a CPE was increased by focusing on a specific economic policy of so-called structural reconstruction aimed at 'industrialization and concentration' based on the 'law of increasing returns' without any limit. This policy was marked by the goal of exploiting available resources as well as creating the largest economies of scale possible for the country. But this policy did not adequately incorporate information on the optimal plant size. The optimal plant size was derived mechanically from the patterns observed in the West and represented an unrealistic reason for the steady increase of the plant size. These large facilities focused the small Czechoslovak economy in a single direction and led to the artificial formation of an indivisible single plant with a natural or technical monopoly (sometimes, an oligopoly) in the domestic market (even in food industry, publishing houses, etc.). The hierarchical structure of the CPE also generated institutional (control) reasons for the formation of an administrative monopoly.

Concurrent to the socialization period of the 1950s with its organizational restructuring and concentration of production, the magnitude of growth in the organizational units gradually accelerated. In an attempt to more easily manage the hierarchy of the CPE and to better coordinate industries and firms, economic authorities decreased the number of enterprises while increasing their size. In Czechoslovakia, between 1958 and 1980 (with an interruption between 1964–66), the share of employment for state-owned industrial firms with less than 500 employees (with non-existence of private firms in manufacturing) fell from 13 percent to 1.4 percent (see Table 2.4). In 1988 the average size of state-owned industrial firms (over 1,600 firms), that employed over 3 million employees (nearly half of labour force) was 3,100 workers or 3,400 employees per firm.

As a result of this newly imposed command system, Czechoslovak manufacturing has been experiencing serious difficulties with its international competitiveness. What is feared is an irreversible sharp decline in export manufacturing, that is, gradually decreasing productivity, relative quality, and consequently a loss of market share (see Mejstrik (1990a)). Even though there is variability in the analyses of Czechoslovakia's level of economic development (Zamrazilova, (1990)), the generally accepted range of Czechoslovak GDP is between 53 percent and 83 percent of Austrian GDP for 1985. These figures demonstrate Czechoslovakia's overall lead in economic level (GDP) by nearly 50 percent over Poland and 35 percent over Hungary. However, the 'mature' Czechoslovak economy over the last decade has approached the lowest average figures of total factor productivity (TFP) growth rates among the European Council of Mutual Economic Assistance (CMEA) countries. The deceleration of the growth of factor inputs was not compensated by adequate growth in TFP. The drop in TFP growth, which can be seen in Table 2.5, led to the gradual

Table 2.4 Enterprise size distribution of Czechoslovak manufacturing firms between 1965 and 1988

a. Share of total number of enterprises – NOENSH

	Employment size categories					
	Number of enterprises			Share of total (%)		
Year	<500	500–2,500	>2,500	<500	500–2,500	>2,500
1956	763	721	73	49.0	46.3	4.7
1960	137	523	181	16.3	62.2	21.5
1970	109	560	204	12.5	64.1	23.4
1980	80	562	218	9.3	65.3	25.4
1988	91	586	213	10.2	66.8	25.0

Source: *Historical Statistical Yearbook* ČSFR, Prague, 1985, *Statistical Yearbook*, 1989.

b. Share of total manufacturing employment – EMPLSH/1/

	Employment size categories					
	Number of workers (1000s)			Share of total (%)		
Year	<500	500–2,500	>2,500	<500	500–2,500	>2,500
1956	193.2	826.2	466.6	13.0	55.6	31.4
1960	154.4	745.4	857.9	8.8	42.2	48.8
1970	37.0	729.4	995.0	2.1	41.4	56.5
1980	26.0	751.0	1,052.0	1.4	41.1	57.5
1988	26.0	787.0	1,024.0	1.4	42.8	55.8

Source: *Statistical Yearbook*, Federal Statistical Office, Prague, respective years.

Table 2.5 Growth of total factor productivity (K, L, M) in Central and East European countries (material sphere, average annual percentage change)

Country	1961–65	1966–70	1971–75	1976–80	1981–88
Czechoslovakia	0.4	2.0	1.5	0.7	0.1
German Dem. Rep.	0.7	1.5	1.3	0.8	1.1
Hungary	1.2	1.6	1.6	0.5	0.3
Soviet Union	0.9	2.1	0.7	0.5	0.5
Poland	0.9	1.1	2.2	−0.6	0.2
Bulgaria	1.7	2.2	2.0	1.4	0.8
Romania	1.2	1.0	3.1	1.5	0.7

Source: based on *Economic Survey of Europe*, 1984–85 and 1989–90 (United Nations 1985 and 1990) and on 'Statisticka rocenka CSSR', Hajek, Janackova, and Nachtigal in Mejstrik, 1990c.

deceleration of average annual rates of growth of the net material product – see Mejstrik (1990b).

The decline in the competitiveness and performance of Czechoslovak manufacturing can be more clearly seen through its fall in export capabilities. According to Mejstrik (1990c), in the period of 1965–86 in various branches of manufacturing, prices per unit of weight of Czechoslovak exports to the EC market developed quite differently from those of competing countries. We analyzed OECD data from International Trade by Commodities. Essentially, these price ratios were characterized by a decline of the Czechoslovak prices relative to those of their competitors. The most notable and prolonged decrease in these ratios of average prices per unit of weight has occurred in the engineering industry. Because of the low quality of Czech and Slovak products the average export prices per unit of weight for products exported by Czechoslovakia to the EC have dropped from 52 percent (1965) to 25 percent (1986) of the prices attained by other countries' exports in the EC. The worst situation has been in high-tech industries (for example, electronics), while the low-tech industries (for example, metallurgy) have performed better. The corresponding figure for metallurgy was 73 percent in 1986. These trends were accompanied by a decrease of Czechoslovak export shares of trade in the EC machinery market: 0.35 percent (1965) to 0.14 percent (1983).

Although these negative trends were recognized in the 1960s and 1970s, the government did not respond adequately. The Prague spring economic reform was interrupted in 1968 by Russian occupation, and the totally unchanged command system of CPE was re-implemented but its performance gradually decreased and the system itself degenerated. A full macroeconomic description is given in Prust *et al.* (1990).

The economic reform was seen as inevitable even by the communist government before the November 1989 revolution. The previous government (as summarized by Dlouhy *et al.* (1990)), reduced the role of central planning somewhat, announced plans to break up large enterprises, permitted the creation of certain private enterprises as well as joint ventures with foreign majority holdings, reduced the foreign trade monopoly of the state, allowed enterprises to retain some foreign exchange from exports, gave employees a voice in the selection of managers, established a wholesale price system based on average cost plus a 4.5 percent return on capital, and introduced a foreign exchange auction. However, the institutional changes were superficial.

After November 1989, the prevailing opinion held that mainly institutional factors can account for the decline of Czechoslovak domestic and international performance and competitiveness. Therefore, radical adjustment measures have been taken to restructure the economy and society as a whole and to meet world standards of production. These were made possible by revolutionary developments in Czechoslovakia in 1989 fortunately with very limited interference by the USSR (see Gati (1990)).

1.2 Behavior of monopolistic firms

Economic reformers face a market dominated by large state monopolies or oligopolies, which were created and maintained by administrative action rather than economic determination. The Czechoslovak economy has almost no private sector, even less than Hungary or Poland.

The coalition structure made possible by the still existing artificial monopolies and oligopolies, developed its own system of barter exchange: an informal distribution network of resources, where formal monetary cost plays a secondary role. The trump card in an exchange is the ability to deliver a deficit product, also known as 'natural revenues', such as industrial materials in short supply, or a 'natural' bonus like vacations. In this situation, the customer attracted a producer of goods in short supply by offering something like vacations for families of the producer's managers and in turn, received delivery of the goods which he had demanded.

Furthermore, it is necessary to emphasize that the traditional assumption of top–down planning is largely a fallacy. The collusion of formal and informal interest groups creates an illusion of 'plan struggle', so often depicted by Western analysts of CPEs. In reality, the collusive oligopoly decides on a distribution of resources and benefits primarily from the internal rewards of the 'mafia'. (This conception was originally discussed by Mlčoch (1989), unofficially published between 1980 and 1983.)

The system of the CPE is more complicated. In fact there is a 'reversed pyramid' in the sense that power is held at the enterprise level rather than the center. The center can be an instrument in the hands of the directors of influential firms in strongly monopolized or oligopolized industries such as the car industry, metallurgy, chemistry, mining, or energy. The traditional top–down pyramid model still applies to industries where there are many suppliers. This is contrary to the standard pyramid model of the command economy which features a strong center prevailing over industries with many producers (agriculture, building, textile, glass industry).

In order to grasp the diversity of the CPE economic system one should take the behavioral characteristics of firms and government into account. The government or the economic center's primary interest is to keep a certain level of discipline in the managed system, and to increase its power (the level of control) over producers. Another interest is to minimize the efforts necessary to govern.

It is in the producers' interest to obtain an advantage at the cost of other producers by 'persuading' the ministry officials to grant them exclusivity of production. They often extort the center, to try to influence the plan constraint instead of fulfilling the original plan. The center planners were assessed according to the proportion of supervised enterprises, which succeeded in fulfilling the plan. This hierarchy of interests led to a common interest of supervisors and supervised units. The position of 'principal and agent' is in this sense exchanged. One can easily see the analogy of regulatory takeover or regulatory capture theories, which depicts actors in the regulatory process as having narrow, self-interested goals – principally job retention or the pursuit of re-election, self-gratification from the exercise of power.

It is important to note that neither of the parties involved with decisions concerning production, the producer and the center, is interested in the rate of return. Their power is given by the relative weakness of their counterpart. In monopolized or oligopolized industries producing intermediate goods, the power of producers prevails. In the 'self-sufficient' CPEs they are irreplaceable, because the government has no real and rapid alternative in the short run. In order to survive in governmental posts (when everybody can be removed by the political center, that is, by the communist politburo) the center yields to the pressure of industrial giants. The easiest solution in such a situation is changing the plan target which can be indirectly, but strongly manipulated by large enterprises.

The structural rigidity even leads to the preference for bottlenecks by the producers or suppliers of intermediate goods. There is an inverse relationship between the performance of a large firm producing intermediate goods and its bargaining power with the center.

1.3 Behavior of small firms

The situation of small firms in an industry with producers of the same commodity or substitutes is quite different. Here the power of the center prevails since they can fire managers. The managers of large firms cannot be dismissed, because the economic power of these firms enabled them to be appointed to central or regional commitees of the Communist Party (if they played an active role also there), which was a nearly irreversible decision. The power of a small firm on the other hand would be derived from its informational advantage in comparison with the center. But because of the diverse nature of this sector, the ability of a small firm to extort the center is excluded. It is understandable that the relative power of firms in different parts of the economy leads to quite different behavioral characteristics.

The main goal of the small producer in the CPE is a positive evaluation of his productive performance by the center. The indifference curve of the center's objective function is the plan (plan constraint), which forms the lower boundary of its production set. It represents the level of danger, under which the manager of the firm could be dismissed (see Hlaváček (1987)).

The small producer's primary interest is the fulfilment of the plan, which gives rise to inefficiency: the producers produce the minimum quantity of goods dictated by the plan. They are permitted to behave this way because there is a shortage (or the absence, in fact) of information at the center about production possibilities.

The second reason for this counter-effective behavior of producers (also relevant for the monopolistic large firms) is the technology of the planning process. The lack of information in the center is caused by both objective and subjective factors. The producers are interested in a soft, and therefore easy to fulfil, plan, which minimizes the risk of non-fulfilment of the plan. Every relevant piece of information gives the center the possibility to increase the figures in the plan.

The essential information needed by the center is the real production situation (position) of producers. Owing to the lack of information, the center is able to make the plan for the year (t) only by multiplying the result (that is, output) in the year (t−1) by an index greater than one. The producer with more effective production in the year (t−1) will have suffered, because his plan for the year (t) will be tighter. In this way, the 'survival of the fittest process' leads to the elimination of those managers who are relatively effective.

To summarize, producers in the CPE minimize the risk of manager's dismissal, which is given by the threat of not being able to fulfil the plan in the following year. That is why a typical producer in the CPE prefers such a production situation, which maximizes the difference (reserve) between the real output and the maximum attainable output with given inputs. This type of producer ('homo se assecurans', that is, 'the producer securing himself') was analyzed in theoretical studies by Hlaváček (1987) and Hlaváček and Třiška (1988).

2. The distorted price system

The prices in the CPE contained practically no relevant economic information. The flow of production volumes was of primary concern. Only after that were prices determined to provide evidence of commodity flows for book keeping. Regarding the impossibility of bankruptcy in the CPE the prices were calculated to cover the costs plus a margin (cost plus principle). The prices in the CPE had a function of plan variables such as volume of subsidy, limits of inputs, planned (required) volume of profit, etc. The prices cannot be understood without respect to these additional parameters. The situation regarding prices was identical to the other variables of the plan: they were determined by the relative bargaining power of enterprises and the center, which in turn was influenced by the 'market' structure of the industry (monopoly, oligopoly, or competitive structure).

Prices in the CPE did not contain information about marginal rates of substitution or marginal utility. Persistent excess demand for practically all commodities contributed to the fact that prices played only limited roles in resource allocation. Allocation was carried out by rationing, distorted by privileges on both a political and interfirm basis ('barter' exchange). In a traditional CPE, prices were controlled by the center, but the enterprises were interested in them only in conjunction with other instruments for softening the plan; therefore prices became a form of subsidy. As we explained above, this was particularly true for intermediate goods markets, where both agents (firms) lived with soft budget constraints.

A slightly different situation existed for consumer goods, where the customers faced hard budget constraints and prices played a partially normal market role. But even in the case of consumer goods there was excess demand, and the prices did not reflect full costs as a result of the CPE failure to deliver full information (search, transaction costs, evaluation of time wasted by queuing in some spots, bribes, etc.). Domestic producers also confronted agents with hard budget constraints when they exported goods to OECD markets.

The situation of firms selling to customers with hard budget constraints (domestic consumers, OECD partners) was different. Such a firm had a strong position when bargaining with the center. In the first case, production for the consumer market, it could manipulate the center with the threat of political instability. In the second case, production for international markets, the firm had a strong position because the center needed foreign currency.

This strong enterprise position caused the center to extend subsidies, which often took non-standard forms. For example, the government financed the research and development of the firm or provided government orders at high prices (transfer pricing). Analyses show huge dispersion in the profitability of producers of the same or comparable commodities (see Novotny (1990)). Political support for subsidies was especially strong in Slovakia.

A good example of state paternalism is given by 'Syndrome Ikarus', described in the 1980s by a protagonist of Hungarian reform, József Antall. The state felt compelled to retain the important source of foreign hard currency earned through the sales of the state bus company. Producers of components asked for prices that in sum exceeded the price of the bus. The state reacted with the introduction of a system of double prices, which provided subsidies both for the final producer and for the producers of components. Such 'syndromes' destroyed price information.

An important consequence of the lack of information in prices is uncertainty by Western investors and Czechoslovak commercial banks when comparing and assessing the producers' assets and liabilities. Even a high rate of return on capital, resulting from conditions of low quality of price information, is not evidence of a firm's ability to survive in market conditions, especially when compared with historical rates of return. When comparing and evaluating firms for privatization, the authors prefer up-to-date and expected cash flow methods since they have slightly better explanatory power. In this case, cash flow analyses can contain a re-evaluation of market prices.

3. The reform trap

We believe that under state ownership a price mechanism based on demand and supply interplay cannot function efficiently. State ownership effectively eliminates the pricing mechanism. In the case of an industry with small firms, the prices do not carry the information about the marginal efficiency of production because of firms' 'anti-profit' objective function. In industries with monopolistic conditions, the bargaining power of a producer in the CPE can force the center (under conditions of price control and excess demand) to increase the price and thus alleviate the plan constraint when measured as the total amount of money received for the goods they produce.

What do we understand from the notion of a 'reform trap', introduced by J. Zieleniec (1990)? Prevailing state ownership, without privatization, corresponds in fact to centrally planned allocation. The attempt to implement market forces in an economy with prevailing state ownership is a waste of energy. Instability in the new 'hybrid' leads to a return to the practices of the CPE. The term reform trap expresses a situation in which only two stable systems of allocation exist: the market-oriented and the centrally planned economy. The many unsuccessful reform attempts in Eastern European and in Chinese economies provide evidence that mixing the two economic systems does not work.

To some, it may be puzzling that CPE management did not improve even with the advent of computers. The reason is simple: aversion to objective information in the center (see J. Hlaváček *et al.* (1988)). The aversion is illustrated by the fact that the decision-maker at the center maximizes his/her power when he/she makes decisions based on arbitrary criteria. Ideally, if the good firm received more inputs, its director could attribute it to his/her ability. On the contrary, if an inefficient producer attained a higher than proportionate amount of resources, and therefore an advantage over his/her competitors, the firm's director realized that he/she was obliged to the center. The knowledge of this gratitude increased the firm's dependence on the center (within the limits given by the 'reversed pyramid of decision making' in the CPE).

Radical economic reformers in Czechoslovakia recognized that the only way to escape from the reform trap was through large privatization. The theory of the reform trap implies that the third way defended by gradual reformers often rooted in ideas of 1968 inevitably leads back to the CPE.

4. Conditions for escape from the reform trap

4.1 Behavior of firms after November 1989

The revolution of November 1989 abolished the system of central planning in a short time, and rapid improvements in efficiency were expected. However, the old economic climate proved to be persistent and the producers' objective functions have not become profit maximization until now. Why?

The reason does not lie, in our opinion, in the unchanged and slow-changing decision-making mentality of the (mostly pre-communist) managers. Nor is it the partial price liberalization. The main reason for the persistent inefficient behavior is the paternalism of the center: the interest of the center in the survival of SOEs (see Kornai (1978)) caused by state ownership of firms. The center has tended to help firms and to prevent them from going bankrupt. There have been hardly any bankruptcies in Czechoslovakia to date.

The center in the CPE used to help firms by granting direct subsidies. Direct subsidies were declared to be a main cause of the inefficiency of allocation. To improve efficiency the system of direct subsidies has been reduced and replaced by indirect subsidies: credit.

Indirect subsidies reflect the implementation of the state paternalism in a situation with negative real interest rates because of inflation (for example, in the first half of 1991 the ceiling of the nominal interest rate was lower than 24 percent, but inflation was close to 60 percent p.a.). The commercial banks have not been subject to market forces. The low ceilings on interest rates set by the center cause a demand surplus in the money market. To combat this, the center should have re-introduced administrative credit ceilings in the first quarter of 1991. The commercial banks are, however, unable to incorporate risk into their decisions, which especially hampers small firms with promising projects.

In this situation, the decision-making concerning the allocation of credit has been partially made in government institutions (that is, the Ministries of Industry and of the Economy). The dialogue between the center and a particular producer leads to the distortion of information. In this situation, profit maximization is once again not the firms' optimal strategy: firms profit from falsely representing their productive capabilities and tend to position their productive capabilities close to the low boundary of the production set (which is given, distinct from the CPE, not by the plan constraint, but by the central regulation of the budget). Firms are usually uninterested in profit maximization, because by pretending they are unable to produce a given quantity of a good (in a situation without bankruptcies), they can profit by receiving direct or indirect subsidies.

Small privatization and the passage of time are not sufficient preconditions for the solution to the situation of state enterprises.

Changes must also be made in the structure of Czechoslovak firms. The average size of a firm in Czechoslovakia is several times larger than the firm's average size in the same branch in market economies (see MacDermott and Mejstrik (1990)). New small private firms are able to take some of the monopolistic profit of the large state-owned firms, but, as a consequence of their small size, they do not take part in setting prices and quantities. In the existing situation, small private firms contribute only 1 percent to the net material product and face a large number of medium and large state-owned enterprises.

Rapid 'large-scale privatization' is certainly the only solution to these problems. At the most rapid speed one must assume that it will take at least two years. There will be a high level of uncertainty in the Czechoslovak economy during this period. No stable labor, capital, or money market will exist. This climate will lead to low innovative activity, and competitive ability relative to Western firms will decline further. One cannot exclude the possibility that political influences will force the government to provide direct subsidies again – and the subsidies would cause a return to inefficient behavior of producers and a distorted price system. The danger of paternalism probably increases with the average size of firms. We can recommend a maximal (and from a technological point of view, acceptable) division of firms before beginning the 'large privatization'.

Short-term administrative problems and pragmatism could cause the leaders of 'large privatization' to prefer to privatize the original giant enterprises as a whole (for example, the case of the metallurgy company POLDI Kladno). These units are easier to evaluate, because the separate divisions have no individual accounting. It would also be very difficult to split the assets and liabilities among the new small units. But private owners might be able to split firms more efficiently, and in some cases the divestitures of conglomerates will increase the price of separable parts.

We think that the splitting of enterprises should take place. But the question of timing remains. Sometimes the split will come before privatization, and sometimes after. In the end, we expect another wave of mergers within the privatized firms caused by their bankruptcies because of the low efficiency and insolvency of many firms.

4.2 Points of departure for privatization

The economic reality of the CPE is a special mixture of the two 'industrial structures' mentioned before: a normal and a reversed pyramid. Besides the large monopolies and oligopolies, something similar to 'a competitive fringe' from the market economy exists. The two principles can coexist.

The informal coalition structure is deeply rooted: behavioral problems cannot be easily changed by the simple, formal transfer of the economy to a market-based one. Barriers include not only those common in developed market economies, but also barriers resulting from both a complete lack of guaranteed supply and very little market and resource information. As already shown over the past decade in Yugoslavia, Hungary, and Poland, partial reforms such as cuts in state subsidies and liberalization of prices of certain product groups can help decrease the hostility of the environment. However, partial reforms lead to a system of mutual lending and subsidization within the coalition, which causes other problems. One should notice, that in Czechoslovakia, mutual lending was rather limited until now in comparison with the other East European countries and there is no intention to develop interfirm credit besides generally accepted debt notes. Unfortunately the latest development led to a vast amount of illegal interfirm credits in a form of late payments of accounts payable (the estimated volume of it in July 1991 was 80 billion koruna).

Even the formal break up of enterprises does not dissolve the coalition structure. In fact, in such a small economy as Czechoslovakia's with many non-tariff barriers, the individual units of former state firms would become monopolies in their own right. Thus, Czechoslovakia is faced with a monumental task of creating basic competition. It can hardly be drafted as an inward-oriented policy of the small Czechoslovak economy.

The main controversy in Czechoslovakia has been debated between *gradualists and radicals* over the speed, depth, and tools of the transition process. Some external supply and demand shocks (cut of oil supplies and oil price increases, CMEA mutual foreign trade denominated in convertible currency, the collapse of the Russian and East German markets, etc.) accelerated public discussion in the direction of the radical transition package, adopted by the federal government in May 1990.

Because it is in Central Europe, the ČSFR mainly follows EC patterns of economic and legal organization in order to be prepared for its affiliation to the EC.

4.3 Basic steps of transition

As was shown by Zieleniec (1990) and described above, price liberalization alone is insufficient to escape from the reform trap since the state retains ownership of the firms.

In order to achieve a dynamic market environment, Czechoslovakia must experience radical institutional adjustments. The basic legislative measures are twofold: separating the political and economic power of the state, and separating public and private law. Several dozen interim acts were passed by the National Assembly in the spring of 1990 including an amended Business Code and a joint venture law. Since June 1990, the newly elected National Assembly has been able to elaborate upon the previous law and pass major measures which took effect on 1 January 1991 (for example, Foreign Exchange Law, the

State Agencies Responsibility Law, the Price Law, the Private Enterprise Law, the Restitution Laws, and the Small and Large Privatization Laws). Some delay, caused by nationalist tensions coming from some Slovaks, has been slowing the necessary adjustments.

A redistribution of the responsibilities of central agencies was also accelerated by these nationalist tensions. Now, there is a tendency to organize economic life mainly in the autonomous Czech and Slovak republics within the federation. The federal, Czech, and Slovak budgets will rely on clearly delineated fractions of revenues from taxes. Specific government agencies are being created: an Internal Revenue Bureau with local branches and a bureau for anti-trust policy. The related costs should be covered by cuts from the existing central planning system's bureaucracy.

Simultaneous to the privatization process, significant movement towards the market system involved renewing the role of liberalized prices. The command economy viewed prices as an often manipulated instrument of evidence based on individual firm's costs and an agreed mark-up supplemented by individual subsidies, etc. One should take into account that the existence of an aggregate equilibrium (no monetary overhang) does not mean that there was a Walrasian global equilibrium and equilibria in all markets. Numerous shortages indicated particular microeconomic disequilibria, distorted prices, resource misallocations, and inefficiencies. These disfunctions of the command economy might only partially be explained by the macroeconomic notion of repressed or hidden inflation because of their mutual compensations.

Why was an aggregate equilibrium possible in the CPE under the condition of many partial disequilibria? It was caused by the fact that an aggregate equilibrium was not called for from 'below', but by an aggregation of partial non-cleared markets from above. The state plan started from the key material balances (in natural units), which represented, *de facto*, the actual past year results multiplied by the planned growth rate. In this way the CPE was able, under relative price stability, to secure a macroeconomic balance. The CPE was, however, unable to ensure microeconomic equilibria, that is, to balance all markets. The resultant allocation inefficiency rapidly weakened the economy.

To liberalize prices in a highly monopolized small-sized economy, such as Czechoslovakia, could harm the important macroeconomic objective of ensuring stable prices with free markets. Only if free markets were to be renewed simultaneously, and only then, can prices and quantities be determined by market forces, by supply and demand, to the maximum possible extent so that the economy can allocate resources efficiently and in the way that is responsive to individual tastes.

Promoting the domestic private-sector development (through privatization and new private establishments) combined with allowing competitive imports should help to create a sufficiently competitive environment when accompanied by restrictive macroeconomic policies. These major measures can only be successful as part of a package of simultaneous policies. The prerequisite for import competition is a convertible currency, of course. Note, that in the gradualists' opinion currency convertibility and liberalization according to a sequential creation of a competitive market should be postponed.

The *liberalization of prices* of goods and services (except state-controlled transport and public utility tariffs, health care charges, oil products, etc.) with a slightly adjusted tax system have come into effect since 1 January 1991 together with further liberalization of imports and exports promoted by limited exchange rate convertibility.

The optional government price control accounted for 15 percent of GNP at the beginning of the year and was lowered to 10 percent in May 1991 and to 5 percent in January 1992. The reintroduction of general import tariffs (in fact an introduction of 20 percent import surcharges) provided a temporary cushion to price liberalization. The tariffs and existing subsidies have been and will be gradually lowered and real free trade will increasingly be allowed. Unfortunately, the originally intended sequencing 'in one simultaneous package' was not adhered to because of political pressures in the National Assembly, which postponed some inevitable reform measures. What was missing? At a minimum, small-scale privatization and anti-trust policy (there had been no anti-trust law) was absent. Especially in retail trade, besides the real adjustment reflecting subsidy cuts, state-owned monopolies misused the liberalization for short-term profits. They set a high retail margin even for foodstuffs which caused both double-digit price increases and the dissatisfaction of consumers and producers in the first month of liberalization. This will probably accelerate the establishment of new private businesses in the long run, which take into account demand restriction but which have been unable to supply enough goods until now. The demand for overpriced foodstuffs fell by 30–70 percent and some producers started to break up retail monopolies. Inevitably, the price response is taking effect. This can be documented by only a 2 percent price increase on a month-to-month basis from April through June 1991 and zero from July through October 1991. Another step in price liberalization of foodstuffs in November may lead to price increases again, but only to a small extent.

With existing price liberalization (as of 1 January 1991), there will be an increase in the insolvencies of many firms, which reached up to 120 billion koruna. In December 1991 several banks received 50 billion koruna in state bonds of Funds of National Property, which allowed them to partially write off bad debts to enable their smooth privatization. Some industries and some regions are threatened more than others, which could force the government to extend further subsidies in order to avoid a further increase of unemployment. A related measure is the individual or regional subsidy, which would spoil the increased quality of price information needed for privatization.

In addition, 5 percent of all prices of goods and services (for example, rental flats) are controlled by the center. Another principal informational distortion is land rent, which in a CPE is often close to zero, and systematically biases firm equity assessments.

The only way to radically improve the quality of price information is to further open up the economy. Of course, bankruptcies in many industries may follow, especially in those firms producing commodities which are imported. There must be a necessary trade-off between the improvement of information and a threat to the privatization process.

Besides the market of goods and services a similar liberalization happened in the labor market for wages (supplemented by a specific regulatory tax-based wage policy; unfortunately this policy had not yet come into effect in 1990, when slightly falling labor productivity had not stopped the moderate rise of wages), in the money market for differentiated interest rates reflecting supply and demand for different components of money supply, and in the land market, etc.

The *liberalization of imports and exports* proceeds under conditions of a rapidly changing territorial structure of trade in favor of the West (50 percent is a current share). The share of the USSR decreased from 30 percent (1988) to 25 percent (1990), the same happened to the whole Eastern European territory and Germany will probably assume the top share sometime this year.

Foreign trade reorientation cannot be accomplished without some form of convertibility. The former system individualized foreign exchange retention quotas (70 percent in 1990) and led gradually to the dollarization of the Czechoslovak economy, when the medium of exchange between the domestic and foreign markets (US dollar, DM) overrated the medium of exchange among the domestic market agents (koruna) in 1990. Many firms were willing to trade only when the domestic trade was denominated in dollars, because they could import everything without respect to domestic excess supply.

The interconnection of domestic and foreign markets was eased by the overnight introduction of *the limited convertibility of koruna* (called 'internal convertibility' in Czechoslovakia); that is, liberalization of current account transactions for domestic residents (with free repatriation of profits). The foreign currency accounts of the firms were cancelled. Hard currency revenues must be deposited in the banks and converted into koruna accounts at the current exchange rate. The firms were forced to sell foreign currency because of their domestic need for liquidity. The forced conversion has been accompanied by the possibility for resident firms to buy necessary amounts of convertible currency at the current market rate for commercial imports. Even if the control of capital flows is maintained, this solution opens the problem of capital flight through both the under-invoicing of exports and over-invoicing of imports. Latin American experience shows that firms keep part of their deposits abroad. Even such a half-way measure to convertibility has been guaranteed by stand-by credits of about 2 billion dollars from international financial institutions to keep the exchange rate as stable as possible.

Discussions about what *initial level of the foreign exchange rate* was to be chosen were conducted. In January 1990, the official exchange rate for most transactions was uniform (around 16.50 koruna per USD). It was significantly lower than the tourist rate (around 25 koruna per USD) and foreign exchange auctions rate (around 33 koruna per USD). There was a long-standing tendency for auction rates to fall from 120 koruna per USD since the beginning of these auctions in August 1989. Firms had originally used foreign exchange auctions as a way to partially protect their profits from heavy taxation (75 percent) and to use the purchased currency which was entered as a cost of purchasing imports. The black market tourist rate was not much higher than the official tourist rate; the black market substituted for inadequate exchange offices.

As a result, a debate about the speculation effects of 'leads and lags' opened when devaluation expectations motivated firms to postpone cash payments from abroad and to pay in advance. That caused liquidity problems on the macrolevel and the policy response had to follow immediately in October 1990, two months before the expected transition package. The initial level of the foreign exchange rate devalued by 54 percent to 24 koruna per USD, which caused some additional cost inflation pressures, that were captured by complementary measures from the reform basket (anti-inflationary policy, import competition, etc.). A second devaluation in December 1990, by 16 percent to 28 koruna per USD equated the exchange rate with the tourist rate, which increased the rate to 32 koruna per USD. In Czechoslovakia most of the fears of immense devaluation-push inflation were based on simulations with inadequate I/O models of foreign trade flows. Models with behavioral equations, however, were not available.

The actual development of the exchange rate level has confirmed original expectations of radical policy-makers. As it was initially devalued to its equilibrium level and pegged to the basket of five Western currencies, and supported by the restrictive policy, its level has been kept unchanged for the year 1991 without a deficit of balance of payments. Because of the higher rate of inflation in ČSFR in comparison with Western Europe, the real exchange rate has decreased. It provides a stable macroeconomic environment for the privatization process and leads to the more favorable conditions for domestic investors.

4.4 First remarks on microeconomic response

Recent empirical evidence has shown that behavioral formulas of firms are changing slowly and unpredictably.

Firms are afraid of closing down. The decision to cease operation will be made by the ministry responsible for the specific firm during the first stage of the transition period. Firms which suffer from primary insolvency are supposed to be closed first. Primary insolvency is defined as inability to sell a sufficient quantity at market prices to cover production costs and the repayment of loans. Secondary insolvency is the result of the insolvency of customers who do not pay for goods and services delivered.

But this categorization has a harmful effect on the economy. First, the identification of inter-firm loans and debts is difficult to clearly ascertain. Second, an interesting paradox is apparent: firms sell products to insolvent customers for higher prices even though their products cannot be sold for the original, lower prices to solvent customers. Firms thus seek to avoid the list of primarily insolvent firms. The reason for this is that under the conditions of central decision-making, firms are categorized into primary and secondary insolvent firms.

The other phenomenon, which is atypical of a market economy in the long run, is continuing to run divisions with losses, if their products can be sold to solvent customers. The *parent* ministry uses the ability of a firm to earn money for wages as another criteria in the decision to close one of their firms. The firms which endeavor to restructure are at a disadvantage because they experience much more financial distress in the short run, because they must cut some of their output to enable them to create the opportunity to build new product lines. This attempt also contributes to limiting their revenues and increasing their debts. In both cases the problems result from the surviving elements of central decision-making.

Unfortunately even writing off 50 billion koruna of bad enterprise debts in December 1991 has not changed this microeconomic climate.

5. Facilitating the expansion of domestic private firms

Since the law on private shops was enacted in January 1989, we have seen some expansion in the number of private entrepreneurs. However, only single individuals and their relatives were allowed to operate the business. A new national registration office exists and local town halls and councils are building Internal Revenue Offices. In anticipation of the full legalization of the private sector after the November 1989 events, membership grew during January of 1990 from 86,900 to 148,500 members in the Czech and Slovak Federal Republic. By January 1991 there were 1,072,500 registered entrepreneurs. A breakdown of the 920,981 entrepreneurs, registered to 30 June 1991 reveals the following figures:

2.3 percent in agriculture and forestry
27.6 percent in industry
24.8 percent in building

2.9 percent in transportation and communication
17.2 percent in trade
0.1 percent in science development
2.0 percent in hotels and recreation
7.9 percent in repairs and services
2.6 percent in education, culture, health care.

As we can see, there appears to be strong development within the service sector, but few healthy prospects for the formation of a private manufacturing sector. Of those who are willing to venture into manufacturing, most are primarily interested in exploiting existing shortages rather than in introducing new and innovative products. Many prospective entrepreneurs in Czechoslovakia do not see the opening of markets as an incentive to implement progressive, technological equipment or innovative methods of production, but rather as a continuation of past production practices in a shortage economy.

It must be clear that in an economy with distorted and rapidly adjusting prices it is much more profitable for new entrepreneurs to invest in many market niches inherited from the past than to invent new products and processes. In other words, the first wave of entrepreneurial spirit is driven by the removal of inefficient allocations. New market motivation can contribute to more efficient uses of existing technology through research and development rather than to stifle technological advances.

Moreover, principal barriers to investment in new technology still exist. There is a definite lack of available capital for investment. Not only are credit policies still in the hands of state bureaucrats, but personal savings in Czechoslovakia, with few exceptions, are virtually non-existent.

The government has taken the first steps to facilitate the development of the private sector. A new law on private enterprises was passed by the parliament in April 1990. The main benefit of this law is that it removes all legal limitations against the number of employees hired and the extent of property acquired by a private firm. However, there is a large implicit barrier. If a firm has more than 25 employees and a yearly income of over 500,000 Kčs, then it must register as a large firm, and be subject to the same regulations as a state firm. More specifically, the firm is subject to a double rate of taxation and internal administrative procedures dictated by the state.

Furthermore, little attention has been paid to several existing entry barriers, the most severe of which we will discuss. Above, we mentioned the serious shortage of available start-up capital for private entrepreneurs. For the foreseeable future, firms will be subject to relatively high tax burdens and to a general shortage of private savings. Although the central bank was formally separated from its control over the commercial banking sector, these 'commercial' banks are still fully owned by the state, and there has been little discussion in the ministries for the imminent need to create a private banking sector.

In fact, in concurrence with the 'tight monetary policy', regulations on credit have actually increased over the past months. It is difficult for small firms to acquire capital, because it is very costly for banks to provide them with relatively small loans and to assess them (they have no past reputation or credit history). The banking sector is still very weak and uses a 'museum of financial instruments'. As a result, to receive a payment from the local bank takes more than one month and involves two different banks. For financially weak small entrepreneurs the lack of liquidity can be disastrous.

In addition, the state demands that private firms guarantee a relatively high minimum wage and subjects them to a steep progressive tax on wage increases. The result is a rigid wage structure, which further raises the firm's costs.

The liberalization of foreign trade and overnight introduction of limited convertibility for domestic residents beginning on 1 January 1991 rapidly helped to open world markets.

Reformers in Czechoslovakia are gradually realizing the need for an industrial policy which actively fosters the development of small private firms in the manufacturing sector. Czechoslovakia needs a distribution of firm sizes, which would efficiently foster technological change and meet the proliferation of consumer tastes. Structural barriers, such as those described above, must be removed if individuals are to have access to the economic opportunities of the market. This entails more than the legalization of private businesses, the implementation of anti-trust policies, and the reduction of bureaucratic red tape.

6. Foreign investment and external shocks

In Section 4 we depicted the liberalization of imports and exports supported by limited convertibility as an important component of the reform package. It is not the full picture. Most Czech and Slovak goods are low-quality machinery and defense equipment which are exported to developing and East European countries. These markets have shrunk dramatically because of the limited availability of credits for those (sometimes illiquid) countries.

In conjunction with the transformation of Czechoslovakia, new markets are opening. New trade and cooperation treaties with the EC and with the USA are examples. The necessary flexibility of exporters increased in 1990, when the monopoly of 50 state-owned trading companies was broken. In 1990, 2,756 firms were authorized to conduct foreign trade activities and more restrictions were lifted. Presently, all incorporated firms are authorized to conduct foreign trade. However, the bureaucrats in the ministries still limit convertible imports and exports (most notably the export of raw material and semi-manufactured goods) through cumbersome licensing. The export and import licenses and quotas should be, in the authors' opinions, replaced by more effective tariff adjustments or general technical and ecological standards.

The low gross indebtedness of Czechoslovakia, which is now 8 billion USD is managable (with 20 percent of exports going towards servicing the debt). In addition, Czechoslovakia has gross reserves of gold, foreign exchange (2.4 billion USD) and other assets in convertible currencies (5.4 billion USD). As a result, the Czechoslovak *net external debt in convertible currencies was only −0.2 billion USD at the end of 1989* (Czechoslovakia has been a net creditor to many developed and developing market economies).

Some 30 percent of Czechoslovak assets are frozen in non-performing loans in developing countries but part of these claims could be repatriated through oil imports from Arab countries instead of Soviet oil.

An even larger problem with regard to the Soviet oil supply is that since 1991 this oil must be paid for with convertible currencies and is available in decreasing quantities. This is an extremely serious supply shock. In 1991, the USSR promised to deliver only one-half of the originally contracted volume, in physical units equal to 7.5 million tons. The Soviet regional problems pose a certain threat for reliable supplies. One should also take into account that this monopolistic supplier traditionally bought Czechoslovak goods in exchange for imported oil. Finally, the USSR operated the main oil pipeline. The Adriatic oil pipeline temporarily used by Russians to export oil to the Adriatic sea tankers is once again at Czechoslovak disposal and breaks the danger of a natural monopoly, but unfortunately the Yugoslavian crisis has limited this advantage.

Unfortunately the Gulf crisis led to an embargo on contracts to repay Iraqi debt by oil supplies. This caused another supply shock deepened by the high world spot price of alternative suppliers. The financial burden for the Czechoslovak economy has been close to 2 billion USD. This could consume part of the foreign reserves originally set aside for the koruna's overnight convertibility. Now, additional foreign loans must be secured in spite of previous intentions not to do so. Fortunately oil prices have fallen or there would have had to have been another devaluation.

Since 1991, all mutual foreign trade within the CMEA has been denominated in convertible currency and actual world prices. This may decrease the terms of trade by 50 percent and deteriorate the balance of payments by at least 2 billion dollars (another supply shock). This simultaneous effect could be more important than the effect of an overnight introduction of limited convertibility. Regarding the lack of convertible currency in the USSR, the quality of Czechoslovak products, and the demand structure of the USSR, the interim solution is a barter trade for approximately one-third of oil supplies. It is sometimes very costly, especially if made with representatives of oil-producing regions and with respect to the negative motivation of Soviet producers, heavily taxed by the federal and republic governments. Barter is often excluded by the federal and republic clerks, who are afraid of keeping all transaction proceeds on the local level.

Another devastating external demand shock is the global collapse of the Soviet market. The Soviet and (formerly) East German markets for Czechoslovak products could be cut in half this year. The same collapse applies, to a lesser extent, to the other East European countries. The global recession in the Western market will contribute to this external demand shock. That will partially restrict aggregate demand, which would then allow some softening of the tight, restrictive domestic policy and alleviate the necessity for a surplus budget. In fact it already happened when interest rates, import surcharges, and turnover taxes were decreased by two points.

The difficult reorientation of trade from the collapsed East to a depressed West requires much better market research and improved export performance (supported by last year's devaluation etc.). Passive adjustment to the cost of indebtedness is not a cautious solution to the Czechoslovak problems. Only reasonable stand-by and other loans can facilitate smooth adjustment. To cover the costs of supply shocks and convertibility introduction, Czechoslovakia has received 1.8 billion USD from the IMF for 1991. Another 2 billion USD should be provided by the G24, the EC and by commercial banks to balance expected deficits in the current account and balance of payments. The gross indebtedness might increase to 11–12 billion USD, but the debt service will still be manageable. After the first quarter of 1991 the situation looks even better and part of the stand-by loans will probably not be used.

All of the external shocks may mean a serious threat to the existence of many Eastern export-oriented firms and an obstacle for privatization, of course. To reverse the shift of the aggregate supply curve westwards (inwards) with inevitable inflationary and recessionary impacts, *the supply side should be revitalized.* The data provides clear evidence of greater supply elasticity in market economies with a competitive private sector, which is another reason to speed up the privatization.

Foreign investors could play an important role in this process. A stable Czechoslovak economy in the center of Europe allows them to start here and either 'go East' (the large Eastern European market and especially the Russian market which is well understood by Czech and Slovak businessmen who usually speak Russian) or 'go West' (an opportunity considered mainly by Japanese, who value the relatively skilled labor, low transport costs, etc.).

The relevant legislation is being adopted gradually. Even more important than the reliable supplies of high technology or innovative products is an up-to-date (imported or transferred) organization and management system. This will allow domestic firms to restructure to meet the unknown standards of Western markets and marketing techniques.

The important steps in the right direction are represented by the adopted legislation regarding FDI (amendment to joint venture law) and relevant bilateral agreements on FDI protection and profit repatriation. In the simplest case, it is legal for foreign investors to own 100 percent of a company. This is very similar to German and Austrian laws. As for each joint venture one must wait for the approval of the office of the Ministry of Finance. Besides the assessment of the financial soundness of proposed investment projects from the domestic and foreign point of view, the field of interest is also assessed. Some strategic sectors are more protected such as banking services (where an approval of the State Bank is needed). The joint-venture screenings have been rather cumbersome until now.

By the end of 1990, the uniform foreign exchange retention quota required selling 30 percent of convertible currency revenues to the banks. Importers producing for the domestic market without sufficient exports could obtain convertible currency at the foreign exchange auctions. 'Limited convertibility', introduced on 1 January 1991, has started to rectify the situation.

Under bilateral investment protection agreements (BITs), profit transfers abroad are free and guaranteed by the government. Local currency financing is available for joint ventures. A minimum of 5 percent of gross profits must be contributed to a single reserve fund, which must be maintained at a minimum of 10 percent of the joint venture 'shareholder equity'. Joint ventures contribute the same percentage (50 percent of the payroll) as domestic firms to the social security funds. There are tax deductions for the joint ventures: they pay profit tax of 40 percent (compared with a profit tax rate of 55 percent for state and other enterprises) and dividends are taxed usually at 25 percent.

The basic problem for joint ventures is identical to the unresolved privatization issues for residents. Acquiring an asset from the SOE or other state property (that still prevails) by a joint venture means there must be partial or full privatization of this asset in favor of foreign investors. How to overcome this obstacle? As proposed in the interim solution, the large-size enterprises must be approved also by the government and only the minority of the SOE assets should participate in joint venture. Capital asset evaluation, however, is a problem in and of itself. The claims of former property owners, whose holdings were expropriated in the past, should be respected in the form of preferential access in the purchase of shares. The final solution of FDI questions related to privatization is the subject of the National Assembly, but joint venture establishment in the proposed, restricted form should be started immediately. Furthermore, the final privatization law will widen opportunities.

As a result, by August 1991, 2,964 joint ventures had been approved, with a total capital invested of 26.4 billion koruna. Most are very small; only 22 joint ventures have equity of more than 100 million koruna. In order to separate those new establishments with foreign direct investment from privatization of SOEs and alleviate conditions for FDI with participation by Czech and Slovak nationals in joint ventures, the government allows the joint ventures to incorporate directly without any approval.

Recently, the first deal between Volkswagen and Skoda car company was completed; VW promises to invest nearly 5 billion USD and ultimately to acquire 70 percent of Skoda shares.

7. Conclusion

A radical transition to a market economy has been started. Unfortunately the negative impacts of external supply and demand shocks are indistinguishable from the positive impacts. The population is ready to support the privatization, but there is a lot of pessimism regarding its immediate results in 1992.

There will, of course, be necessary social costs involved in closing enterprises, such as growing unemployment. These problems must be anticipated and social policy adjustments quickly made. The population may better tolerate it now, rather than if the measures are postponed.

References

Blinder, A. (ed.) (1990), *Paying for Productivity*, The Brookings Institution, Washington, D.C.

Colleen, Duncan (ed.) (1990), *German Reunification. Privatization of Czechoslovakia, Hungary, and Poland: Implications for Western Business*, New York University Press.

Dlouhy, Vladimir, Dyba, Karel and Svejnar, Jan (1990), *Czechoslovakia: Recent Economic Developments and Prospects*, Paper for AEA/ACES Meeting, Washington, D.C.

Dyba, Karel (1989), 'Growth, Structural Changes and Openness of the Economy', *Politicka ekonomie*, No. 5 (in Czech).

Ehrlich, E. (1987), *Absolute and Relative Economic Development Levels and their Structures, 1937–1980*, Budapest.

Gati, Charles (1990), 'After Communism, what? The Political Agenda in Central and Eastern Europe in the 1990's', Third US–Czechoslovak Roundtable on Economic Relations, Washington, D.C.

Griffith, W. (ed.) (1989), *Central and Eastern Europe: The opening Curtain*, Westview Press.

Grosfeld, Irena (1990), *Privatization of State Enterprises in Eastern Europe: The Search for Environment*, Delta, Doc. No. 90–17, Paris.

Hajek, Mojmir, Janackova, Stanislava, and Nachtigal, Vladimir (1990), 'Total Factor Productivity Trends in Czechoslovakia: A Comparison with Advanced Market Economies', in: Mejstrik (ed.) (1990b).

Hanke, Steve H. (ed.) (1987), *Privatization and Development*, International

Centre for Economic Growth, ICS PRESS, Institute for Contemporary Studies, San Francisco, California.

Hanusch, Horst (ed.) (1988), *Evolutionary Economics*, Cambridge University Press.

Hlaváček, Jiří (1987), 'Homo se assecurans', *Politicka ekonomie*, Prague.

Hlaváček, Jiří and Třiška, Dusan (1988), *Producers' Criteria in Centrally Planned Economy*, Institut of economics, Prague.

Hlaváček, Jiří, Kysilka, Pavel, and Zieleniec, Josef (1988), 'The Aversion to Objective Information in CPE', *Politicka ekonomie*, Prague (in Czech).

Kornai, Janos (1978), *The Economics of Shortage*, North Holland.

Kornai, Janos (1990), *The Road to a Free Economy, Shifting from a Socialist System*, Norton and Company, New York.

Kouba, Karel (1990), *System Changes in Czechoslovakia*, Paper for US–CS Roundtable, Washington, D.C.

Kriz, Karel (1989), *When One can and cannot use Effective Restrictive Policy*, State Bank J., December (in Czech).

Marer, Paul (1989), 'The Economies and Trade of Eastern Europe', in: Griffith (1989).

MacDermott, Gerald and Mejstrik, Michal (1990), *Czechoslovak Competitiveness and the Role of Small Firms*, Paper for the conference at the WZB, Berlin.

Mejstrik, Michal (1990a), 'Where are We Headed: The Case of Czechoslovakia', in: Colleen (ed.) (1990).

Mejstrik, Michal (1990b), *Innovation and Technology Transfer*, (Proceedings of conference), Institute of Economics, Prague.

Mejstrik, Michal (1990c), *The Transformation of Czechoslovakia to a Market Economy. The Possibilities and Problems*, Seminar on Privatization, UNDP, Warsaw.

Milanovic, Branko (1989), *Liberalization and Entrepreneurship Dynamics of Reform in Socialism and Capitalism*, Armonk, M.E. Sharpe, New York.

Mizsei, Kalman (1990), *Experiences with Privatization in Hungary*, World Bank Conference, Washington, D.C.

Mlčoch, Lubos (1989), *Behavior of Czechoslovak Enterprises*, Research Paper No. 348, Institute of Economics, Prague (in Czech).

Nachtigal, Vladimir and Dedek, Oldrich (1987), 'Disaggregation of the Rate of Total Factor Productivity', *Politicka ekonomie*, No. 2 (in Czech).

Nellis, John (1990), *Privatization in Reforming Socialist Economies*, Conference on Privatization in Eastern Europe, ICPE/EDI World Bank/UDNP, Ljubliana.

Novotny, Zbynek (1990), *Comparison of Producers in Building Industry*, UEOS Bratislava (in Czech).

Ordelt, Dusan (1991), 'Menovy kos cs.koruny', Hospodarske noviny, 17/1.

Prust, Jim *et al.* (1990), *The Czech and Slovak Federal Republic: An Economy in Transition*, Occasional Paper No. 72, IMF, Washington, D.C.

Ramanadham, V.V. (ed.) (1990), *Privatization in Developing Countries*, Routledge, Chapman and Hall, New York.

Schaffer, Mark (1990), *On the Use of Pension Funds in the Privatization of Polish State-Owned Enterprises*, LSE mimeo.

Vrabec, Vaclav (1991), *Znarodneni 1945* (Nationalization 1945), Dejiny a soucasnost 1, Praha (in Czech).

Vuylsteke, Charles (1989), *Techniques of Privatization of State Owned Enterprises. Volume I. Methods and Implementation*, World Bank Technical Paper Number 88, the World Bank, Washington, D.C.

Young, S. David (1990), *Business Valuation and the Privatization Process in Eastern Europe: Challenges, Issues and Solutions*, INSEAD, Fontainebleau.

Zamrazilova, Eva (1990), 'International Comparisons of Economic Development Levels Between East and West European Countries', *Jahrbuch des Ost-Europa Wirtsschaft*, November.

Zieleniec, Josef (1990), 'Czechoslovakia on Crossroads', *Archy*, No. 1, Lidove noviny, Prague.

3

The decision-making structure of Polish privatization

Jan Szomburg*

1. The background of the law on privatization

The history of Polish privatization begins in September 1989, with the creation of the first post-communist government in East Central Europe. For the first time in the region, privatization became a practical problem and work was begun to formulate both a general privatization strategy and a legal framework for the process as a whole. In July 1990, after nine months of discussion the parliament passed the basic law on privatization. This law established the legal framework for privatization, but was unaccompanied by a government program defining the nature of the strategy to be pursued. The next half year was devoted to the definition of this strategy, and to the resolution of particular practical problems such as the preparation of five state enterprises for public sale. 1991 was above all a year of practice. Based on this practice however, the privatization program has been broadened and enriched by new paths and forms.

By the end of 1991, some 1,000 state enterprises (not counting the 'small privatization' of retail trade) had been privatized. A little over half of them were enterprises dissolved through bankruptcy procedures according to the Law on State Enterprises, and their assets were sold off by state-appointed receivers. About 353 enterprises were privatized by the 'liquidation technique' according to the Law on Privatization. In these privatizations, the state enterprise is liquidated and its assets leased to a new corporation created primarily by the management and labor of the old state firm. Some eighteen enterprises were sold to foreign or domestic buyers through trade sales.

* Translated by Tony Levitas

Another six firms were sold through public offerings. Poland remains the only post-communist country to have privatized firms using this method, aside from one example in Hungary. In addition to these privatizations, another 350 firms were commercialized, meaning they were given normal corporate governance structures and had their assets capitalized. These firms currently remain owned by the state, but commercialization is to be the first step towards their privatization (although there is no timetable). Many of these firms are to be included in the program of mass privatization. Some 8,000 firms still remain in the state's hands. The vast majority of them will eventually have to be privatized.

The problems and particularities of Polish privatization can only be understood within the dual context of the self-management system of enterprise control that Solidarity forced upon the Communist Party in 1981, and the weakness of the political structures that accompanied systemic change. The collapse of communism meant that for the first time privatization could be treated as a practical problem. But the collapse left a political vacuum of sorts. Not only was there no established party system, but also there were simply no parties, only vague umbrella groups that pushed one or another political orientation. Worse, the public had a general aversion to politics and after forty-five years of communist rule thought of politics as something dirty, if not also harmful. Indeed, the only institutional structure of any weight was an extremely cumbersome trade union whose internal unity had been built more around opposition to communism than around the articulation of specific social interests or programs.

As such, the first post-communist government had no reliable partners with which to discuss absolutely key systemic questions such as privatization. In fact, the only organized group capable of articulating a position on privatization was the self-management movement and the political lobby that grew out of the Employee Council system of enterprise management. This group was over-represented in parliament (because of the way Solidarity had chosen candidates in the partially free elections of June 1989), was influential in the economic press, and had very dynamic activists. The lobby represented the interests of the work-force, the insiders. Not surprisingly, it supported a decentralized model of privatization which *de facto* amounted to proposals for the creation of employee-owned enterprises. Meanwhile, the government had an essentially technocratic vision of privatization based on the British model of selling enterprises through public offerings. It also hoped – in the interim – to reassert state control over self-managed firms through the creation of a specialized government agency.

Throughout the spring, the conflict between the state and the Employee Council movement played itself out in parliament around the law on privatization, and without the participation of other organized interests. The conflict was resolved through a compromise over how privileged the work-force would be in stock purchases, and over the degree of 'social' control over privatization itself. On 13 July 1990, the parliament passed the basic law on privatization and created the Ministry of Property Transformation (MPW). The material interests of the work-force were recognized in the law by provisions that allowed employees to buy up to 20 percent of the stocks at half price, so long as the preferences per worker do not exceed the average annual earnings in the five basic sectors of the economy.

The question of social control over privatization was resolved by the creation of a two-tier decision-making system. At the top, parliament, and by extension the state, was given the right to define annually the basic direction of privatization and to determine where the proceeds from privatization were to go. At the bottom, wide powers were granted to the enterprises themselves with respect to the decision over whether to be privatized or not. Moreover, these rights were dispersed within the enterprises among the managing director, the Employee Councils, and the general meeting of the work-force,[1] all of whom had to agree to privatization before it could begin.

This division of powers not only left the decision-making structure of self-managed enterprises in place, but also extended to firms the right to veto decisions over privatization. In self-managed firms, the Employee Council and the general meeting of the work-force have the rights that are normally held in a joint-stock company by the Board of Directors and the meeting of the general stockholders. As in a joint-stock company, these institutions have the right to make decisions about division of profits, creation of new units, investments, and hiring and firing of directors. But, in a self-managed firm, these institutions are controlled solely by employees, and not by the owners of capital.

This model of firm governance was forced upon the regime in 1981 by Solidarity. The union's intention at that time was to take power away from the communist state by giving the Employee Councils the rights held by the branch ministries and the central planners. The struggle between the union and regime over self-management had both political and economic elements. Politically, self-management was a way to fight against the omnipresence of the communist nomenklatura. By giving control over management selection to the Councils, Solidarity hoped to enlarge and protect the sphere of freedom and autonomy that the union had won for itself and for society as a whole. Since, according to the governing ideology both power and property belonged to the working people, the self-management movement was in effect demanding the practical fulfilment of constitutional promises. The union, in short, was using official propaganda to legitimize a more general political struggle for social autonomy.

Economically, the self-management system was understood as a way to free firms from the directives of the central planning agencies. The elimination of these directives was considered a necessary precondition for the development of market relations. Firms were not only to be politically released from nomenklatura control, but to be self-managing and self-financing as well. These three elements of self-dependence, self-management, and self-financing were symbolized in the slogan '3 × S'. And this slogan became the rallying call of the trade-union movement with respect to economic reform and the division of powers within the firm. Self-management seemed to answer the question of how to rationalize the behavior of state firms when wide-scale privatization was politically inconceivable. Or more exactly, it was an answer to the question of what would be a politically acceptable modification of the economy's structure that at the same time provided at least the possibility for increasing the role of the market.

The declaration of Martial Law in December 1981 did not overturn the self-management legislation passed three months earlier. It did, however, make possible the reassertion of state control over firms through other means. Throughout the 1980s, and with differing degrees of intensity the outlawed labor movement attempted – without much success – to use the letter of the law to reassert control over factories. With the political collapse of the communist state, and the collapse of the Party's ability to control firms through extra-legal means, the *de jure* status of firms all of sudden became a reality. As such, Polish state enterprises in 1992 are state enterprises in name only. Nowhere in the world, and never in history, have there been such autonomous state firms.[2] The state does not control managerial selection, and can no longer make decisions about profits, investments, wages, or production profiles. Indeed, 1990 saw the legal strengthening of the autonomy of state enterprises: for the first time their economic interactions became regulated by the civil code and not by administrative law.

In sum, the privatization process began in Poland in a situation characterized by the following elements: first, the extreme decentralization and dispersion of rights of ownership and control, second, the strong political and psychological attachment of employees to the idea of self-management, employees who shared a general feeling that the 'firms are ours', and third, the extremely weak capacity of the state to supervise and monitor the behavior of the firms.[3]

The law on privatization perpetuated this division of decision-making powers between the formal owner – the state – and the employees of the firm – management and the Employee Councils. Moreover, it further dispersed the rights to make decisions about privatization across various institutions within the state apparatus. City and provincial governments, branch ministries, the MPW, the Prime Minister, and his Advisory Council on Property Transformation were all given partial powers over the privatization process. Let us look at the content of these dispersed rights and powers.

In communist Poland, cities and counties were not legally independent entities, either as units of democratic self-rule or as owners of municipal assets. Public utility companies were owned and controlled by the national government and not by the localities in which they operated. In 1990, cities were given legal identities, and some 2,500 new, democratically elected administrative units were created. These new municipalities were in turn given title to some 1,500 state enterprises. Unfortunately, some of these firms performed normal commercial functions and should not have been considered public utilities.

But, in any case, the right to make decisions about the privatization of municipal enterprises is not shared with the MPW. Instead, the municipalities have the powers that are elsewhere held by the Privatization Ministry and the so-called founding organs of firms: the branch ministries and provincial authorities that had been responsible for exercising the state's ownership claims under the centrally controlled system. Municipalities share their powers over privatization only with insiders, that is to say with management and the Employee Councils in accordance with the basic law on privatization. In all other firms, 1 of the 49 provincial authorities or 15 branch ministries exercise the ownership rights of the state *vis-à-vis* enterprises. Provincial governments are responsible for some 4,500 – mostly small and medium-sized – firms. The branch ministries are responsible for about 3,500 larger ones.

The division of powers among the MPW, the Founding Organs, and the Employee Councils differs depending on which of the two paths to privatization (foreseen in the basic law) is followed. One path ('capital') allows firms to be transformed into joint-stock companies of the Treasury and then sold to investors either in public offerings or in trade sales. The other path ('liquidation') allows for a state firm to be dissolved and its assets leased or transferred – in whole or in part – to a newly created corporation.[4] Irrespective of the path, however, the governing philosophy of the law is one of consensus. All parties to the process legally have 'something to say' in the matter and generally must agree both on the decision to privatize, and on the path of privatization.

The law, however, also provides for the possibility of forced, state-led property transformations in cases where enterprises are first to be transformed into joint-stock companies and then sold to outside buyers. The law reserves for the Prime Minister the right to force firms to submit to privatization plans drawn up by the MPW. But even in such cases of state-led privatization – considered exceptional by the law – there is still a legal obligation to obtain the opinion of management, the Employee Council, and the Founding Organ of a firm. The possibility of transforming the status of an enterprise against the will of its employees or the founding organ is thus politically weakened by the need to obtain the opinions of those involved. In the case of firms privatized through liquidation/leasing arrangements the legal possibilities of state-led action are even weaker. So although the theoretical possibility of forced privatization exists, the political cost of resistance at the enterprise level has prevented it from being carried out.

Leaving aside this still unused possibility, the initiators of the process may be either the enterprise itself or its founding organ. The MPW is empowered to transform an enterprise into a joint-stock company only after receiving the written agreement of the managing director, the Employee Council, and the founding organ of the firm. Indeed, the Employee Council can give its approval only after a general meeting of the work-force has discussed the issue. The founding organ may initiate the process. Or the initiators can be the managing director and the Employee Council of a firm. But in either case all three parties must be in agreement before the MPW can approve the plans. If the Minister of Property Transformation refuses to agree to the proposed transformation the representatives of the firm can bring the matter to the courts.

In liquidation privatizations, the Employee Councils have the sole right to initiate the process. If their proposals are refused they can take legal action. To make matters more complicated, the general roles of the MPW and the founding organs are reversed in liquidation/leasing privatizations: in capital sale privatizations the founding organ must agree to the proposals, but it is the MPW that supervises, organizes, and makes the final decisions; in liquidation/leasing procedures, it is the MPW who must agree to the proposal, but it is the founding organ that has the first right of refusal, and the legal responsibility for supervising the execution of the plans.

Since the founding organs are legally responsible for privatizations carried out through liquidations, units within them had to be created and trained to deal with privatization. In practice, there has been a lot of variation in how these units were constructed and how well they have functioned. Initially, either the provincial government or the branch ministry empowered an individual to deal with privatizations. This person then established a working group that eventually became an office within the provincial government or the Ministry.

In sum, the law on privatization passed in July 1990 gave Poland a highly dispersed and decentralized decision-making structure for privatization. The intention of the legislators was that privatization should be dependent on the will of internal actors and should take place through a consensual procedure in which insiders, the founding organs, and the MPW all come to agreement. In practice, this intention has entailed the dispersion of property rights throughout the administrative apparatus responsible for the process: the MPW, 49 provincial governments, 15 branch ministries, and 2,500 municipalities – to say nothing of the firms themselves – have varying degrees of competencies with respect to the decision to privatize, its form, and its procedural rules. From the purely praxiological point of view, this is obviously not an optimal solution. From the social point of view, it is a 'soft' solution intended to minimize conflicts and ensure that the potential tensions created by privatization do not accumulate.

2. The functioning of the decision-making structure and the dynamics of privatization

2.1 Privatization through capital sales

Immediately after the passage of the July law, the government became painfully aware that employees were not particularly interested in capital sale privatizations, and that the provisions in the law for preferential employee stock purchases were insufficient to encourage firms to initiate privatization procedures. As an added incentive to privatize, the government modified the wage tax system. Firms were told that if they became joint-stock companies of the Treasury the penalty tax for exceeding wage norms would be reduced by 20 percent. When firms became more than 50 percent privately owned the tax would be abolished altogether. Moreover, firms expected that after commercialization they would not have to pay the so-called dividend – or capital tax – required of other state enterprises.[5] These incentives proved sufficient to encourage some firms to begin the privatization process. By the end of 1990, 30 enterprises had become joint-stock companies of the Treasury.

In the first half of 1991, the economic situation of state firms deteriorated radically, in part because of the collapse of Soviet trade, in part because of the cumulative effects of the government's fiscal, monetary, and tariff policies. With this deterioration, a new motive for privatization emerged within firms: the desire to relieve themselves of the responsibility for self-management and operational independence. Worker groups that had fought for autonomy now want to talk about their future to the new state, which has however lost interest in the meantime. It is, in short, a desire to return to the presumably protective umbrella of clear state ownership in the hope that the state would not allow its firms to go bankrupt, would reduce their debts, and might even help in finding foreign creditors. Thus, despite the fact that commercialization entailed the elimination of the Employee Councils, more and more firms announced their willingness to become joint-stock companies of the Treasury. By May, some 150 firms had been commercialized, and by November 1991, 300.

In general, then, the division of rights with respect to capital sale privatizations has not caused serious social tensions. On the horizon, however, two different types of conflicts can be foreseen. First, it is possible that a large number of firms immediately threatened by bankruptcy will try to commercialize themselves in order to force the state to take direct responsibility for their futures. The MPW, however, can defend itself against such an eventuality because both the spirit and the letter of the law foresee commercialization as the beginning of a process that is to end in privatization, and not simply as change in the governance structure of state firms.

Second, it is possible that there will be conflicts with firms in relatively good economic condition over their willingness to participate in the mass privatization program. Here it is possible that because of the speed with which the mass privatization program must be carried out, the Prime Minister will be compelled to use the state's residual ownership rights to force these firms into participation. The probability of this scenario, however, is low because 10 percent of these enterprises' stocks will be given to employees free of charge and this will probably prove sufficient for winning the backing of insiders.

2.2 *Privatization through liquidation*

The functioning of the decision-making structure for firms privatized through liquidation is both more complicated and more interesting. Of the 353 enterprises that were privatized through liquidation procedures, 283 of them were lease/buy-out arrangements in which the leasing firm was created primarily by the employees of the former state firm. Twenty-one firms were liquidated and sold to outside investors and 13 were contributed to existing private firms in which the state received shares based on the value of the contributed assets. The remaining 40 or so have been liquidated through a bankruptcy procedure according to the law on privatization, with most of the assets split up and sold. In practice, this meant that private Polish investors have had relatively little access to the primarily small and medium-sized state firms that are using this procedure for privatization.

Thus, privatization through liquidation has so far had a very one-sided character both with respect to the form – leasing arrangements – and with respect to the final owners – predominantly, the employees of the former state enterprise. The law states that leasing may be undertaken only by firms for which a plurality of stocks is initially held by employees of the former state enterprise, though not necessarily in equal proportions. At the same time, these stocks must be transferable. The newly created firms may, however, invite outside investors to participate, and the outside investors are free to acquire controlling interests.

In virtually all cases of privatization through liquidation, the initiative comes from the enterprises themselves; the founding organs virtually never initiate the process. The legal, political, and organizational situation of the founding organs is too weak for them to carry out an active policy of selling-off small firms to outside buyers. Indeed, attempts by the Founding Organs to sell enterprises to buyers of their own choosing and not those of the firm have been met with resistance from the Employee Councils and ultimately with threats to bring the matter before the courts. Blackmail of this type has forced some founding organs to retreat from a more aggressive effort to sell small firms to the private sector.

Only privatization plans that met with the approval of both the Employee Councils and the founding organs have been realized in practice. Typically, a coalition of insiders, including management, the Employee Councils, and the unions, pushes the procedure forward. Curiously, this is a coalition of parties who earlier were often in conflict with one another. The coalition is created in order to achieve the best bargaining position with the founding organ and to win the best conditions for the sale or lease of the assets. Generally, the founding organs and the MPW have required that the initial capitalization of the new enterprise be equal to at least 20 percent of the value of the former state firm's assets. But this value and the conditions of the lease are open to extensive bargaining.

In sum, it is fair to say that this method of privatizing small and medium-sized enterprises has a rather closed character. It has not permitted the full exploitation of the entrepreneurial reserves of the country, because it makes it difficult for domestic and foreign private capital to participate in the process. This does not mean, however, that all firms privatized through liquidation procedures have dispersed or completely employee-owned capital structures, or that their governance structures did not undergo fundamental changes. For example, there are many in which the controlling package of stocks is in the hands of management and the stock ownership of other workers is not concentrated enough to negatively affect decision-making. Indeed, it may even facilitate greater employee effort. In firms where employees are not capable of raising the founding capital of a new enterprise themselves, they often try to find outside investors. Sometimes these outside investors immediately acquire a controlling interest in the firm.

In some firms, however, ownership is rather widely dispersed and there is no clearly dominant voice. Occasionally, the performance of such enterprises deteriorates after privatization, and will only improve once the turnover in shares allows for the emergence of a strategic investor. Both the sale of stocks and the ability of an employee-owned firm to enter into joint ventures increases the possibility of attracting foreign capital and improving management. But, economically speaking, the improvement of performance, brought about either by the sale of stocks or the creation of a joint venture, could have taken place earlier without the intermediate step of creating a largely employee-owned entity.

In May of 1991, the MPW presented parliament with draft legislation designed to speed up the privatization of small and medium-sized enterprises. The legislation was to strengthen the legal, political, and organizational position of the founding organs so that they could more aggressively assert the state's property rights. On the one hand, the organizational capacities of the founding organs to develop their own privatization plans were to be increased by giving them new resources. On the other hand, the law on privatization was to be amended, and the right of the Employee Councils to reject privatization initiatives coming from the founding organs eliminated. The hope was that by strengthening the position of the founding organs the state could move away from the passive politics of waiting for firms to initiate privatization, and towards a more active process of selling enterprises to outside investors. This legislation was not intended to completely displace privatization through liquidation and leasing procedures controlled by employees. It was, however, intended to shift the proportions of ownership towards outside investors and to create new and faster means of privatizing small and medium-sized enterprises. Unfortunately, parliament rejected these legislative proposals.

Conclusion

The fundamental weakness of post-communist Poland's political infrastructure has made it extremely difficult to attain a workable social consensus about the nature of privatization. In conditions approaching something like a political vacuum, it is very hard for social groups to articulate their opinions, interests, and political positions. And without such articulation it is virtually impossible to forge a socially acceptable program. The absence of appropriate political 'tools' and avenues of communication has meant that despite four waves of discussion about privatization and a year of practice, no basic consensus has been reached. The most spectacular example of the political system's inability to articulate interests and forge them into a common strategy is the question of reprivatization. Here, despite the fact that everybody understands that delay in this area constitutes one of the most important barriers to privatization and to the entrance of foreign capital, there is still – after two and a half years of discussion – no legislation in this field. The most important consequence of this political failure to achieve a general social consensus at the level of the state has been the vague dispersion of property rights through society at large, and the painfully slow necessity of achieving consensus at the micro level: in other words in the case-by-case privatization of firms.

Notes

1. In firms employing more than 300 people, the general meeting of the work-force is composed of delegates.
2. But see L. Szakadat's and E. Voszka's discussions of the position of enterprises in Hungary in this volume. (Editors' note.)
3. This weakness is exemplified by the fact that the state no longer has an organized system of information about 'its' enterprises.
4. The privatization of firms through liquidation procedures can take three basic forms: the sale of the entire enterprise or parts of it, including through bankruptcy procedures; the in-kind contribution (for an

ownership stake) of all or part of the assets into a new corporation; or the leasing (with or without buyout) of all or part of the assets by a new corporation. In practice the vast majority of these procedures are ten-year lease/buyout arrangements with firms created by the employees of the old enterprise.

5. In fact, this has been handled on a case-by-case basis, with the dividend actually being reduced only in a minority of instances.

PART II

Privatization plans, policies, and results

4

Spontaneous privatization in Hungary

Eva Voszka

Introduction

One of the most significant changes in the Hungarian economy in the last three years was the appearance of thousands of new market actors (mainly companies) and new owners. This chapter analyzes the historical preconditions of this development and, using recent empirical research, describes the main ways of establishing companies, the motivations behind transformation, and the methods of changing the structure of ownership and legal forms. Special attention is devoted to the so-called 'spontaneous privatization', to its methods and its consequences.

This chapter argues that despite the political turnover, there has been a remarkable continuity in legislation, decision-making mechanisms, and governmental intentions with respect to the transformation of ownership relations. The chapter shows that 'spontaneous privatization' is not privatization in the strict sense of the word. It means rather commercialization with mostly state institutions ('holdings', enterprises, and banks) as new owners. This process has not been unambiguously spontaneous either, considering the direct and indirect influence of state organs even in the first period. Nevertheless, Hungary's freely elected government tried to centralize the decision-making power in transformation and privatization of state enterprises. This attempt ran into difficulties because of an earlier decentralization of ownership rights to enterprise management, which led to increased power relative to the central controlling organizations. Thus, the second period of the ownership changes, the so-called 'centralized period', did not square with its name either.

Perhaps the most significant change in Hungary's economy in the last three years was the rapid growth in the number of market actors. The new units were established mainly in company form, which means that new owners appeared on the scene. Who are these new owners? What were their motivations to create companies? Does this process indicate the privatization of state assets? This chapter tries to answer these questions on the basis of empirical research,[1] focusing its analysis on big industry during the period of 1988–mid-1990.

The first section describes the main lines of changes in the organizational and ownership structure. One is the so-called 'spontaneous privatization', the transformation of state enterprises into one or more companies, usually without involving private capital. Following a depiction of the legal and informal preconditions and the continuity of development in the second section, the third analyses the characteristic features of spontaneous privatization. We argue that this process cannot be considered as privatization in the strict sense of the word. Nor is it purely spontaneous, as we show in the fourth section, which examines the role of the state in the changes.

1. Main lines of the transformations, 1988–90

Before we examine the reasons for and the results of the transformation of company structure, a brief summary of the extent, the main sources, and the forms of expansion of company form is in order.

The number of economic units[2] in the Hungarian economy increased from 10,000 to nearly 30,000 between 1988 and 1990. These numbers reflect a rate of growth of 50 percent in 1989 and more than 90 percent in 1990 (see Table 4.1). Nearly all of this rapid expansion was growth in the company forms, primarily the limited liability company, while the number of state enterprises and cooperatives remained practically unchanged. The change has been most spectacular in trade, transport, and industry.

This process has significantly changed the range of sizes of economic units. The proportion of the smallest organizations, employing 20 people or less, reached more than half of all units in 1990, starting from less than 20 percent in 1988. The number of organizations with 300 or more employees has not changed but their proportion has fallen from 25 percent to less than 10 percent of the total (see Table 4.2). Most of these large units are enterprises and cooperatives, while on the other hand the rapidly expanding group of small units belongs to the limited-liability company form (see Table 4.3).

To what extent has this process meant the expansion of the private sector and/or the privatization of state property? At this point, the terminology has to be made clear. The term privatization will be used in this chapter in the strict sense of the word: transferring ownership of property to private physical or legal persons. The expansion of the private sector may, of course, be independent of those ownership changes. Private units can emerge without using any former state assets. On the other hand, the establishment of a company does not necessarily mean either the expansion of the private sector or of

Table 4.1 Number of economic units in different branches

	1988	1989		1990		1991 II. quarter	
		Total	Former year = 100 %	Total	Former year = 100 %	Total	Former year = 100 %
Industry	2,839	4,092	144.1	7,528	183.8	10,759	142.9
Building	1,586	2,293	144.6	4,232	184.6	6,109	144.4
Agriculture	1,564	1,684	107.7	2,112	125.4	2,787	132.0
Transport-communication	147	291	198.0	752	258.4	1,246	165.7
Domestic trade	879	2,025	230.4	6,475	314.8	11,538	181.0
Foreign trade	100	325	325.0	1,120	344.6	2,690	240.2
Other service	3,696	4,526	122.4	7,251	160.2	9,917	136.8
Total	10,811	15,236	140.9	29,470	193.4	45,046	152.9

Source: Central Statistical Office

Table 4.2 Number of economic units – organizational forms (% of all units)

	1988	1989	1990	1991.III. quarter
Enterprise	22.0	15.8	8.0	5.1
Company:	8.8	34.3	66.0	77.7
– limited liability company	4.2	29.4	62.3	74.6
– share company	1.1	2.0	2.2	2.2
Cooperative	63.6	46.4	26.0	17.2
Other	5.6	3.5	0.0	0.0
Total	100.0	100.0	100.0	100.0

Source: Central Statistical Office

Table 4.3 Size of economic units – number of employees (% of all units)

	Less than 20	21–50	51–300	More than 300	No data	Total
1988	18.7	14.5	28.2	23.3	15.3	100.0
1989	33.5	15.7	22.7	17.2	10.9	100.0
1990	55.9	14.0	15.2	8.8	6.1	100.0
1991.III.quarter	65.9	12.5	11.5	5.3	4.8	100.0

Source: Central Statistical Office

privatization. It can be simply the transformation of a state enterprise into a state-owned company (commercialization) or the transformation of a private unit (for example, former small entrepreneurships, private, 'small' cooperatives or partnerships) into a private company.

So, in our analysis of the basic data, we should distinguish between truly new units and mere changes in form, and among private companies, state companies, and companies of mixed ownership. Unfortunately, the registration information concerning the first question is uncertain and registration of the ownership structure was suspended in the Central Statistical Office (KSH) in 1989. We can only make an estimate of the extent of different types of changes.

According to the data published by the KSH, nearly half of all economic units were founded 'without any precedents', that is, they had not been included previously in the records of the KSH in any other form, and did not indicate a legal predecessor. We can suppose that the majority of them, at least those in the small categories (under 20 employees) are new private units.[3] This means that at least 10 percent of economic organizations existing at the end of 1990 were private firms.

To interpret this figure, two remarks should be made. First, although the number of private firms increased rapidly and their proportion became rather high, their size and the weight of their activities in the overall economy remained small. According to the official estimate of the KSH, small firms (the majority of which are probably private firms) employ 15 persons on average, have an annual output of less than 20 million forints, and have a share in industry of 3 to 4 percent.[4] The share of the whole private sector in the GDP – including agriculture, services, and the second economy as well – is usually estimated at 10 to 15 percent in 1990–91.[5]

Second, we have to point out that most small private firms were presumably established by the pooling of private capital, in other words they emerged independently from the privatization of state assets.

There is another group of companies that represents not only the expansion of the private sector but privatization as well: joint ventures with foreign capital. According to the data of the KOPINT DATORG consulting firm, at the beginning of 1990 there were 1,590 joint ventures in Hungary, with a foreign investment of about 30 billion forints.[6] According to a recent announcement by the Registration Court, nearly 4,000 joint ventures were founded in 1990 with more than 70 billion forints of initial capital. The foreign investment involved is about one-third of this sum.[7] The total amount, 50 billion forints (30 plus 20 invested before 1990), is 2.5 percent of all state property, estimated at 2,000 billion forints. This is the lower limit of the extent of privatization. An extreme upper limit can be calculated from the total property of all companies (115 billion forints)[8] which would imply a 6 percent share.

The problem is that there are many companies which are entirely or majority state-owned. This means that in addition to the establishment of new private enterprise and joint ventures with foreign capital, a third way of founding firms has to be taken into account, namely, the creation of subsidiaries or the disintegration of state-owned enterprises into several companies. The usual method has been the transformation of factories, plants, central divisions (trade, computing centers, products design) attached to large enterprises into independent joint-stock or limited-liability companies. Most of their shares have remained in the hands of the original state enterprises of which these units were part. New shareholders, if there were any, were generally state-owned banks and business partners of the given enterprise – again state firms.

This process of transformation will be discussed later in detail. Here we wish to emphasize that a rather significant segment of newly established companies was associated neither with the expansion of the private sector nor with privatization. Nevertheless, even this type of change, together with foreign investment, was called 'spontaneous privatization'.

There are no reliable statistical data available on the extent of this type of transformation. According to the data of the Ministry of

Industry and Trade, 40 percent of state-owned enterprises in industry, trade, and building were involved in founding companies with 10 percent of their assets, about 82 billion forints altogether.[9] It seems certain, therefore, that only a relatively small part of state property was organized into companies, although the process affected nearly one half of state enterprises. According to our estimate,[10] the number of companies in which a state-owned enterprise is a (partial) owner is between 3,500 and 6,000. A significant part of this group is made up by joint ventures with foreign investment; the rest does not represent privatization as the new owners are state organizations as well.

To summarize, the rapid spreading of the company form in the Hungarian economy is the driving force in increasing the number of market actors and in decreasing the size structure. There are three main types of companies with various participants and with different relationships to the private sector and to privatization. About 40 percent of companies (mainly small ones) are entirely private units, without significant links to the selling of state assets. Roughly one-fourth of companies are joint ventures with foreign capital. If the Hungarian partner is a state enterprise, this means privatization has taken place. The last third of companies is estimated to be entirely state-owned, and the transformation here has resulted in neither the expansion of the private sector nor in privatization. Despite these considerable movements, the total share of the private sector and the extent of privatization are both modest. The first is estimated at 10 to 15 percent of GDP and the second at 2.5 to 6 percent of state property as of late 1990.

In order to understand why the changes took place in these forms and degrees, the preconditions of the process are worth examining.

2. Historical preconditions: formal and informal frameworks

A specific feature of Hungary, in contrast to other East European countries, is that all types of property and organizational changes have antecedents in the last decades.[11]

The first line of change described above is the establishment of private firms. Small-scale private activity was permitted in Hungary as early as the 1960s, first in agriculture and later in other sectors. In addition to the legal forms of small private businesses, there has been an extended second (or shadow) economy.[12] In the early 1980s a new impetus was given to the expansion of private firms by a legislative order that permitted new organizational forms and linked preferences in regulation to their usage.

As a result of all of these developments, a great number of small entrepreneurships and the half-legal, shadow economy forerunners of private units emerged. A considerable proportion of the new units registered in 1988–90 can presumably be attributed to the legalization or the changing of the organizational form of these units.[13] This implies that the true growth in number of companies over the last two or three years is less dramatic than official statistics would seem to show. Still more important, thousands if not millions of Hungarians taking part in small entrepreneurships or in the shadow economy became familiar with entrepreneurial skills and self-reliant attitudes.

The second main line of change, the introduction of foreign investment, also has a significant history in Hungary. The first legislation in this field was passed in 1972. Administrative control over the founding of joint ventures with foreign partners was eased considerably. Financial incentives were then extended to foreign investors in several stages during the 1980s.[14]

However, the most interesting and complex issue is the third type of change: that of the formal and informal position of state enterprises. The basic idea behind the Hungarian reforms, beginning with those in the 1960s, was always to increase the independence of enterprises from state control. Among other things, this process meant the decentralization of an increasingly significant share of property rights from central bureaucratic organizations to enterprise management. The process began with the abolition of compulsory plan targets, the establishment of an enterprise's right to choose its business partners, and the informal concession of bargaining power to enterprise managers vis-a-vis party and government organizations.[15]

A crucial step towards decentralization of state property rights was the introduction of the 'self-governing enterprise' in 1985. Enterprise councils, employees' general assemblies, and meetings of delegates were established in two-thirds of enterprises.[16] These bodies, which were in practice dominated by enterprise management, received the rights, among others, to determine the organizational structure of their enterprises, appoint chief executives, make decisions about mergers and de-mergers, and establish joint ventures and companies involving state property.

Such types of transformations could be executed according to the pre-1945 laws, which were unused but still in effect. In 1988 the Company Law was passed, providing a new legal framework for the founding of corporations but no special regulations for transforming state enterprises into company form. This need was met by the Conversion Law (sometimes referred to as 'Transformation Law') of 1989, which granted self-governing bodies the right of transformation subject to several conditions. These included raising of capital, entry of new external owners, and leaving 80 percent of the shares to the state property administration as owner.

At that time, such an organization was lacking, so the State Property Agency (SPA) was set up in February 1990 and given the authority to utilize and sell state property. These powers, however, were restricted to the corporate property of units established according to the Transformation Law[17] and to enterprises subject to direct administrative control (that is, not self-governing, without enterprise councils). The SPA mandate did not cover the assets of state-owned enterprises which had been corporatized before. However, the Law on the Protection of State Property passed at the same time, contained prescriptions for enterprises founding new companies with some of their assets, and for the sale and lease of enterprise property. Under this Law, the SPA could prescribe a new asset evaluation and an open tender, or it could veto the contract.

But by that time, several hundred deals (transformation of state enterprises into company form with or without private partners) had been completed in the process of the 'spontaneous privatization'. Thus, by the time of the political turn (the potential beginning for a mass privatization process), most state property rights had already devolved to enterprise and company management. The inheritance of the former political system in this respect was not one of strong and stable state ownership, but of dispersed property rights divided among different types of organizations.[19]

In fact, there are many features of continuity in the Hungarian process. First, there is continuity in legislation, governmental aims, and in the behavior of other participants. One of them has already been mentioned: the former government's attempt to regain its lost central powers over the enterprises by setting up the SPA. The previous government had also prepared a set of laws, including laws on small privatization and competition, that were passed by the new government without significant changes. Although it was not given any great publicity, it has been documented[20] that official proposals in autumn 1989 already suggested a radical reduction of state ownership, a wide-ranging privatization. Thus there was also no clear line of division concerning the concepts of a new ownership structure.

Second, debates on the allocation of property rights are also not entirely new. As early as the 1960s and 1970s, there emerged proposals aimed at separating the roles of owners and managers by establishing new, but entirely state-owned institutions (joint-stock companies, holdings, pension funds). Although the concept of privatization in its narrow sense (that is, the transfer of state property into private ownership) first appeared in proposals by some experts and in programs of some of the new opposition parties at the turn of 1988 and 1989, in many cases, this meant simply the continuation of the same institutional forms, only with private owners. Moreover, not only the ideas, but also the real changes could be interpreted as a continuous process: state enterprises being reorganized into companies, then selling their shares to private proprietors.

Last but not least, continuity can be observed in the introduction of market elements in other fields of the institutional system and in the deregulation beginning in the late 1960s (for instance, the abolition of compulsory plan targets, easing of price and wage regulation in the state sector, and permission of small-scale private activities). Since the mid-1980s, commercial banks have been established, and bonds and bills of exchange have appeared. In 1988, a personal income tax was introduced, the system of turnover tax was simplified, and the profit tax became uniform for all firms. Social insurance was (at least formally) separated from the central budget. Imports have been gradually liberalized. And, in the first months of 1990, legislation was passed on trade in securities and the establishment of a stock exchange.

When evaluating the process of transformation, we must consider the fact that all these steps were taken before the free elections, by the old government. Summing up the preconditions for ownership transformation that the new political regime found in place, there were several elements of continuity: the intentions of the two governments, the existence of some market institutions, and the entrepreneurial behavioral patterns in wide groups of citizens, including enterprise managers. All these features are the result of the relatively liberal system of the last twenty years and the economic reform process in Hungary. The same factors are responsible for the decentralization of property rights from central state organizations to economic units, that is, the limitation of the power of the state as an owner. These preconditions not only provided the framework for transformation at its earliest stages (in 1988–89), they have also continued to influence the Hungarian transition since the free elections in 1990.

3. Spontaneous privatization: methods and interests

Spontaneous privatization was the term given in Hungary to the transformation of state enterprises into companies, when initiated and carried out by the firms themselves. According to the Enterprise Law (establishing the enterprise councils), the Company Law, and the Transformation Law, the enterprise self-governing bodies – in practice the top management – had the right to found companies making use of state assets. In many cases, they took only a minor part of the property into joint-stock or limited-liability companies, while the original state enterprise continued operations with the remaining assets.

In several dozen other cases, however, large state enterprises founded individual companies with each of their factories, plants, and even administrative departments. The former enterprise center was left only with the function of asset management. Although they called themselves 'holding companies', they preserved the form of a state-owned enterprise, either under direct state control or in self-governing form. Thus, the holding itself had no new owners, no shareholders, but could now exercise ownership rights over the newly created companies.

Usually, these 'holding companies' held a majority share in the new companies which were founded on the basis of the factories or subunits of the former large enterprise. At this level, new owners appeared as well; apart from foreign investors, they were state-owned organizations: banks and enterprises that had the right to buy stock in other partners' firms, or to make a debt-equity swap. At least during this period, domestic private investors seem to have played little role in the organizational and ownership changes of state-owned assets.[21]

According to Maria Csanadi's analysis of the balance sheet data of 57 enterprises which in 1988–89 were the first to engage in this type of transformation, this group was heterogeneous. Sub-branch division, size of assets, market structure, liquidity, and profitability indicators of the companies concerned were rather varied. The changing environment seems to have caused similar reactions in very different organizations. The question is why? What motivates state enterprises to reorganize themselves into companies?

First, the starting point was often an agreement between the managers of the large enterprises with the managers of their subunits. These two groups decided on the evaluation and division of assets and liabilities, as well as on the new ownership structure. They, and not the founding ministry or any state organ, negotiated prices with potential new owners. Facing serious financial and market problems, the top management sought to compromise with factory management, based on the common interest of survival. What were these common interests?

For enterprises in an unstable financial situation with large debts, the advantages of transformation are obvious. One method of creating financial stability through transformation is to convert credit into shares, making a debt-equity swap with banks or other creditors. A second method is to concentrate all financial burdens in the 'holding company'. The sub-companies are then debt-free on foundation and can continue production even if the holding company goes bankrupt.

Another motivation for transformation, characteristic not only of units near bankruptcy, is the desire for independence. This factor became more important for enterprise centers because of their increasing need to find new markets and products. The new organizational system gave independence to plants, once they were transformed into separate joint-stock or limited-liability companies (independent legal entities). Yet by maintaining majority ownership of the former enterprise center, the original enterprise may be kept intact. The enterprise center can thus determine the new organization and prevent the division or sale of the enterprise into individual units. As the previous administrative entity of the enterprise is replaced by legitimate ownership rights, it becomes more difficult to attack this unity both from inside and outside.

The protection against external, government intervention is also an important motivation for transformation. For instance, government intervention could manifest itself in the form of a transfer of an enterprise to direct state control (through suspension of the enterprise councils), the division of an enterprise into several units, or as a privatization initiated by state administrative organs. The corporate form provides some protection against this. A company cannot be taken under direct state control and cannot be split up by the government. Its shares can only be sold by its owner, for instance the former enterprise center. These are additional ownership rights for the 'holding' management. In this sense, the 'spontaneous' transformation of state enterprises into companies can be interpreted as a stage in the battle between the central state organizations and enterprise management for ownership rights.

Nevertheless, companies did not wish to sever all ties with the state. On the contrary, one of the secondary aims behind transformation was to obtain preferences. From 1988 to 1991, every new economic unit, including those founded with assets from a state-owned enterprise, received a 50 percent reduction in their profit tax for a period of three years from the founding date. However, this tax preference has been discontinued since the beginning of 1992.

Finally, when business partners and banks become owners of the new companies, they may bring wider contacts, opportunities for greater choice, and price bargains. Owners' connections and interrelationships between companies and banks can lead to exclusive purchase and sales relations, elimination of competition, and differential treatment, regardless of efficiency considerations.

Thus, from an enterprise's point of view, the establishment of companies may act to restructure production and organization (by eliminating debts and involving new owners), but it can also be a means of conserving previous structures through the administration of purely formal changes. In other words, transformation may be a defensive maneuver in part. Similarly, it may assist organizational decentralization in some cases, but in others strengthen centralization through newly created ownership relations. It may loosen the connection with state administration, but maintain redistribution channels, extend the range of business partners, or reduce competition. Thus the intention to establish companies may mark a step towards market-oriented behavior, but it may also represent an attempt by state enterprises to survive without making any considerable change in their orientation and to preserve those elements of the previous economic mechanism that were beneficial to them. These contradictory aims differ not only across the various types of enterprises, they also co-exist within individual organizations. The actors have not consistently followed particular aims, but rather have fluctuated among them. So the presence of the company form itself indicates neither progressive nor conservative motivations on the part of the enterprises. Neither does it guarantee market orientation in the actual changes following the transformation.

A similar duality characterizes the interests of new owners: other state enterprises, banks, and foreigners. The most important interest of partner companies that buy shares in a transformed firm is a long-term contract for selling or buying their products and services. This motivation often implies helping the enterprise which is undergoing transformation to survive. In other cases, there may be a situation of 'forced ownership'. Because for smaller units it is crucial to receive orders from large buyers, investment in the large company, even if the sum is only symbolic, may be a prerequisite for doing business.

The motivation of increasing profits through stock holding has also appeared among Hungarian firms, but these motivations are more typical of foreign investors. The interests of foreigners, of course, do not exclude obtaining preferences from the government (which may even be attained through direct agreements), as well as maintaining or creating a monopolistic position.

Banks as owners may have different motivations. Speculation on share prices, keeping the companies' accounts, and swapping of debts for shares are among the market-type motivations. The debt-equity swap helps to clear their balance sheets (by formally abolishing non-performing credits), as well as to raise the probability of returns and mobilization of frozen capital (if the shares can be sold). Since these opportunities are uncertain, the swap also involves semi-market elements: chasing such investments and mutual exchange of favors. Finally, banks have been 'encouraged' to acquire property by the government, which has either explicitly exercised control as majority owner of the banks or used the traditional, informal methods of 'persuasion' and preference. The market type of motive seems to be characteristic of small banks, the semi-market type typical for large commercial banks, and the last typical of the State Development Institute, which is directly dependent on the central budget. However, these motives have often been found together within the same organization and transaction.

The last group of organizations concerned in the establishment of companies is that of state administration. In 1988–89, government representatives at various levels were preoccupied with avoiding widespread bankruptcy of state enterprises. But they have faced the same alternatives as the parties concerned, that is, to cancel or reschedule part of the debts, to shrink the organization, or to split it up. The transformations into company form were first considered merely a continuation of the enterprises' struggle for independence. Conversion of debt into shares was considered equivalent to debt cancellation. However, the government could find no better solution. Furthermore, the corporate form may be advantageous for the government. In the short run, it helps the enterprise to survive (without the troubles of re-structuring), it saves central resources, and in the long run it may contribute to positive change in the structure of the economy.

This duality in the motivations of governmental organizations not only reflects the traditional conflict of branch and financial interests (ministries), but also the problem of the role of the state. The state as owner is interested in protecting enterprises and in maintaining and preserving their monopolistic position. On the other hand, as the representative of the public interest, it should guarantee the framework of competition and concentrate on increasing overall efficiency, even if this involves the contraction of some enterprises and the loss of control over others. This dilemma is not a new one, but it assumed paramount importance in the course of debates about privatization. However, the government's effort to decrease state ownership presumed a prior re-centralization of dispersed ownership rights. The government's motivation to recentralize also involved power considerations and the desire to increase revenue from the sale of state assets.

In summary, the company form has spread rapidly even in the state owned sphere, because all of the concerned parties hoped that their particular interests would thereby be furthered. The conflicting interests in company foundation do not exclusively, or even primarily, indicate the diverse efforts of different participants (factory, enterprise, financial institutions, branch ministries). What is more important is that, within a single organization, the foundation of companies seemed to be the appropriate solution to conflicting interests. These can be summarized as both traditional (natural, preserving structure and organization) and profit-oriented efforts. This duality is characteristic of the transforming units, of investors, and of state organizations, and may not necessarily be clearly connected to particular enterprise groups, professions, or positions. The major advantage of the company framework is its flexibility. This is why it could be used both as an escape and as a practical method in the transformation process. As a feature of continuity, it may be one of the symbols of 'peaceful transition'.

4. Spontaneity and the role of the state

The process called 'spontaneous privatization' was spontaneous in that most enterprises did not follow state directives when founding companies, but rather initiated and carried out the process themselves. Governmental organizations were nonetheless active participants in the changes, even before the establishment of the State Property Agency. Thus, the process was not spontaneous in the sense that it would have taken place without any external impetus.

The government encouraged privatization by pressuring enterprises with tight credit and reduced subsidy policies. Positive encouragement also contributed to the process. As discussed above, initially all companies received tax concessions, although later tax preferences were limited to joint ventures with foreign capital. Strict wage controls were abolished for all companies. Debt-equity swaps can also be considered a form of preference.

The state sometimes directly initiated the transformation, especially in cases of bankruptcy. However, the methods and results of these transformations seem to have been only moderately successful. Buyers did not have to compete, assets were undervalued, and the sale price was often criticized. (Tungsram, Ganz Mavag, and Minosegi Cipogyar are prominent examples.) In other cases, state organs were unable to sell the assets due to a lack of interest (for instance, Peti Nitrogenmuvek). In still others, the state bodies blocked the contracts that the enterprise had drawn up because they were not satisfied with the price or the guarantees presented by the potential buyer (Nagykanizsai Sorgyar). The most controversial cases were those in which foreign capital was involved, and therefore state property was really privatized, creating the possibility of a real 'loss' of state property.

Government organs were able to interfere in company foundation through several other channels. The establishment of joint ventures with foreign investment was long dependent upon a license from the authorities. They could also decide on the transformation of units under direct state supervision, those not among the group of self-governing enterprises. Sessions of enterprise councils were always attended by a representative of the ministry, which meant that the supervisory body received information on enterprise plans in advance. Finally, the top management of the firms often consulted the state administration, even if they were not formally obliged to do so.

The governmental organs involved in such cases, however, usually remained rather passive. There are many instances of enterprises under direct state supervision deciding on transformation mainly through internal agreements, while units with enterprise councils did not act without the intermediary role of the government. This shows that the enterprise council was not the cause but rather the consequence of the enterprise management's increased rights. The law on self-governing forms did not create their power, rather it strengthened their power by formalizing decision-making rights. Likewise, the existence of self-governing forms was not the cause of spontaneous privatization. The lack of formal granting of ownership rights to enterprises would not have modified the transformation methods significantly. Rather, it would have simply limited the process to a smaller circle of companies.

At the same time, efforts made to centralize ownership rights may be criticized on the grounds of efficiency and of efficacy. Efforts of this kind occurred under the previous government, before the 1990 elections, for instance the establishment of the State Property Agency and the enactment of the Law on Protection of State Assets. Nevertheless, this attempt to recentralize ownership rights represented the most spectacular change in the intentions of the new government. Its first and most important question was not to work out a comprehensive privatization program or to identify new owners (buyers), but to identify the current real owner (the seller). The government's answer was that it owned the property in question, not the enterprises. The

Antall government has therefore attempted to restore central power through an increase in the status and functions of the SPA to give it more control over transactions. The stated goals of this re-centralization were to provide better protection of state property and to accelerate the pace of privatization.

Formal centralization of decision-making mechanisms, placing the SPA under the Government's supervision and extending its authority, however, did not lead to any clarification of roles. In autumn 1990, the SPA considered the most important result of its activities to be the fact that it had not upset the speed of enterprise-initiated transformations. It was stressed that the firms were ready to cooperate and often requested state assistance themselves.[22] Ironically, the primary concern of enterprise managers is to identify the SPA officials who regulate the firm's transformation, to discover his or her knowledge, goals, and interests, and to work out appropriate arguments and bargaining strategies to realize the enterprise's particular aims.

Thus, attempts at re-centralization increased the dependence of the firms on the state, promote their traditional reflexes to adapt themselves and profit from the vagaries of state administration. In this situation, all elements of transformation and privatization (form, schedule, selection of owners and managers) may be part of a bargain. The indistinct boundaries of state and enterprise decisions recall the interrelationship of economy and politics of the pre-reform period. Deals are again being made by government offices, bodies, committees, and secretariats, in accordance with their own power or financial situation, while responsibility is not clear, and the actual influence of enterprises is strong. This new centralization trap hinders the achievement of the state's goals in their original form, even if they were to exist as coherent policies. Centralization on the governmental level actually strengthens the bargaining positions of the enterprises. Just like the old mechanism, this leads to mutual dependence and exposure.

5. Some conclusions

Continuity in the transformation of the ownership structure is a characteristic feature of the economic transition in Hungary. Elements of continuity include the development of market institutions, legal frameworks, the system of regulation, and the attitudes of broad groups of the population. All three main lines of transforming the ownership structure (founding new private enterprises, starting joint ventures with foreign capital, and establishing companies based on state assets) have historical precedents. Some date as far back as the late 1960s. Others emerged or accelerated in the mid-1980s. The period from 1988 to 1990 was also characterized by these elements of continuity. Despite political changes, government policy changed little, and there were no drastic deviations from the pattern of developments in the transformation of the ownership structure. The last Government of the old regime worked out many elements of the methods, direct and indirect incentives, and legal frameworks for the transformation and privatization of state property. In its first six months in power, the new government followed the same path, with one considerable exception: the attempt to centralize ownership rights and thus the rights to sell or transform enterprises.

In spite of these efforts, continuity can be considered in the line of real change as well. The primary method of transforming state enterprises, 'spontaneous privatization', was not privatization in the formal legal sense of the word. Most new owners – apart from foreign investors – remained state-owned units: the former enterprise center, other enterprises, and banks.

The founding of companies and the modification of ownership structure do not necessarily go together. They may also be realized separately. State assets can be sold to private individuals without a corporate form, and a state company can be transformed into company form without involving any private capital. In the last few years transformation without privatization has been typical in Hungary.

Nevertheless, one has to take into account that transformation into company form may also contribute to privatization. The appearance of asset valuation and securities, that is, the opportunity to divide assets into smaller parts, makes it easier for new, genuinely private owners to participate in the company. Equally, dividing former enterprises into smaller, independent companies facilitates accurate accounting of revenues and losses. This may provide an additional incentive for private persons or their companies to buy shares.

However, this process may also have a reverse effect. The development of a complicated network of corporations, that is, the spread of the 'limited-liability company owned by another limited-liability company owned by a joint-stock company', may hinder the widening of privatization. The identity of the owner, the potential seller, again becomes uncertain in this structure. If the incentives of the parties concerned do not promote further steps toward privatization, neither can anyone from outside, including the formal owner, the state itself.

The transformation of state enterprises into company form was not initially privatization in the strict sense of the word in many cases. Nevertheless, it can be considered as privatization in a special sense. Converting traditional enterprises into companies means transferring additional rights to the management of holding companies: they may sell and buy assets, securities, and play the role of owners *vis-à-vis* the management of the companies in which they hold shares.

The expansion of the rights of managers has been an important element in economic reforms over the last twenty years. Up to 1990, the changes in ownership structure can be considered as ownership reform. This reform did not change the ultimate legal owner, but it did modify the exercise of some ownership rights. It was reform in the sphere of interests: compromise reached through the simultaneous efforts of various participants was typical in this process as well. Finally, it was a reform in its methods. The ideas were still formed in discussions among experts by positional fights between government organs. Their bureaucratic, partial interests were hidden behind efficiency and technical arguments, just as before.

Last but not least, 'spontaneous privatization' was not spontaneous in the sense that it would have take place without any external impetus. State organs influenced the process through positive and negative incentives. Moreover, many of them were active participants in decision-making even before the State Property Agency was established. And since spontaneous privatization was not really spontaneous, the centralized nature of later transformation efforts, initiated by the new government, was not really centralized. Inherited conditions prevented successful recentralization by purely administrative or legal means. For the same reasons, the future of the transformation of the economic and ownership structure is likely to depend more on the behavior of economic agents and social forces than on any government intentions.

Notes

1. The chapter is based on empirical research carried out in Penzugykutato RT (Finance Research Ltd.). The authors of the case studies were Maria Csanadi, Galina Lamberger, Attila Havas, Sara Pasztor, Janose Revesz, and Eva Voszka. A comprehensive study was written by E. Voszka (Tulajdon – reform; Ownership – reform, 1991).
2. 'Economic unit' is the most general term used in this chapter for all forms of entrepreneurships, enterprises, cooperatives, companies, partnerships, etc. The term 'enterprise' refers to directly state-owned (by a ministry or local government) economic units, while a 'company' can be a transformed state enterprise with various types of owners or a new private unit. For more detailed data see Sara Pasztor: *A Fovarosi Cegbirosag Adatainak Elemenze*, 1991, and Eva Voszka, op. cit.
3. The partial data of the Registration Office confirm this estimation; see Pasztor, op. cit.
4. Central Statistical Office (KSH) Information Material, Oct. 1990.
5. According to another report from the KSH, the contribution of small ventures to the GDP was 15 percent in 1988. No reliable data for the past two years are available. Because the KSH conducts an incomplete survey of establishments with less than 50 employees, these estimates are usually considered very conservative or unreliable.
6. KOPINT-DATORG: Report on business cycles, 1990/3.
7. Ceghirnok (Report on firm registration), April 1991.
8. Brief report on company balance sheets of 1989, Taxation and Financial Control Authority (APEH), 1990.
9. Unpublished data from the Ministry of Industry and Trade as of mid-1990.

10. See Eva Voszka, op. cit.
11. A version of this part of the chapter was written as a background study for 'Privatization in Hungary, Poland and Czechoslovakia', by Paul Hare and Irena Grosfeld, 1991.
12. Gabor R. Istvan and Peter Galas: *The 'Second' Economy*, 1981.
13. There are no reliable data. The KSH registers only the units with legal entity status, while most of the small firms transformed did not belong to this category.
14. See Chapter 9, this volume for an extensive discussion.
15. See for instance Erzsabet Szalai: 'Gasdasagi mechanizmus, reformtorekvesek es nagvallatati erdekek' (Economic mechanism, reform intentions and interests of big enterprises), 1989.
16. This involved only about one half of state property and about one half of all employees, because some large units, particularly in heavy industry (oil, aluminium, coal mining, and steel), remained under direct control.
17. The Transformation Law applied only to the founding of a company from a whole enterprise.
18. Erzabet Szalai, op. cit.
19. A privatizatios kormanybiztos eloterjesztese, Nov. 1989.
20. Maria Csanadi: *Nelyek es miert?* (What enterprises and why?), 1991.
21. Data to precisely quantify the extent of private participation do not seem to exist. To the extent that the domestic private owners are legal persons, these assets should be counted among those of private companies. Managers seem to have enhanced their incomes more through transfer pricing arrangements than through asset-grabbing.
22. SPA, Nov. 1990.

References

Central Statistical Office, (1990) 'Information Material,' Budapest, October.

Csanádi, Mária (1991), *Mely vállalatok és miért?* (*What enterprises and why?*) Pénzügykutató Rt.

Csanadi, M., Lamberger, G., Havas, A., Pasztor, S., Revesz, J., and Voszka, E. (1991), 'Case Studies,' Financial Research Ltd., Budapest.

Gábor, R., István and Galasi, Péter (1981), *A 'második' gazdaság* (*The 'second' economy*), Budapest, Közgazdasági és Jogi Könyvkiadó.

Hare, Paul and Grossfeld, Irena (1991), 'Privatisation in Hungary, Poland and Czechoslovakia', Discussion Paper No. 544 (April), London, Centre for Economic Policy Research.

Havas, Attila (1990), *A Minöségi Cipögyár átalakulása* (*The transformation of Minöségi Cipögyár into a company*) Pénzügykutató Rt.

Kopint-Datorg (1990), 'Report on Business Cycles', Budapest, March.

Kornai, János (1991), A privatizáció elvei Kelet-Európában (The principles of privatization in Eastern Europe), Közgazdasági Szemle, No. 11.

Lamberger, Galina (1990), *A Ganz Mávag átalakulása* (*The transformation of Ganz Mávag into companies*), Pénzügykutató Rt.

Major, Iván (1991), 'Privatization in Hungary: Principles and Practices', Working Paper No. 20. Stockholm Institute of Soviet and East European Economics.

Matolcsy, György (ed.) (1991), *Lábadozásunk évei: A magyar privatizáció* (*Years of convalescence: the Hungarian privatization*), Budapest, Privatizációs Kutatóintézet.

Milanovic, Branko (1990), *Privatization in Post-Communist Societies*, The World Bank, Washington DC.

Móra, Mária (1990), *Az állami vállalatok (ál)privatizációja* (*Pseudo-privatization of state enterprises*), Budapest, Gazdaságkutató Intézet.

Pásztor, Sára (1991) 'A Fövárosi Cégbirósag adatainak eleménze' (Analysis of the data of the Registration Office in Budapest), Pénzügykutató Rt.

Pásztor, Sára (1990), *Az Ápisz társasággá alakulása* (*The transformation of Ápisz into Companies*).

Révész, Jánosné (1990), A Budaflax átalakulása (The transformation of Budaflax into a company), Pénzügykutató Rt.

Soós, Attila K. (1990), 'Privatization, Dogma-Free Self-Management and Ownership', *East European Economics*, Vol. 28.

Stark, David (1990), *Privatization in Hungary: from Plan to Market or from Plan to Clans? East European Politics and Societies*, Vol. 4, No. 3.

Szalai, Erzsébet (1989), *Gazdasúgi mechanizmus, reformtörekvések és nagyvállalati érdekek* (*Economic mechanism, reform intentions and interests of large enterprises*), Budapest, Közgazdasági és Jogi Könyvkiadó.

Szalai, Erzsébet (1991), 'Integration of Special Interests in the Hungarian Economy: the Struggle between Large Companies and the Party and State Bureaucracy', *Journal of Comparative Economics*, Vol. 15, No. 2.

Voszka, Eva (1991), 'Kötéltánc – A Ganz Danubius társasággá alakulása', Külgazdaság No. 10., 'Rope Walking, Ganz Danubius Ship and Crane Factory – Transformed into a Company', *Acta Oeconomica*, Vol 42, (3–4).

Voszka, Eva (1991), *Tulajdon–reform* (*Ownership-reform*), Pénzügykutató Rt.

5

The role and impact of the legislature in Hungary's privatization

László Urbán

Introduction

The term 'privatization' is used in a very broad sense in Hungary, and consequently it will be in this chapter also. It refers to a wide range of transactions, including the 'transformation' of the legal form of the traditional state enterprise into a corporation or a limited liability company, as well as increasing the ownership share of agents other than the central government through sale or increase of stock capital. These new owners can be domestic or foreign private persons or companies, employees, or institutions such as banks, social security funds, or even local governments. A privatization can take place in one transaction, for example a 100 percent sale to a foreign investor, or it might involve a series of transactions that extend over several years. However, all of these transactions can be included under this umbrella-term 'privatization' in the sense of the *process* of decomposition and denationalization of traditional state enterprises.

It is a very important peculiarity of the Hungarian privatization process, that although there are rules, these rules serve only as a framework within which there is always room for bargaining among participants. This is the major difference between the centralized, distributive schemes for privatization in Poland and Czechoslovakia, and the case-by-case mechanism of 'spontaneous' or management-initiated transactions dominant in Hungary. In Hungary, the legal framework is applied in the case of each enterprise by different actors, and, as a consequence, almost every case is different. This chapter discusses typical cases, but one must not forget about potential variations.

Every country in Eastern Europe is trying to work out ways to go through this process. In each country, a government agency or ministry is being created as a key institution to design and/or implement the job. In Hungary this is the State Property Agency (SPA). However, the SPA is not the only decision-making institution for privatization in Hungary. In fact, since its establishment in March 1990 the SPA has not been very successful in implementing privatization of state enterprises. Out of 20 enterprises included in the first 'active' program of the SPA in late 1990 only 4 smaller enterprises had been completely privatized by the end of 1991. Its primary function has been the supervision and control of transactions initiated by the management of state enterprises, within the legal framework set by the legislature.

It has been this so-called 'spontaneous privatization' that has produced the second best record of privatization in the region, after Eastern Germany. By the end of 1991, there had been a complete transformation of over 200 enterprises with about 400 billion forints (Ft) value of assets. In addition, partial transformation of enterprises could have involved assets of a similar magnitude (exact data is not available).[1] Together, these two groups probably represent about 20 percent of the total number of state enterprises and 30 percent of the total value. As an average, about two-thirds of the stocks of these transformed companies are still in state hands (owned temporarily by the SPA, or by state enterprises), but about one-third belongs to new owners. The spontaneous privatization and the role of the SPA have been primary topics of analysis in literature written on Hungarian privatization, but the role of the legislature has been neglected so far.

What kind of role can the legislature play in this privatization process? The obvious answer is, of course, *setting the legal framework for the process*. However, this answer does not tell us how much influence the parliament as an institution, separate from the government, has on the process.

The Hungarian political system is a parliamentary one. The current government is supported by a three-party coalition including the Hungarian Democratic Forum, the Smallholder Party, and the Christian Democratic Party, altogether controlling about 58 percent of the seats in the one-chamber legislature. In parliamentary regimes, the government majority is supposed to vote along the line of the government's policy; the executive and legislative branches are not really separate. However, even in a parliamentary system, legislators tend to have their own interests, somewhat different from those of the government, which might result in a kind of division of labor between the two institutions, not only with respect to the forms of their activities but also with respect to the policies they are pursuing. This is even more likely in the case of a coalition government. Of course, government institutions must operate within the legal framework created by the legislature, but the question arises, does the legislature simply approve whatever is suggested by the government, or does it play an active role? Does the legislature make decisions affecting privatization transactions directly, or it is only regulating the environment for the actors?

The first section of this chapter presents the legislative actions that are having a direct impact on the Hungarian privatization process. On the one hand this means creating a legal framework for the process; on the other, it means administering the transfer of entitlements. The legislature can either transfer property free of charge to a new owner, or can sell it and determine how to distribute the revenue. Both kinds of decisions are made in the Hungarian parliament, and both can serve as means of benefitting some social groups. How much revenue can be expected from privatization, and for which purposes will it be used? This question is addressed in the second section. The third section discusses some implications, limitations, and dangers of the influence of the legislature on privatization.

Legislative actions

The privatization process in Hungary had already begun in 1987, well before the free parliamentary elections in 1990. Decentralization of state enterprise assets into newly created companies represented the first cases of the so-called 'spontaneous privatization'. This process was not controlled by any government institution and resulted in some scandals; the assets contributed by state enterprises to the newly created corporations were deeply undervalued, benefitting the private partners excessively.

In June 1990, the newly elected legislature passed two new laws: on the *State Property Agency* (SPA) and on the *Protection of State Property*. The law on the SPA not only assigned controlling power and responsibility to the SPA, but at the same time removed the institution from the direct supervision of parliament and put it under the control of the government (the members of the board of directors are nominated by the Prime Minister, not elected by parliament, as when the SPA was originally established in March 1990). The SPA then became a government agency. These laws did not prevent 'spontaneous privatization', but required the approval of the SPA as a precondition for any privatization transaction (for instance, transformation of an enterprise into a corporation, or selling or contributing a significant portion of its assets). Together with these two laws, the parliament also passed a resolution on the so-called 'Property Policy Guidelines' which was supposed to determine, on a yearly basis, the privatization strategy to be followed by the SPA.

These first legislative actions on privatization only approved the proposals submitted by the government. The representatives of the government coalition supported the government's proposal to place the agency responsible for the implementation of privatization under the control of the government. However, the parliament maintained its right to determine the guidelines for the operation of the SPA, and the SPA must submit a report of its performance to the parliament once a year.

The first guidelines were passed in March 1990 and were supposed to be replaced in October 1990 by new guidelines for 1991. However, instead of submitting new proposals, the government suggested extending the validity of the old guidelines until the end of September 1991. This was approved by the parliamentary majority in September 1990. Since these guidelines were to be the parliament's major instrument for controlling and influencing the privatization policies of the SPA, by approving the government's suggestion they deprived themselves of this power. In October 1991, when the government asked for a further extension of the validity of the same guidelines, the parliament did not agree. However, they decided not to pass new guidelines either, because they wanted to discuss them together with a package of new laws on privatization in February 1992. Therefore, there were no valid guidelines between November 1991 and February 1992.

However, this does not mean that the parliament left itself no instrument with which to affect the privatization process. The SPA had been given responsibility for transactions when state assets are either directly sold or contributed to newly created corporations. In either case, these are supposed to be *business* transactions. But at the same time, the parliament made decisions about *free transfer* of property of state enterprises for new owners, through new legislation.

There are several legislative acts on free transfer of state assets. Hungarian privatization is very often distinguished from the privatization taking place in the other East European countries by the dominance of *sale transactions* as opposed to the *free distribution schemes* planned in other countries. In fact, there is a substantial amount of free transfer involved in the Hungarian practice as well.

The first legislative acts involving free transfer of property were passed by the old parliament, before the free elections. The so-called 'Transformation Act', passed in 1989, contains a paragraph which prescribes that 20 percent of the stock of a state enterprise completely transformed into a corporation must be used to issue special stocks for the *employees* (including managers) of the company. This kind of special stocks can be bought by the employees for a preferential price, with up to 90 percent discount. Through another regulation, the Property Policy Guidelines guaranteed that up to 15 percent of the equity of the corporation created from the assets of state enterprise can be sold to employees with a maximum of 50 percent discount. A new proposal on employee stock ownership was submitted to parliament in January 1992 that, if passed, would likely increase the employee ownership share. These provisions constitute only a framework, and there are a lot of individual variations among cases. In the case of a 100 percent buy-out by a foreign investor, employees might not become owners at all, and at the other extreme there are examples of employee (including managers) buy-outs.

Another kind of free transfer was first guaranteed in the 'Transformation Act', applying to cases of complete transformation, which was later reinforced in the Law on Local Governments in 1990. This law, adopted by the parliament under consensus agreement (because it required two-third majority to be passed), states that local government units are entitled to an ownership share of enterprises transformed into corporations. The law specifies that the value of the transferred stock must be equal to the value of the land used by the company on the territory of the local government concerned. Of course, the local governments are free to sell their stocks at any time, which they are often asked to do, for instance if a foreign investor wants 100 percent ownership. In these cases the final result is that there is a split of the revenue collected from the sale of assets between the SPA and the local governments involved.

Special legislation was also passed by parliament enabling former owners whose property was taken away by the communist regime to receive some compensation. This is different from 'reprivatization', because the law did not call for returning specific assets to their original owners. Rather, compensation will take the form of 'compensation bills', which can be used to buy assets from the public sector, including land for agricultural production. This formula was invented to avoid the harmful consequences of reprivatization on the stability of property rights. Although compensation will be regressive (lower proportion of value is given for larger claims), and cannot exceed 5 million Ft (60,000 USD) per person, it is estimated that it may consume about 50 billion Ft value of assets of state property. The Constitutional Court declared unconstitutional certain parts of the first version of the Law on Compensation passed in April 1991. This version did not treat all kinds of property identically, for example in granting a higher percentage of compensation for nationalized land than for other kinds of property. A revised version of the law was passed in June 1991, and the deadline for submitting requests for compensation was December 1991. This first law on compensation provided eligibility for those whose property was taken away after 1949, but only for physical assets (land, house, shop, company). This will be followed by other laws that favor those whose property was taken away between 1939 and 1949 and those who were deprived of their life or freedom for political reasons.

The first compensation bills appeared in early 1992. The bills are planned to be traded on the stock exchange, but not earlier than the summer of 1992. They are expected to increase the demand for stocks of privatized companies.

Probably the largest package of free transfer of property will take place when the Social Security Fund(s) (SSF) will be given at least 100 billion Ft value of stock. Currently there are two funds: the Pension Fund and the Health Fund. SSFs are guarantee funds to be set up to back social security payments (pensions, medical insurance, health care system). These liabilities are being covered from payroll taxes on a 'pay-as-you-go' basis. This stock transfer is still only a plan and will be implemented gradually. Once enterprises are transformed into corporations and partially privatized, the remaining shares owned by the state are accumulated by the SPA. The SPA is to prepare portfolios of these stocks, including only minority shares in each company, to be turned over to the SSFs. The SSFs need to be given assets, because even the already very high social security payroll taxes (50–60 percent) are not sufficient to cover the current expenditure for pensions and other social security benefits. The Hungarian social security system does not have accumulated funds of assets as a guarantee behind its obligations. These funds can be established only from free transfer of assets from state property. The funds will be required to maintain the value of the portfolio and must not simply consume them. As a consequence of these transfers, SSFs could become important actors on the Hungarian stock exchange (as holding companies), by trading stocks to optimize the composition of their portfolios.

Although this chapter is primarily concerned with the privatization of productive assets, it is worthwhile to underline the importance of *real estate*. The only valuable asset possessed by many enterprises is their real estate: the land and buildings they are using.

Among the privatization decisions of the parliament there is one in particular about certain kinds of real estate. Many buildings owned by churches, especially Catholic and Protestant Churches, were nationalized by the communist regime. Legislation passed by the government coalition returns most *church property* to its original owners. Advocates of this legislation argued that churches play an important role in social life and they cannot fulfil their function without this kind of support.

A related matter is the privatization of apartments owned by local governments. Strictly speaking, this is not a parliamentary issue, but decisions on this are in the hands of the elected bodies of local governments (city councils), so there are important similarities. Local governments are the owners of *state-owned apartments*, in which many people in major cities live as tenants. This could be a large value of assets. At the same time, rent is not set at the market rate, which is still a difficult political question. Because rents are so low and because there is such a large number of these apartments, local governments do not have sufficient funds to keep these houses in good repair. A few years ago they began selling them to tenants, for about 10 percent of the estimated market value. After the municipal elections in 1990, some local governments have considered selling these apartments for somewhat higher prices (but still far below market value), but they met with protest from tenants. The final outcome is still unclear and will vary among different municipalities.

After this overview of legislative actions which have a direct impact on the privatization process, let us now turn to the consequences. First, what are the implications on collectable revenue?

Privatizable enterprises: collectable revenues

In calculating the revenue that may be obtained from privatization, the sales price of assets to be sold must be estimated. But some groups of enterprises will not be privatized, while others are unlikely to produce net revenue from their privatization. In these cases, we shall refer to their book value. For the rest, we shall estimate their business value in order to calculate how much revenue can be collected from their sale, taking into account free transfers prescribed by laws and also calculating the costs of the process.

The total number of uncorporatized state enterprises in Hungary was about 2,000 in 1990. The total book value of their assets was approximately 1,900 billion Ft (26 billion USD). From the viewpoint of revenue collection, these enterprises can be divided into the following sub-groups.

The government is selecting approximately 100 enterprises with a book value of 530 billion Ft *to remain majority state-owned for the long term*. These enterprises will be corporatized, and outside investors will be permitted a minority ownership share in some of these companies, but not by purchasing stocks. They must instead increase the stock capital, which means that there will be no revenue collected by the government. These companies will be regrouped within newly established state holding companies.

In 1990, 400 enterprises with a book value of about 350 billion Ft were *loss-makers*. At least half of these enterprises must be liquidated. Their assets will be sold piece by piece and the proceeds will go to creditors. The other half may be sold after restructuring. There is a plan to create a 'turn-around holding' (under the supervision of the Ministry of Industry) for this purpose, but it is doubtful that a public company will effectively restructure itself. Even in the best case, it is unlikely that there will be net revenue collectable from the privatization of these enterprises.

About 600 enterprises with a book value of 300 billion Ft are *small enterprises founded by local governments*. Each is employing less than 300 people and has a book value of less than 300 million Ft. Some of these enterprises provide public utilities and will be given to their respective municipalities, according to the Law on Local Governments. A special program has been introduced for the remaining small enterprises, to accelerate privatization. Due to the low profitability of these enterprises, the total collectable revenue from their sale is expected to be approximately 50–60 billion Ft.

The *remaining 900 state enterprises* with a book value of 700 billion Ft must provide the source for the free transfers described above, because bankrupt enterprises cannot be used for this purpose. Let us examine the implications of parliament's decisions on the revenue collectable from the privatization of these enterprises.

As mentioned above, when a state enterprise is being transformed into a corporation, a certain share of stocks, or the revenue from its sale, has to be given to the *local governments* that have jurisdiction over the territory where the plant of the enterprise is located. About 8–12 percent of the value of each enterprise is being transferred on the basis of this regulation. The relative share of this portion within the total value of the enterprises is increasing, because the profitability of the enterprises is declining while the value of the real estate is increasing.

The costs of the preferences offered to enterprise *employees* during privatization are averaging around 10 percent of the value of each firm. These preferences can be provided in the form of free transfer of stocks, as a discount on the sale price to employees, and/or as a severance payment for those being laid off.

These two factors together (the rising proportion of revenue due to local governments and the cost of employee preferences) decrease the *book value base of the sellable enterprise stocks to 550–570 billion Ft* (80 percent of 700 billion = 560 billion).

Table 5.1 summarizes the above.

Table 5.1 Sellable enterprises

	Number	Book value (billion Ft)
Total	2,000	1,900
Long-term state	100	530
Loss-makers	400	350
Local government enterprises	600	300
Remaining sellable	900	700

How can we estimate *sale price*? The experience of the completed sales controlled by the SPA has been that the sale price of an enterprise was about seven times the before-tax earnings. Of course, there is a large variance among cases, but we are only concerned with aggregate value. Since total earnings before tax of these 900 enterprises was approximately 90 billion Ft in 1990, the total sale price can be expected to be around 650 billion Ft, which is approximately equal to the total book value.

The revenue collectable from the sales must also be reduced by the following items.

Costs of the privatization process, primarily fees paid for the services of different consulting companies (auditing firms, lawyers, investment banks, brokers, etc.), are around 6–8 percent of the total value of an enterprise.

It is very difficult to estimate the *costs of cleaning up the environment*. The situation in Hungarian industry is not as severe as in the other countries of the region, but the costs can be expected to be around 5 percent of the value of each enterprise. In one case it amounted to over 30 percent of the revenue collected from the complete sale of the company. The SPA has suggested setting up an environmental guarantee fund from 5 percent of the collected proceeds.

The *preferences given to employees* through various forms can be estimated at around 10 percent of the value of each enterprise.

These three factors together suggest a 20–25 percent loss of revenue from the total sales revenue from the viewpoint of the government. If we subtract the estimated loss of revenues from the total expected price, we can estimate a total revenue of about 450 billion Ft for the SPA from privatization.

However, we have not calculated the 'compensation bills' yet, which accounts for another 50 billion Ft. The remaining 400 billion Ft must serve as a basis for the free transfer of stocks for the Social Security Fund(s) (100 billion Ft is planned).

Table 5.2 summarizes the above.

Table 5.2 Collectable revenue

	Business value (estimated, billion Ft)
Total collectable revenue (900 firms)	650
Costs of privatization	50
Environmental guarantee fund	30
Local governments share	50
Employee share	60
Compensation	50
SSF	100
Net collectable	310

What we are left with is in the best case around *300 billion Ft* net collectable revenue, the use of which has not yet been determined by any legislation. The government's announced policy was initially that the revenue collected by the SPA from privatization must be used primarily for *reducing the total accumulated domestic debt* owed by the treasury to the central bank. If we compare this 300 billion Ft with the total domestic debt of over 1,200 billion Ft, it is obvious that this goal can be only partially realized. Nonetheless, the members of the government coalition in the parliament still believe that they can collect large revenues from privatization. They hope to use these not only for reducing the domestic debt, but also to *extend the compensation program* to former political prisoners, to provide *new funds for entrepreneurs*, to create new jobs in *undeveloped regions*, to *develop infrastructure*, etc.

That the government's attitude is similar can be seen from the central budget for 1992. The budget borrowed 15 billion Ft from the SSF in 1991, which is supposed to be paid back with a package of stocks of partially privatized companies or from the proceeds collected from privatization. The Treasury is also planning 20 billion Ft as current revenue for the central budget from privatization of state enterprises for 1992. With both of these items the government wants to reduce the visible amount of central budget deficit, but in fact, these items are only new forms of financing a portion of the current deficit. Privatization is regarded as a source of additional income covering some government expenses which cannot be covered with revenues from taxes.

Implications, limitations, and dangers of the involvement of the legislature

The legislature's decisions have consequences that affect more than the amount of revenue from privatization. These decisions are clearly dominated by *political goals*. The most important questions are who gets what, when, and how much? These questions are, of course, the essence of politics in any country. Politicians favor free transfer of property because they hope to attract voters. They also would like to regard proceeds from privatization as additional money to spend.

The popularity of the government parties has continuously declined since the parliamentary elections in 1990, and they hope that these distributive decisions will reverse this trend. The Law on Compensation was crucial for the second largest government party, the Smallholder Party. The law concerning the return of real estate to churches had similar importance for the third party in the coalition, the Christian Democratic Party. All parties in parliament were in favor of free transfer of assets, at least before the local elections of 1990, which benefited local government interests. They hoped in this way to gain popularity. Plans to further extend subsidized transfers of property to employees are also being worked out. Those plans are spearheaded by the largest government party (Hungarian Democratic Forum), which is hoping to thus bolster its electoral support.

Which political party will benefit, and by how much, from these decisions are questions that can only be answered in the future. However, the prevailing attitude toward privatization cannot be maintained for long, because the value of the assets (and thus revenues), the transfer of which has not yet been determined, is decreasing rapidly. In fact, distributive decisions will affect only that group of enterprises remaining after we eliminate those enterprises not stated for privatization, and those which are clearly not viable and must go bankrupt. Decisions concerning both the transfer of entitlements and the allocation of revenues from sales are limited by the total value of the assets of this group of enterprises. If the economic viability of these companies is the top *economic priority*, then the dangers of overdistribution (resulting from the politician's view of privatization as a distributive game) become clear. There is a real possibility that politicians will not recognize the consequences of their distributive decisions until it is too late.

What is the danger here? Political choices concerning who should be the winners of the 'distributive game', or who should be assigned property rights, do not always contribute to the economic viability of the enterprises. Local governments, company employees and government holding companies will not necessarily manage the property more efficiently than the state did under the old regime. One could argue that politically motivated initial assignments of property rights will have only distributive consequences, and that allocative efficiency will depend primarily on how well defined the property rights become,[2] and how competitive the emerging markets will be. However, experiences of political democracies show us that we cannot really anticipate that politicians will be active only in the initial assignment of property rights or that they will be removed from the conflicts resulting from the operation of the market economy. If politicians intend to play an active role in choosing the initial owners, we can expect them to intervene later also, in favor of their constituents. The same is true with respect to the proceeds from sales. If politicians become accustomed to spending more money than that which they can collect from taxes, they will continue to look for this kind of opportunity.

What are the implications of the decisions of the legislature? In one sense, these decisions are creating additional 'purchasing power' for privatizable assets, which can increase the speed of the process of privatization to the extent that they are transferring entitlements from the government to individuals and institutions. However, this is not always true, because there are additional negotiating and bargaining costs which also result from these laws. Thus, the transaction costs might offset the gains from the presence of additional demand. For instance, if the local governments have veto power over the valuation of the land used by the enterprise on their territory, it could result in long disputes and could even stop the whole process. In addition, although the transaction costs of the introduction, distribution, and trade of 'compensation bills' cannot yet be estimated, a new nationwide bureaucracy had to be built for this job.

Various political actors are struggling to influence the Hungarian privatization process. The three key actors in the center are the SPA, the Ministry of Finance, and the government coalition parties in parliament. Moreover, managers, employees, and investors also try to influence and lobby decision-makers through various means. We have already discussed the motivations of legislators. The SPA was made responsible for control over 'spontaneous' transactions. This control function, however, sometimes becomes active, when the SPA actually determines the privatization plan of an enterprise. The Ministry of Finance is continuously criticizing the SPA for the slow pace of privatization. The motivation behind this criticism is basically twofold. On the one hand, the Ministry of Finance is responsible for the central budget, so they would like to see as much revenue from privatization as possible. On the other hand, the Minister of Finance, as the person in charge of economic policy-making within the government, would like to have the authority to make key decisions on privatization himself. He would like to see the SPA as an agency implementing privatization transactions based on decisions made by the Ministry of Finance. Of course the Minister is aware of the fact that he cannot really provide guidance for hundreds of transactions, so he is in favor of decentralization, providing an even greater role for 'spontaneous' privatization. At the same time, however, he wants to maintain the role of the SPA as a controlling institution over the process. Unfortunately, there is a trade off between control over the process and its speed. If the SPA wants control, it will require time to collect the information necessary for this job, which will naturally slow down the process.

It seems that a workable compromise was found in the newly launched program of 'self-privatization'. Small enterprises employing less than 300 people each can be privatized without the direct controlling participation of the SPA. The enterprise must be privatized by one of 84 consulting firms who have signed contracts with the SPA which enable them to act on the SPA's behalf (within the given legal framework), as privatizing agents for these enterprises. If the program proves to be a success, it could be further extended to larger enterprises.

Conclusion

What kind of role is the legislature playing in the Hungarian privatization process? This Hungarian process is often perceived as differing from those of other countries in Eastern Europe by the dominance of sales as opposed to free distribution. But the Hungarian parliament has passed and is planning to pass laws that involve a substantial amount of free or preferential transfer of state property to new (private or institutional) owners. What then is the difference?

The Hungarian parliament chose not to intervene in the privatization process as drastically as the legislatures of other countries of the region. The managers of state enterprises are not excluded from the process. They are actively involved as privatizing agents at the enterprise level: they are the most important initiators of individual transactions. This gives the Hungarian privatization its unique character. The role of the parliament is to set and shape the legal framework for these transactions, but these are being carried out on an individual basis. In other East European countries the logic is the opposite: political decisions are prescribing universal schemes to be followed by groups of enterprises.

In Hungary it is still the sale transaction, not the free transfer which gives the framework for the individual cases, even if only a portion of the stock is being sold. This allows the government to collect some revenue from privatization. However, once this revenue is collected, it soon becomes caught by the redistributive logic of politics and is increasingly being used to finance current public expenditures.

Notes

1. Eva Voszka's chapter in this volume contains an estimate. (Editor's note.)
2. These are the implications of the so-called Coase-theorem. R. Coase: 'The Problem of Social Cost', *The Journal of Law and Economics*, 3 (1960), pp. 1–44.

6

The different paths of privatization: Czechoslovakia, 1990–?

Jan Mladek

Introduction

The aim of this chapter is to describe those methods of privatization that are either being currently implemented or are in preparation for implementation in Czechoslovakia in the near future. Privatization is a complex economic and social process deserving of thorough and well-rounded study. It is a key issue in economic reform, or more precisely in economic transformation. This chapter is meant to provide readers with as much inside information as possible, and data is provided wherever possible.

Sections 2 and 3 describe reprivatization and privatization, and comprise the core of this chapter. Section 2 contains a thorough discussion of reprivatization (restitution) and the laws regulating it. In Section 3, the standard methods of privatization are described as well as the special scheme of voucher privatization.

The remaining sections discuss the particular problems of reprivatization and privatization in different branches and different categories of property. Agriculture and cooperatives, which pose perhaps the greatest dilemmas for Czechoslovak reformers, are discussed in Sections 4 and 5. Section 6 explains the impasse in housing reform. The roles of wild privatization and foreign privatization are covered in Sections 7 and 8. The special problem of political party property transformation is elaborated in Section 9. And finally, an Appendix provides readers with background data on the performance and structure of the Czechoslovak economy.[1]

1. Reprivatization

Reprivatization is the return of property to those who owned it prior to its nationalization after 1948. Currently, the predominant categories of property being reprivatized are houses, restaurants, hotels, workshops, stores, and small factories. It is important to note that in 1948, the state already dominated ownership, so that 82.3 percent of the 'means of production'[2] were state owned, 4 percent were owned by cooperatives, and only 13 percent were private. The contribution of the private sector to economic performance was 33.4 percent of the whole net material product,[3] 95 percent of agricultural production, 13.7 percent for industrial production, and 15.3 percent for construction.[4]

These properties are being taken from the state and legal persons (mainly state enterprises, cooperatives, etc.), and from physical persons only in those cases where they violated the law valid at the time in obtaining the property.

Eligibility for reprivatization is restricted to physical persons who are resident Czechoslovak citizens whose property was nationalized between 25 February 1948 and 1 January 1990. Legal persons (excluding the churches), foreigners, and Czechoslovak emigrants living abroad are ineligible.

Reprivatization has been the subject of a long and continuing discussion. Initially, there was the question of whether or not to reprivatize at all. This was followed by lengthy debates on what to privatize, to whom, from whom and how. In this section, I shall recount these discussions as they unfolded chronologically, in order not only to acquaint the reader with how each of these questions was raised and resolved, but also to provide some insight into why the scope of reprivatization has become so wide.

Reaching a decision on the question of whether or not to reprivatize at all was very difficult, as were subsequent questions of 'to whom' and the complicated problem of 'how' to do it. At the beginning of 1990, while the majority of reform economists supported privatization, they did not support reprivatization. They believed reprivatization would be too costly and too time-consuming. It would lead to thousands of court processes over property claims, further complicated by the fact that in many cases property claims were not clear. For instance, multiple claimants for one piece of property have appeared, confusing the issue of the legitimate owners. It was considered easier to begin privatization with a clean slate, that is, without facing the long waiting periods necessary to determine whether a piece of property would be reprivatized before it became free for privatization.

Gradually, however, public opinion regarding reprivatization changed. The metamorphosis began with the debate over the rehabilitation of former political prisoners. Punishment for those imprisoned had often included the confiscation of their property, and virtually everyone agreed that this property should be returned to them. But, people argued, if property is returned to individual political prisoners then it should also be returned to the Catholic Church, especially since many clergymen were among the political prisoners. The first reprivatization law, No. 298/1990 – On Regulation of Property Relations of Religious Orders and Congregations and the Olomouc Archdiocese, resulted from these arguments.

The expropriation of the Church's property followed a unique path in Czechoslovakia in the early 1950s. Clerical orders were simply dissolved; monks and nuns were sent to camps, prisons, or factories. There were no formal decrees (unlike other cases) concerning the nationalization of Church property. This property was simply confiscated by the state and its organizations. In 1948, the Catholic Church owned vast amounts of land in Czechoslovakia (6 percent of all agricultural land and numerous other estates, including churches, parishes, and monasteries). Eight hundred of these properties, mainly monasteries, were expropriated after 1950 (the beginning of the communist campaign against the Catholic Church).

In the first round of reprivatization, it was decided that 74 of these would be returned to the Church and its religious orders. Because of the complete lack of documentation, those 74 properties briefly described in the law were simply declared property of the Catholic Church.[5] An additional 176 are included in the amendment to the law No. 298/1990 which was discussed in summer 1991 but postponed because of numerous difficulties with the first 74 properties. If passed, this would conclude the reprivatization of Church property. The remaining roughly 550 properties were not even demanded by the Church because they were either destroyed or in bad condition. This reprivatization of properties to the Catholic Church was also dampened by the hostility it engendered from the Protestant Churches.

At present, the question of Church agricultural land remains open. And even with properties which have been privatized so far, many problems remain to be solved. There are many schools, museums, and health service facilities housed inside monasteries, and the relation between them and their new owner, the Church, is often complicated.[6]

With law No. 298/1990 effectively initiating reprivatization, it was clear that some reprivatization had become necessary. The question became to what extent reprivatization should be pursued. It seemed simplest to start with the last government and branch ministry decrees on nationalization, laws which were issued after the year 1955, mainly because this was the well documented last wave of nationalization. Furthermore, there were practically no political objections to this kind of reprivatization because at stake were small pieces of real estate such as rental houses, pubs, shops, restaurants, workshops, stores, car services, etc. The majority are family firms. The number is estimated at 80,000. Everyone felt that it would be very troublesome to sell this kind of property in an auction since the former owners were often still living in the same house with his/her former shop, pub, etc. That is, the continuity of ownership in these cases was usually not completely broken.

On 2 October 1990 the law No. 403/1990 on Relieving the Consequences of Some Property Injustice (Small-scale Reprivatization Law) was approved. The essence of this law is the return of or compensation for property nationalized after 1955. Compensation was to be paid in cases where the property was sold to another private person or was destroyed. Former property owners were given a period of six months (1.11.1990–30.4.1991) to petition the current user (in the majority of cases, a state organization) for their former properties. The current user is then obliged to return the property to the former owner, except in the case of a dispute at which point the court would be consulted. Court services and notary services were free for claimants. On the other hand, state organizations were required to pay to the Ministry for Privatization 3,000 CSK (100 USD) for each day of delay resulting from their actions. But those claimants who failed to apply in time will have nothing returned to them. Overall, law-makers attempted to protect former owners against the hostility of state organizations.

While at first the procedure seemed relatively simple, many problems soon arose. Only a few days after the enactment of the new law (after 1 November 1990), reformers encountered the dilemma of what to do with around 170 villas that had been nationalized and then used by foreign embassies in Prague. Many countries threatened to expropriate Czechoslovak property in their countries if 'their' villas were returned to their former owners. The parliament quickly amended the law and excluded those villas from reprivatization. The former owners were given securities instead. Then, in April 1991, another amendment to the Small-scale Reprivatization Law was passed that returned those real estates used by embassies to the former owners, but with the requirements that those owners must then rent them for a minimum of ten years to the current users (the time for application is longer in this case, up to the end of September 1991). The same ten-year rule of forced rental agreement was also applied to social, medical, and cultural bodies that were housed in facilities in privatized real estates.

The small reprivatization is now finished except for an unknown number of court disputes about claimed property. Small-scale reprivatization was the first big penetration into the monopoly of state property. It helped in the development of a private retail-trade sector by enabling private entrepreneurs to immediately open either their own reprivatized shops or more readily buy or rent space from persons receiving property through the scheme of small-scale reprivatization.

One problem for this mode of reprivatization is the case of destroyed property. In cases where the property had been destroyed, money compensation was to be paid to the claimant, but the valuation of this property was determined from an old decree of 1964. Official prices and derived compensation were thus usually much lower than today's market price. The time elapsed would only be taken into account by simply adding 3 percent (with no compounding) to the value for each year. Many questioned the justice of this law because of these methods of valuation and discounting.

Another political dispute is caused by the problem of nomenclature cadres purchasing expropriated real estates for low prices from the state. The law generally treats all purchases by physical persons as good faith transactions, if violation of laws valid at the time of transaction is not proven. Former owners of such properties were to be compensated only up to the level of the official price, which again is usually far under the true market price.

The next step in the reprivatization effort was the law No. 87/1991 on Out-of-Court Rehabilitations or the Large-scale Reprivatization Law. It states that physical property that was nationalized or expropriated from Czechoslovak citizens (physical persons) between 25 February 1948 and 1 January 1990 but not included in the small-scale reprivatization scheme would be returned to its former owners. (Excluded from this scheme are land and forest which present special problems and are dealt with in a special law, the details of which are in Section 6.) Former owners were again given six months from 1 April 1991 to apply for their property. In the case of more than one owner, the whole property would be returned only to those former owners who had applied in time. Any partial owners who did not file their claims within this six-month deadline lost their claim to the property. If nobody applied by the end of the six-month period, the property would be sold in auction or privatized using some other method.

Very dramatic public discussion of the reprivatization issue started only with the debate over this large-scale reprivatization law (beginning of 1991). The whole discussion was reopened and reprivatization was connected with the question of the rehabilitation of former political prisoners and other victims of the communist regime. Discussions were often very emotional and economic arguments were often mixed with political, legal, and moral ones. This left opponents of the large scope of the reprivatization effort in a difficult political position. All attempts to limit the scope of reprivatization were taken as attempts to prevent the rehabilitation of the political prisoners and other victims of the communist regime.

The key questions concerned the scope of reprivatization, specifically the relevant time frame and set of persons who would be included in this reprivatization scheme. With respect to time, many different cut-off dates were suggested. There were propositions to go back to 1945 or even to 1939.[7] The proposal for using 1939 was designed to return the Jewish property which had been expropriated from the Jews who were sent to Auschwitz. This property had been given to German, Czech, or Slovak owners, usually those who helped send the Jews to concentration camps. Furthermore, much of this property was nationalized from these recipients only after the communist *coup d'état* in 1948. In the end, however, this kind of property was completely excluded from the reprivatization scheme.

The principal motivation for using 1948 as the cut-off was to avoid the problem of the property belonging to the Sudeten Germans who were expelled from Czechoslovakia in 1945–46 by the Czechoslovak government with the agreement of the victorious powers of World War II. If the cut-off line were to fall before 1948, the German issue would have to be addressed, opening an extremely sensitive political problem. Therefore, it was decided that the final cut-off would be 25 February 1948, the day of the communist coup in Czechoslovakia.

Yet another dramatic problem was the question of whom to include in the reprivatization scheme. Should Czechoslovak emigrants be included? The conclusion was that only to those who return and take up permanent residence in Czechoslovakia would property be returned. There was an attempt to reopen the issue in September 1991, but the Federal Assembly rejected the proposal to amend the law on large-scale reprivatization.

Then there was the issue of legal persons, beginning with joint-stock companies. One of the original proposals included compensating stockholders for their holdings prior to nationalization. Finally, this proposal was rejected because it was thought to be administratively unmanageable. Initially and throughout most of the reprivatization process, the philosophy that property in-kind is to be returned but financial losses are not to be compensated has been followed (communism was taken as an uninsured catastrophe). It was believed that this distinction would minimize bureaucratic red tape and expedite the privatization process. Later, however, some provision for compensation in the case of destroyed properties has been enacted.

Czechoslovakia (aside from the former GDR) has the largest reprivatization scheme of all former socialist countries in Central and Eastern Europe. Large-scale reprivatization has delayed small- and large-scale privatization, because in many cases property rights are unclear, and it was often necessary to wait six months to determine whether the former owner of a property would make a claim. Despite the fact that the share of private firms was not high in 1948, as mentioned above, the majority of firms have at least a small part of their property which is under reprivatization. The fate of this old private property must be determined before privatization can begin. The administrative problems involved in handling property rights are enormous. The Czechoslovak legal system is under terrible strain, not having been designed to handle such large transfers.

Another problem is the attempt by some of the former owners of property to push for a cut-off earlier than the 25 February 1948 deadline. This is especially the case with the old nobility. Their castles were usually nationalized between 1945 and 1948, but the contents much later. There are even cases of members of the old nobility taking the furniture and pictures from publicly opened castles.[8] The largest noble families sent representatives from abroad to become Czechoslovak citizens, with a clear aim to lobby for returning family property. This kind of reprivatization is giving little or no gain to economic performance and at the same time is undermining political support for economic reform.

3. Privatization

In 1983 81.9 percent of capital assets were under state control in Czechoslovakia; another 10.5 percent were in cooperative hands, and only 7.6 percent were in private hands.[9] The share of the private sector in net material product creation in 1989 was 3.6 percent, that of cooperatives 12.6 percent, and the majority of production – 83.8 percent – was produced in state enterprises.[10] From these numbers, it is clear that the task for economic transformation is huge. By comparison with privatization programs in the West, Czechoslovakia's must proceed much more quickly. For example, if the Czechoslovak privatization had the speed of the British program in the 1980s, complete privatization would not be finished for 600 years. This led reformers to the development of a 'non-standard' approach to privatization: the so-called voucher privatization. The whole process of privatization was divided into small-scale and large-scale privatization. The first one was developed earlier to privatize first of all shops, restaurants, hotels, small firms, and other smaller items. The method of privatization in this case is public auction; it is described in Section 3.1. The remaining part of privatization is called large-scale privatization and includes, beside standard methods like tenders, auctions, direct selling, and selling of shares on stock exchanges,[11] also the non-standard approach of voucher privatization; all of this is the topic of Section 3.2.

3.1 Small-scale privatization

Small-scale privatization was allowed by law No. 427/1990 on the Transfer of State Property and Some Goods to Other Juristic or Natural Persons. The main idea is to sell smaller property directly to private persons in Czechoslovakia in an auction.

The original aim was to sell 100,000 to 120,000 items in this program. But in October 1991, the Czech minister for privatization Mr Tomás Ježek declared on TV that the small privatization program will be finished with the selling of only 23,000 items, 13,000 of which are already sold and 10,000 prepared for auctions. This does not mean that the original goal of privatization was abandoned. The items from small privatization will be moved into the auctions and tenders of the large-scale privatization, which permits selling property with obligations, which was a troublesome brake for small-scale privatization. Nevertheless at the moment the further developments are not quite clear because politicians' and officials' statements are often rather contradictory.

Before the approval of this law, there were many complicated discussions. Employees in shops and hotels wanted special rights during the auctions. They wanted closed rounds of auction 'just for employees'. Trade unions in the retail trade threatened industrial action, strikes, etc.

At a special meeting of all three governments (Czech, Slovak, and Federal) 'economic' ministers (ministers responsible for different economic branches and issues) were nearly outvoted by 'non-economic' ministers who favored the employees' closed-round auctions. The economic ministers prevailed with the idea that the auctions will be open to all Czechoslovak citizens in the first round and to everybody in the second round. Nevertheless this original proposal included special access to loans for employees for up to 50 percent of the starting price with a low interest rate. Quite surprisingly, parliament refused all proposals to help employees by special loans. In the final law, there are no preferences for employees.[12]

The auction of the shop must be announced thirty days before it is to occur. The starting price is determined by book value. Auction participants are required to pay a fee of 1,000 CSK (33 USD) for participation and deposit a refundable 10 percent of the starting price or 10,000 CSK (333 USD) at least to take part in the auction.

The auction process is in two rounds. In the first round, only people who are or were Czechoslovak citizens at least some time since 25 February 1948 or legal persons consisting of Czechoslovak citizens, can participate. The participants are restricted by citizenship, since foreign participation in small businesses has been seen as desirable only if Czechoslovak citizens are not interested or do not have enough money to start a business. Government policy is to create an indigenous business class. Legal persons founded in communism are precluded from participating, because it could lead to the transfer of the privatized property back into state or cooperative hands. In the second round, foreigners may participate.

The auction follows the normal procedure, if there are people willing to pay the starting price or more. If not, a type of Dutch auction is utilized if there are at least five participants in the auction: the starting price is progressively decreased by amounts of 10 percent up to 50 percent. This is the case in the first round; for items not sold, a second round is held in which the price can decrease to 20 percent of the starting value.

Publicly, small-scale privatization is perceived as the best method of privatization, because there is the best public control of the process of selling state property. The prices at auction have often been much higher than the starting prices. By 15 September 1991, 13,178 units had been sold in the Czech and Slovak Federal Republic for 11.291 bln CSK (376 mln USD), when the combined starting price equalled only 7.803 bln CSK (260 mln USD). There were 3,189 units, which were sold completely, including both the buildings and the land. Of the aforementioned 13,178 auctions, 2,228 were done in the Dutch way. Most of the rest of the items originally planned for small-scale privatization are supposed to be sold in the auctions of large-scale privatization.

One of the biggest units which was privatized in this way, so far, is the department store, Prosek, (Prague 9) with 6,810 m^2 of selling space and 11,396 m^2 of land. The starting price was 40.5 mln CSK (1.35 mln USD), and the department store was bought for 95 mln CSK (3.166 mln USD), plus it was necessary to pay 41 mln CSK (1.366 mln USD) for the inventory (sold separately).

Very often, only shop (pub, hotel) equipment and not the buildings are sold in this scheme of small-scale privatization. The winner of the auction originally had only the right to a two-year rental agreement of the premises. But in October 1991 this agreement was extended to a five-year obligatory rental agreement. Currently any extension beyond the five-year agreement must be decided between the auction winner and the real-estate owner.

The auction scheme is working quite well for smaller property. In the case of larger property (in Czechoslovakia, valued at more than a couple of million CSK (60,000–200,000 USD), there is the risk of collusion in the auction. If there are, for example, only two real bidders, one way of cheating is obvious: one participant could pay the other for letting him win in the auction and three other people for their formal participation. It thus becomes possible to have state property sold for only 50 percent of the starting price. Domestic savings are limited, and loans are difficult to obtain (current interest rates are 14 percent for these loans and collateral is demanded); therefore people compete hard for smaller property and pay half a million CSK (16,667 USD) for a kiosk with 7 m^2; on the other hand, those who have larger savings can obtain bigger properties relatively cheaply.

This mode of privatization is under close public control, so the real fight is about which property to include in small privatization. Outside the small privatization scheme the possibilities for protectionism, bribing, etc. are much bigger. The old bureaucracy is often looking for foreign partners to establish joint ventures with the best part of their network and in this way, to preserve at least part of their past power. Some foreign firms have nothing against collaboration with the corruptible bureaucracy, which will control the Czechoslovak part of a joint venture.

Despite these problems of shortage of domestic savings and possibilities for abuse, the small privatization by auctions has already helped in the process of market creation especially in trade and services. The auctions will continue, but probably in the framework of large-scale privatization, because it permits selling the property with obligations, which was not permitted under small-scale privatization: probably its biggest shortcoming. Those obligations are of various kinds like an obligation to run the given activity for some time, to fulfil obligations of a previous owner or to train an apprentice. It was probably the most important lesson so far learned from the process of small privatization: it is necessary to privatize not only property, but also the state's obligations!

3.2 *Large-scale privatization*

The law on large-scale privatization is law No. 92/1991 on Conditions of Transferring State Property to Other Persons and was approved in April 1991. But this law did not finish the discussion about large-scale privatization. The law was a compromise between supporters and opponents of the non-standard method of privatization: the voucher scheme. Both standard and non-standard methods of privatization will be used. Standard methods include auctions, tenders, direct selling to foreign investors and selling shares.

Besides those standard methods, however, there is also a voucher privatization planned. One reason for this is the lack of savings among Czechoslovak citizens that could be used to buy or invest in enterprises, and it is believed that using only standard methods would either take too long or lead to too much majority foreign control. Another reason is political; reformers believe that they will obtain political support for the general reform effort by including the citizens in the privatization effort. In practice, the scheme entails distributing the property for nearly free among Czechoslovak citizens older than eighteen. The vouchers are distributed to those who pay a nominal fee (1,000 CSK or 33 USD per head).

The law leaves open the extent to which privatization will be divided among standard and non-standard methods. This will be decided by the ministries of privatization selecting a privatization project for each enterprise prepared by management or other interested parties. The Ministry for Privatization prefers competition of two or more privatization projects for one enterprise. The branch ministry evaluates the project(s), but the final decision is up to the privatization ministry (in special cases up to the government). The privatization project must describe how the state property was obtained, the valuation of the privatized property (book value, except in the case of foreign investors where an estimate of market value is required), the legal form of the new enterprise (trading company, joint-stock company), whether and to what extent investment vouchers will be used, the form of selling, and prices. This means that in the end, the scope of voucher use and other parameters of large-scale privatization will be determined by applications of this rather open-ended law.

The sequence of events in the voucher privatization plan is as follows. At the beginning of 1992 come the first of two 'waves'. Together the two waves are planned to bring about the privatization of some 4,129 enterprises (2,285 in the first and 1,844 in the second). Each wave lasts roughly half a year and consists of 4–6 rounds, which are used for overcoming the valuation problem. The starting price of the state companies, transformed in the meantime into joint-stock companies, is set administratively in terms of vouchers per share: the first approximation of the starting price is calculated through book values of privatized firms and the number of participants in the voucher privatization. The starting price is the same for the shares of all companies, but different companies have different numbers of shares.

In each round, Czechoslovak citizens demand the shares of different companies. If the demand for shares of a particular enterprise is lower than or equal to the supply, the shares are given to those who demanded them and the remaining shares are brought to the next round at a lower price. If demand is only slightly higher and the demand of individual citizens is lower than supply, then sales to Investment Privatization Funds (not to individual citizens) are reduced and the shares distributed. If demand for an enterprise's shares is substantially higher than the supply, no shares are sold in that round and all shares go into the next round at a higher price. Thus, to the next round go those shares that were not sold due to low demand, forcing a price decrease, and those for which demand was too high, forcing a price increase. The whole process of privatization is highly centralized with computers executing all of these comparisons of demand and supply.

There are two ways for citizens to participate in the voucher privatization: as individuals or through investment funds. Investment Privatization Funds (IPF) can be used by those citizens who do not want to invest themselves. Some of them have already been created by state-owned commercial banks; some others are being created by private firms. The citizens will be owners of the shares of the IPF, which manages the portfolio. Investment funds should provide the opportunity to those people who are either unable or unwilling to participate personally and also should help in the creation of control groups in the newly privatized firms.

For the moment, it is unclear how well large privatization will function in practice. The general idea is accepted by the public, at least in the Czech republic, but this could always change. The number of participants 8.2 million people, out of a maximum of 11.5 million, people – all adults above eighteen in ČSFR. For running the 'first wave', 1.6 million people are required just to cover the costs, which are estimated at 1.6 bln CSK (53 mln USD).

There is virtually no regulation of trade with shares and no protection against insider trading. This can bring plenty of problems to the legal and political credibility of the privatization process. For example the Communist Party wants to establish a communist mutual fund.

Members and supporters of the Communist Party are asked to invest their vouchers in this fund, to be used for obtaining control of the best firms about which they have inside information through the communist nomenklatura.

An open question at the beginning of the program in fall 1991 was the supply side. The list of firms to participate in first-wave large-scale privatization, second-wave, and not at all was known, but the share of vouchers in the whole privatization was not yet known (see Table 6.1).[13]

Table 6.1 Privatization plan of ČSFR governments

Under control of	1st wave	2nd wave	No privatization	Liquidation	Total
Czechoslovak government	29	23	76	1	129
Czech government	1,630	1,248	584	41	3,503
Slovak government	626	573	611	40	1,850
Total	2,285	1,844	1,271	82	5,482
% of all	41.7	33.6	23.2	1.5	100

Source: *Ekonom*, No. 43, 1991

The start of voucher privatization was postponed because of unpreparedness on the supply side (slowness in evaluating the enterprises' privatization projects), and the start of the whole program was not until June 1992 and not in January as originally planned. Quite paradoxically, under the *laissez-faire* flag the biggest experiment of social engineering since the communist creation of the CPE in the 1950s is prepared. Hopefully, the results will be better than in the case of communist social engineering experiments.

4. Reprivatization and privatization in agriculture

Czechoslovak agriculture seems to be a puzzle for economic reformers. The country is self-sufficient in food, which is produced on 245 state farms (average size 5,900 hectares) and on 1,660 cooperatives (average size 2,630 hectares). The state farms are producing one-third of agricultural production, two-thirds are produced in cooperatives, and the share of the private sector is negligible. Despite the fact that the Soviet model of collectivization was implemented, the results were not so catastrophic. First of all, the collectivization terror was not comparable to the Soviet case. Czech 'kulaks' were not sent to Siberia, but to North Bohemia or to the cities, from whence it was often possible to return. And, after some time, peasants developed ways to live with bolshevism in cooperatives. It was probably easier than in other countries, because Czechoslovakia was, at the beginning of the experiment with communism, a relatively wealthy country. That is why large-scale subsidization was possible.[14] Furthermore, industry was able to supply machinery, chemicals, fertilizers, pesticides, etc. All of these factors contributed to the relative success (self-sufficiency) of Czechoslovak agriculture in comparison with the past and with other former socialist countries.

The costs of this 'kind of success', however, are high. First, agricultural production is inefficient. Second, the basic means of production in agriculture, soil, is in bad shape. Cooperatives have used the soil without much thought of the future; in fact, they were destroying it. Finally, the highest costs are paid probably indirectly through a heavily polluted food chain and damage to the environment.

On the other hand, the situation of agricultural workers has improved. They are not under pressures similar to those of private peasants. They need not care for their animals every day, seven days a week, all year. On cooperatives and state farms, workers have holidays and work in shifts. Furthermore, the wages in agriculture are higher than the average for the whole economy. In 1989 the average wage for the economy as a whole was 3,340 CSK (111 USD) per month, but in cooperatives it was 3,788 CSK (126 USD) per month and in state farms 3,452 CSK (115 USD).

In this situation of relative 'success', it is very difficult to enact the de-collectivization. The productive assets, which were used forty years ago were usually destroyed or rebuilt as garages, etc. There is practically no discussion in Czechoslovakia about the right of the people to withdraw the land from cooperatives and start private business. Furthermore, the majority of land was private even in communist Czechoslovakia. People had their land taken into cooperatives, but the land was still theirs *de jure*, if not *de facto*. Now, however, they can withdraw the land from coops or ask coops to pay them for using their land. The problem is that few people are eager to go private (some estimates are that 3–5 percent of peasants would like to be private).[15] The question is whether, in a more hostile environment for cooperatives, people will not be more eager to be private.

In this situation, the question has become how to transform the cooperatives into either cooperatives of owners or into joint-stock companies. Should property shares be distributed according to the land and other property given to the cooperatives or according to the labor used for improvement of cooperatives in the last forty years or according to all productive factors (labor, land, capital)? The last option is the most probable; but it will probably be implemented with limits, such as that the one factor can be utilized as the criteria for 15 percent to 50 percent of the distributed property. For this kind of decision, there is an important question: who will decide how to divide cooperatives' property: the law, the current members, landowners? There were 645,552 people working in agricultural cooperatives in 1989, but less than half of them had their own land. On the other hand, there are more than 3 million agricultural landowners of whom only 10 percent are working in agriculture today.[16] This means that if current members were allowed to decide about distribution of property, they would probably prefer the distribution according to labor devoted to the cooperative; if the landowners were to decide the mode of property division, they would prefer distribution according to the land.

Parliament did not reach a consensus about this point in spring 1991 and approved only a narrow version of the law dealing only with land reprivatization: the law No. 229/1991, on Regulation of Ownership of the Land and Other Agricultural Property. This law allows reprivatization of land and agricultural capital assets up to the end of 1992. This means that reprivatization in agriculture was solved, but not the transformation of the cooperatives. Cooperative transformation was postponed and parliament's decision was to solve the transformation of all kinds of cooperatives in one law. This law is being discussed in the winter of 1992; it will contain the rules about transferring today's cooperatives into cooperatives of owners or into joint-stock companies.

5. Transformation of consumer, housing, and productive cooperatives

Consumer and productive cooperatives were producing about 6.6 percent of Czechoslovak NMP in 1989, and employment was 353,205 people, or 4.5 percent of the total labor force. There were about 403 productive and apartment cooperatives in 1989 with an average staff of 453 people. Today, the number is greater, because of the birth of new cooperatives and splits in some large, established coops. Needless to say, the importance of consumer, housing, and productive cooperatives in the total economy is much greater, because their activities are concentrated in services (especially apartments) and were not calculated in NMP. In GDP, the share of cooperatives is higher.

The importance of the problem of cooperatives was for a long time undervalued by reformers. Only in the middle of 1991, after parliament's failure to approve the law concerning agricultural cooperatives, did serious discussion of the issue begin. It was decided by the parliament that the transformation of all kinds of cooperatives will be accomplished in one law.

At the beginning of the reform attempt, there was a suggestion to privatize cooperatives as state-owned firms. The differences between coops and state-owned firms were seen as negligible. Cooperative property was taken under communism as a part of the so-called 'socialist property', and the movement was in the direction of erasing differences between state and cooperative property. Both kinds of property were assumed to merge into the so-called 'all people property'. But the cooperatives found strong supporters, especially among former reform communists from the Prague Spring like Mr Dubček, Rychetský and others (for example, Rychetský, (1991)). Their argument was that cooperatives had a long tradition in pre-communist Czechoslovakia (in 1948, they produced 2.6 percent of NMP, *Historical Yearbook of CSSR*, Prague 1985) and that, in fact, Stalinist communism undermined genuine cooperatives, which should be revived from the old ones. Furthermore, there are legal problems, because a large share of Czechoslovak cooperatives had their antecedents in prewar Czechoslovakia. The cooperative lobby is not only against privatization of its coops, but it asks for the return of the property which was taken from coops in 1952.

Therefore only the reprivatization laws currently apply to cooperatives. They may lose property to former owners, but as legal persons, they have no right to make claims. There is no law which would press them to privatize. Sometimes they are privatizing on their own, like consumer cooperative Jednota, which is trying to sell all shops with a turnover lower than 70,000 CSK or 2,333 USD per month, or to lease the least profitable shops to private persons and trying to run only the most profitable parts of its network. Nevertheless this is the cooperative's decision, and the government cannot force them to do so.

Before the law about cooperatives is approved by the parliament, some consensus about the issue has already been reached. Those who decide about the cooperative transformation are current and former members of cooperatives as well as those who contributed some property into the cooperative. Another agreement is that labor, land, and capital should be the factors according to which property should be distributed, but the share of these different factors is not yet settled. The idea to exclude those who will participate in cooperative transformation from voucher privatization was not accepted in the end.

6. Privatization and reprivatization in housing

Housing was the sector closest to a mixed economy even in the worst Stalinist years in Czechoslovakia. There were some 2 million state-owned flats in 1989, 1 million cooperative flats and more than 2 million flats in private houses.

Housing is perhaps the most neglected area of the reform attempt. Thus far, the only thing which has been done is the reprivatization of houses nationalized after 1948. In fact, even that process continues. The real move away from control in the hands of the state bureaucracy to those of private owners is still a problem. The protection of renters, which was introduced in Czechoslovakia by Adolf Hitler, still survives, including enforced rent ceilings and the practical impossibility of evicting renters. There are still some cases of flats built before the war where the rent is the same in 1991 as in 1936. In the meantime, we have had three kinds of currency, two monetary reforms, not to mention two occupations of the country, and the price has remained constant. There are cases of people who still pay only 100 CSK (3 USD) per month, because the rent was settled before the war. Average rent is some 300 CSK (10 USD) to 600 CSK (20 USD) for 3 + 1 state flats (three rooms and the kitchen, 50 square meters). For the same size cooperative flat, it is roughly twice as much.

Private owners cannot effectively exercise control, because they cannot evict renters (excluding mafia methods) and they cannot increase the rent, because rents are still regulated prices. In the first step before gradual liberalization, administrative rent increases must be performed. The first step should be to increase the rent in state-owned houses to the level of cooperative houses. This was accomplished on 1 July 1992 when the rents in state-owned flats were increased by 100 percent. Additionally, as of January 1992 the prices for services connected with housing were increased by 80 percent for all kinds of flats.

This is not the first plan to increase the rents in state-owned flats, but the earlier ones were rejected by politicians. The impasse is a result of the political business cycle. It is clear to nearly everybody that rents must be increased, but there are too many voters living in state flats. At the moment the government is afraid of the peoples' reaction to rent increases. There have been several price shocks for the average citizen, and another may not be bearable. On the other hand, if this first step towards market prices in housing cannot be completed, there will be many social consequences, since a shortage of housing is a barrier to labor mobility and inhibits other developments of a market economy.

This entire situation is rather strange, because the housing sector was seen in the past by some economists as the most hopeful sector for changes, because there was always mixed economy in this sector. What are the reasons for delays in the housing sector? Why should there not be quick liberalization of prices? The problem is that a rather unfortunate distribution of population developed in the distorted market. There are too many people in Prague and other large cities; there are too many old and poor people living in the centres of the cities, who would normally be living somewhere in the countryside or in the suburbs. Under a free market for housing, poorer people will move from the most expensive and popular parts of cities to cheaper and less popular ones and richer people will move in the opposite direction. This is evident to many of these poorer people, and they are trying to stop or brake the commercialization of housing.

Another problem is that of foreigners who are renting flats and offices in Prague and with whom Czechs are unable to compete in rent prices (average rent for foreigners for a 3 + 1 flat is 300 USD–600 USD, when average Czechoslovak wage per month is about 130 USD). A vicious circle is established in this way. Because the supply of flats and office space is limited, the prices are high; this leads to a cry for keeping a regulation which limits the supply. . . .

The last accomplishment in housing was the passing of the communal property law by the Czech and Slovak parliaments. State-owned flats were given as property to the municipalities. What the practical consequences of this step will be is an open question.

7. Wild privatization

The attempt by the Czechoslovak reformers to avoid wild privatization was unsuccessful. The basic scheme is similar to that in Hungary and Poland, where it began earlier. The director of a state firm establishes a private firm alone, or, more often, in collaboration with some of the leadership of the firm. Taking advantage of their position of power and their specific knowledge of idle productive capacities, they obtain the best resources or most profitable orders of the state company on behalf of their private company. Sometimes these orders are filled using the capital assets and labor of the state enterprise. Leasing is informal, and the prices are symbolic. Furthermore, the employees are much better paid than they would be for the same type of work in a state firm (where the wages are strongly regulated; in private firms employing up to twenty-five people, no regulations apply). Besides leasing and taking over of orders, there is also a transfer of the capital assets from the state firm to private companies despite the fact that this is forbidden.

A very interesting question is why this is occurring. Part of the answer could be the low morality of the former nomenklatura cadres, but this is only part of the story and too simple an explanation. The central reason is the question of control. In the past, managers had, in fact, partial property rights. Although they did not have full property rights, they had control over the execution of the firm.

The reformers did not give special preferences to managers – for example, to be allowed to purchase part of the shares at a discount – therefore, the managers are trying to use their part of the property rights which they maintain and to capitalize on them through their own private firm. This phenomenon, then, is caused not only by moral defects, but also by cracks in the economic reform program. One of those cracks is definitely the incentives of the managers in state enterprises.

8. Foreign privatization

It was clear even for the communist political leaders in the late 1980s that it would be beneficial to have foreign capital for technology and hard currency. At the same time, they were afraid of the influence of

Western capital on the economy and the political system in Czechoslovakia. Joint ventures with foreign participation were an element alien to the centrally planned economic system. The result of this ambivalence was law No. 173/1988 regarding the participation of foreign capital in Czechoslovakia. This law allowed for Czechoslovak legal persons to establish joint ventures with foreign legal and natural persons. Pure (100 percent) foreign firm ownership was prohibited. The communist state strictly controlled each project individually. There were also many problems with the legal system, taxation, transfer of profits, the leading role of the communist party in joint ventures, etc. Nevertheless, even under these complicated conditions, some joint ventures were established. A step forward was the amendment of law No. 173/1988 in April 1990. This amendment allowed foreign ownership up to 100 percent, created a simplified government approval procedure (only the Ministry of Finance's approval was necessary or that of the State Bank for the banking sector), and allowed Czech/Slovak natural persons to participate in joint ventures with foreign legal and natural persons.

General conditions have further improved. Czechoslovakia has signed agreements with many countries on the protection of investment and on avoiding double taxation. The problem of the transfer of profits was solved by temporary measures for 1990, and internal convertibility was introduced on 1 January 1991. Because a joint venture is subject to Czechoslovak law, it has the right to buy hard currency and to transfer profits out of the country. The increase in the number of joint ventures, shown in Table 6.2, is dramatic.

Table 6.2 Joint ventures in Czechoslovakia

Date	Number
31.12.1989	55
31.12.1990	1,200
30.6.1991	2,901
31.8.1991	2,946

Source: Federal Statistical Office, Prague

Nevertheless, if we look at their combined capital, the numbers are not as impressive. Total foreign capital of all joint ventures in ČSFR was 25 bln CSK (833 mln USD), 45 percent of which was of foreign origin: 11.3 bln CSK or 376 mln USD. The majority of joint ventures are small firms, as we can see from Table 6.3.

Table 6.3 Capital of joint ventures in ČSFR (30.6.1991)

Capital above 10 mln CSK (3.3 mln USD)	94 firms
Capital above 100 mln CSK (33 mln USD)	20 firms
Capital above 1 bln CSK (333 mln USD)	6 firms

Source: Federal Statistical Office, Prague

The biggest deal concluded in this area was the merger of the Czechoslovak car maker, Škoda Mladá Boleslav, with Volkswagen, after dramatic negotiations. At the beginning, ten world car makers were competing for Škoda. In the end, Volkswagen and Renault were the last bidders. After a long fight, where financial and political questions[17] played a role, Volkswagen won. During the negotiation about the future partner for Škoda, it was necessary to solve plenty of complicated issues. Employment was a particularly important question. Finally, it was agreed that core employees will stay, but all working pensioners, foreigners, etc. were fired. Other key questions were how to handle debts of the firm and suppliers to Škoda and whether to keep the trade mark Škoda.

9. Political parties' property transformation

The property of political parties and similar organizations was called 'social property' in Czechoslovakia. While the number of such properties was not so large, their political importance continues to be great. Newspapers, publishing houses, and other real estates are included. The process of privatization of these properties began in November 1989. The newspapers were owned by political parties, but controlled by the Central Committee of the Communist Party. At the moment that this control disappeared, people in political parties and newspapers started to behave quite differently.

There were fights for control in many newspapers. For example, the staff of *Mladá fronta*, which was the newspaper of the Socialist Youth Union, refused to work for their former masters and established a joint-stock company. They used the forgotten fact that the property of this publishing house and newspaper were transferred in 1945 to the state and not to the youth organization.[18]

The question of ownership of the Communist Party assets was given top priority. Under strong political pressure, they began to give away their property to schools, hospitals, health centres, etc. An interesting point was that the Communist Party had used a lot of state-owned buildings. It had never entered into their minds that property rights could ever be problematic. What had always been important was who used the property and not who owned it.

Besides these forced transfers of communist property, the Communist Party also tried to save properties by transferring them to cooperatives or to private persons who were loyal to the Communist Party. That is why the government decided to control all transfers of Communist Party property to other persons. At the end of 1990, two laws were passed. One law concerned the return of the property of the Communist Party to the hands of the people of the Czech and Slovak Federal Republic and the second law, the property of the Socialist Youth Union. The property of the Communist Party was valued at 12.6 bln CSK (420 mln USD) on 1 January 1990. In the first half of 1990, 4.5 bln CSK's (150 mln USD) worth of property was removed from their ownership; in the second half of 1990, another 5.4 bln CSK (180 mln USD) was removed. The remaining part was transferred in the first half of 1991.

10. Conclusion

Privatization is a complicated and painful process. The social relations of millions of people are in a period of upheaval. People are uncertain who the winners and losers will be. In order to gain a thorough understanding of what is occurring, it is, first of all, necessary to know how the so-called command economy or socialist economy worked. Many pages describing why it does not work were written. The opposite question, 'Why was it working at all?' is raised only rarely. Can you have a society where there is no private activity and everything is state owned? The answer is obviously 'no'! Bureaucrats, technocrats, economists, nomenclature cadres were taking part of the property rights into their hands and were rewarded for it. Those property rights, however, were not transparent, dividable, and transferable, and this was the main reason why the system worked so poorly. This implies that the privatization process involves the transformation of vague property rights into a very clear form.

This process is and will be very complicated, painful, and with contradictions in all cases. Hopefully this chapter will help in understanding this rather dramatic transformation process and will stimulate other economists to analyze more deeply this complicated development.

Notes

1. I am very grateful for the grant of the Central European University which permitted me to write this chapter. I am also very obliged to Prof. Roman Frydman, Prof. Andrzej Rapaczynski and Prof. John Earle who assisted me with their comments. I am especially grateful to Ms Arlene Geiger, New York and Mr Norman Mullock, University of Michigan, for their editing help and many useful comments. Nevertheless, the author takes full responsibility for the accuracy of this chapter.
2. Terminology of the *Historical Statistical Yearbook of Czechoslovakia* – SNTL-ALFA, Prague 1985, p. 57 – for capital assets in the 'productive' sector.
3. Net Material Product (NMP) consists of the production of the so-called 'productive sphere' (agriculture, industry, construction, freight transport, telecommunications, part of trade) and the output of passenger transport, education, housing, health services; 'non-material services' are not included. Depreciation is also subtracted in calculating NMP.
4. Source: *Historical Statistical Yearbook of* ČSSR, SNTL-ALFA, Prague 1985, p. 55.
5. One of those problems was described in 'Mladá fronta dnes' ('Nuns

versus Children'), No. 103, 3.5.1991, p. 3. The old Prague Monastery was given back to the nuns, who are working in the neighborhood hospital. These nuns would like to live in the monastery again, but the monastery currently houses a school for handicapped children, and there is no place to move them.
6. In the law, specific real estates are declared to be the property of the Catholic Church and its orders, for example 9. Franciscan Monastery Plzen, No. 121 monastery building with the land No. 384, current owner: Czechoslovak state–West Bohemian Museum Plzen, current user: the same, written in the books of Státní Geodesie, Plzen-město under the No. 5660).
7. Not to mention the rather curious story of President Havel, who during his visit to Sweden asked the Swedish government for the paintings and other pieces of art that were stolen by the Swedish army during their occupation of Prague in 1648!
8. For example: 'Nejcenější kusy pryč' ('The Best Pieces Away'), *Rudé právo* 1, No. 134, 10.6.1991, p. 2.
9. *Historical Statistical Yearbook of Czechoslovakia*, SNTL-ALFA, Prague 1985, p. 57, 1983 is the latest year for which capital ownership data are available.
10. *Statistical Yearbook of ČSFR 1990*, SNTL-ALFA, Prague 1990, p. 139.
11. Prague and Bratislava stock exchanges are planned to be opened at the end of 1992.
12. The issue in the case of these small firms is not the number of new owners, but whether there should be preferences or advantages given to employees in the bidding to become the private owner.
13. The numbers of firms are the numbers of privatized administrative units. Because sometimes physical parts of administrative units are privatized separately, the final number of privatized items will of course be higher.
14. The break happened in the middle of the 1960s. After a decline in agricultural production, some pragmatic measures were taken. The peasants started to be more dependent upon current production and more resources were given to this branch. Today, the level of subsidies is estimated by experts in the Ministry of Economy to be 10 percent of gross production!
15. Compare Jan Kostrohoun: 'Peasants are not asked' *Rudé právo*, 30.4.1991, No. 101, pp. 1 and 3.
16. *Statistical Yearbook of ČSFR 1990*, SNTL-ALFA, Prague.
17. On one side, workers in Mladá Boleslav were prepared to strike on behalf of Volkswagen; on the other side, French President Mitterand tried to influence Czechoslovak President Havel in favor of Renault.
18. Today, *Mladá fronta dnes*, is the best-selling newspaper in Czechoslovakia.

References

Chaloupka, O. and Klusák, M. (1991), *Subjektivní dimenze realizovatelnosti privatizafního procesu* (Subjective Dimension of Realization of Privatization Process), working paper No. 1872/92, UUNV, Prague.

Kostrohoun, J. (1991), 'Sedlákà se nikdo neptá' (Peasants are not asked), *Rudé právo*, 30.4.1991, No. 101, pp. 1 and 3.

Kuponova privatizace – informacni prirucka (Voucher Privatization – Information Booklet) Federal Ministry of Finance, Prague 1991.
Mládek, J. (1990), *Privatization, Liberalization and Foreign Participation in Czechoslovak Economy: Current Situation and Proposals*, working paper, University of Namur, Belgium.
Prokop, M. (1991), *Kuponova metoda velke privatizace* (Voucher Method of Large Scale privatization), ASCO, Prague.
Rychetský, P. (1991), Poslání družstva a legislativa, Družstevní noviny 46, 5.2.1991, p. 1.
Svobodová, J., Vaník, S., and Forejt, A. (1990), *Právní encyklopedie soukromych podnikatelà* (Law Encyclopedia of Private Entrepreneurs), Trizonia, Prague.
Švejnar, J. (1989), *A Framework for the Economic Transformation of Czechoslovakia*, PlanEcon Report, No. 52, 29.12.1989, Washington D.C.
Zieleniec, J., Mládek, J. *et al.* (1990), *Československo na rozcestí* (Czechoslovakia on the Crossroad), Prague, Lidové noviny.
Zoubek, J. (1990), *Legal and Practical Framework for Doing Business in Czechoslovakia*, East-West, Brussels.

Appendix

BASIC ECONOMIC INDICATORS

The following tables are presented to provide the reader with knowledge of the background for privatization in Czechoslovakia.

Table 1 Macroeconomic indicators

Year	1987	1988	1989	1990	1–6/91[a]
Real NMP produced	2.1	2.3	2.2	−3.4	−13.8
Real priv. consumption	2.8	4.9	1.6	−1.3	−37.1
Consumer price index (all growth in %)	0.1	0.2	1.4	18.4	49.2
Gross external debt (in bln dollars)	6.6	7.3	7.9	8.1	8.8
State budget surplus (in % of NMP)	−0.1	−2.6	−1.1	0.8	1.8

a: Preliminary estimations

Source: Statistical Yearbooks of Czechoslovakia, Federal Statistical Office, Prague

Table 2 Change in the output of basic Czechoslovak industries in percentages (first half of 1991 over first half of 1990)

Total industry	82.4
Fuel	102.4
Paper and cellulose	95.1
Energy	98.3
Wood and furniture	87.6
Machinery	81.3
Printing and publishing	80.5
Iron and steel	92.3
Glass, ceramics, and porcelain	81.0
Textiles	75.0
Food	78.4
Leather industry	74.0
Electronics and electrical machinery	71.6
Clothing	63.3

Source: Federal Statistical Office, Prague

Table 3 Structure of fixed assets and gross output in industry in ČSFR in 1989 (in percentages)

Branches	Share of fixed assets	Share of gross production
Fuels	10.8	4.1
Power	14.8	4.0
Ferrous metallurgy	9.9	9.0
Non-ferrous metallurgy	2.4	2.2
Chemical and rubber industry	10.5	13.6
Mechanical engineering	18.5	21.9
Electrotechnical industry	2.7	5.5
Metal-working industry	2.9	4.3
Building materials	5.0	3.3
Wood and furniture	2.6	2.9
Pulp and paper industry	2.8	2.0
Glass and ceramics industry	1.8	1.4
Textile	4.3	4.3
Clothing	0.5	1.4
Leather industry	1.1	2.1
Printing industry	0.8	0.6
Foodstuffs	7.0	13.5
Freezing production	0.4	0.5
Other industries	1.2	3.4
Industry total	100.0	100.0

Source: Federal Statistical Office, Prague

Table 4 Registered unemployment in ČSFR

Date	In thousands	In %
31.1.91	119.5	1.5
28.2.91	152.3	1.9
31.3.91	184.6	2.3
30.4.91	223.2	2.8
31.5.91	255.8	3.2
30.6.91	300.8	3.8
31.7.91	362.8	4.6
31.8.91	405.6	5.2

Source: Federal Statistical Office, Prague

Table 5 Number of registered private entrepreneurs as of date given

Date	Federation	Czech Republic
31.12.1987	38,200	–
31.12.1988	51,100	–
1.12.1989	–	65,202
31.12.1989	86,900	–
31.1.1990	148,500	–
31.3.1990	–	109,970
30.6.1990	224,100	163,952
30.9.1990	–	255,851
31.12.1990	462,500	–
30.6.1991	901,700	713,000
31.8.1991	1,072,500	–

Source: Charap, J., Dyba, K., and Kupka, M.: *The Reform Process in Czechoslovakia*, working paper, Prague, 1991

Table 6 Number of private farmers (in thousands)

Year	1930	1949	1953	1957	1965	1974	1988
0–2 ha	754	695	729	759	–	–	–
2–5 ha	444	351	235	180	–	–	–
10– ha	443	456	223	136	–	–	–
Total	1,641	1,507	1,188	1,074	174	59	4

Source: Federal Statistical Office, Agricultural Yearbooks

Table 7 The scope of agricultural cooperatives in ČSFR

Year	1970	1980	1990
0–1,000 ha	5,343	80	55
1,001–2,000 ha	862	606	539
2,001–3,000 ha	55	562	569
3,001–5,000 ha	–	399	421
Total	6,270	1,716	1,656
Average ha per coop	638	2,493	2,591

Source: Agricultural Research Institute, Prague

Table 8 Size structure of state farms in ČSFR

Year	1980	1989
0–4,000 ha	25	28
4,001–7,000 ha	69	80
7,001–10,000 ha	35	33
10,001–12,000 ha	7	8
12,000– ha	14	22
Average ha	6,986	8,432

Source: Agricultural Research Institute, Prague

PRIVATIZATION AND RELATED LAWS

1. Law No. 104/1990 on the Joint Stock Companies
2. Law No. 105/1990 on Private Business
3. Law No. 111/1990 on State Enterprises
4. Law No. 112/1990 on Enterprise with Foreign Capital Participation
5. Act No. 116/1990 on the Leasing and Renting of Non-Flat Space
6. Act No. 176/1990 on Construction, Consumption, Production and Other Cooperatives
7. The Decree No. 177/1990 of the Presidium of Federal Assembly About Some Measures Concerning Property of Political Parties, Political Movements and Social Organisations.
8. Act No. 298/1990 – on Regulation of Property Relations of Religious Orders and Congregations and the Olomouc Archdiocese.
9. Act No. 403/1990 – on Relieving the Consequences Some Property Injustice. [SMALL SCALE REPRIVATIZATION Act]
10. Act No. 427/1990 – on the Transfer of State Property and Some Goods to Other Juristic or Natural Persons. [SMALL SCALE PRIVATIZATION ACT]

11. Act No. 458/1990 – Amendment of Act No. 403/1990.
12. Act No. 497/1990 – on Constitutional Act about Returning the Property of Communist Party of Czechoslovakia to the People of Czech and Slovak Federal Republic.
13. Act No. 497/1990 – Constitutional Act on Returning the Property of the Socialist Union of Youth to the People of the Czech and Slovak Federal Republic.
14. Act No. 87/1991 – on Out-of-Court Rehabilitations. [LARGE SCALE REPRIVATIZATION ACT]
15. Act No. 92/1991 – on Conditions of Transferring State Property to Other Persons. [LARGE SCALE PRIVATIZATION ACT]
16. Act No. 229/1991 – on Regulation of the Relations of Ownership the land and other Agricultural Property

7

Privatization in a hypercentralized economy: the case of Romania[1]

John S. Earle and Dana Săpătoru

Introduction

One of the most perplexing dilemmas and intriguing paradoxes of the economic transformation in Eastern Europe is the seeming contradiction in the roles envisioned for the state during compared with after the transition. A more rapid and complete transition to a market economy, thus a quicker reduction of state control, may be more readily achieved where a strong state can actually force the privatization process. The command system, engaged in what could be called 'centrally planned privatization', continues through the transition, but is thereafter expected to somehow self-destruct or 'wither away', having fulfilled its purpose. Of course, exactly analogous to the 'withering away of the state with the arrival of the Communist Era', a critical problem becomes ensuring that this essential final step is actually accomplished.

An examination of East European privatization experience thus far indicates that the strength and centralization of state power in the transition indeed seems to be greatest in those East European countries adopting the most radical privatization policies. For instance, the centrally planned and initiated programs of Czechoslovakia and Romania can be counterposed to the much more decentralized processes in Hungary and Poland. It is also notable that the former countries had the highest degree of centralization and least experience of partial reforms under the old regimes. Unlike the situation in the latter countries, which dabbled with various versions of market socialism, property rights, and economic decision-making, power in the former remained clearly with the center. Taken together, these observations suggest the hypothesis that this history of having followed a more orthodox communist road may be the very factor that enables these countries to pursue a more aggressive privatization policy. Ironically, in the struggles and ordeals to create a market economy, some advantage may be had by those who started farthest behind in terms of experience with the market, thus a new application of 'the advantage of backwardness'.[2]

Of all the East European countries, this characterization seems to apply best to Romania. As developed in Section 2, Romania's economy under communism was particularly hypercentralized and hyperdistorted, even compared with its neighbors. On the other hand, Romania's program for the transformation of ownership relations, discussed in Sections 3 and 4, is one of Eastern Europe's most dramatic. The program first forces most enterprises to corporatize, next transfers 30 percent of their shares to 'Private Ownership Funds', and finally sells the remaining 70 percent through a variety of mechanisms and newly created institutions. The Privatization Law allows little influence to enterprise insiders and stipulates that the ownership changes be 100 percent completed within seven years.

This radical program, however, is not without pitfalls. The new state institutions founded to develop and implement this policy are analyzed in Section 3, demonstrating the remarkable continuity in the centralization of economic policy. The transparency in the allocation of responsibilities that could have accompanied this centralized policy has unfortunately been muddied by recent revisions to the program, which have created an unclear criss-crossing division of tasks among the institutions. The program of free distribution and subsequent sale of shares of corporatized enterprises is analyzed in Section 4, showing the continuity also in the dependence of policy on individuals and institutions following commands, rather than creating a system of incentives relying on individual motivation and market-type mechanisms. The discussion of the organizational and incentive problems of the program raises the fundamental issue of the transition referred to earlier and to which the concluding Section 5 returns: the difficulty of ensuring that state institutions work to reduce state power, that the state itself acts to replace itself with the market.

The research reported in this paper contributes in several ways to the existing literature on East European privatization. First, most research on this general topic is either purely descriptive or completely abstract. This chapter goes beyond a detailed exposition of the features of the privatization policy to analyze its likely consequences and problems, particularly in the areas of incentives and institutional design. Second, this analysis is embedded within larger comparative and historical contexts: a cross-country comparison of large privatization programs and an historical perspective that relates the particular preconditions of the transition to the particular policy followed. This perspective of 'path dependence' acquires added importance when one considers its possible implications for the shape of the resulting economy, for instance in corporate governance and the financial sector. Finally, Romania has been neglected in most research on the East European transition. This chapter attempts to redress that omission with a clear, complete, and up-to-date analysis of the Romanian privatization program. We hope to have demonstrated that Romania is an interesting and valuable subject for study.

2. Initial conditions for ownership transformation in Romania

Among the so-called 'Soviet satellites' of Eastern and Central Europe prior to the revolutions of 1989, Romania perhaps most closely fit the classical archetype of the socialist command economy. Detailed central planning was carried to absurd extremes by Nicolae Ceausescu, the President and General Secretary of the Romanian Communist Party. The economy functioned almost like a single firm, with most agents simply following instructions and with virtually no reliance on individual motivation to secure desired results.

The 'Law of Proportional Planned Development of the National Economy' was the basis of central planning. Prerequisites for following the 'Law' were 'conscious establishment of necessary economic proportions, imposed by social needs, between branches, subbranches, individual units, and activities of the national economy', management of the economy based on the national plan, and 'the acknowledgement and use of the entire system of the economic laws of socialism'. Socialist planning meant compulsory imposition of all of the following: the objectives and their deadlines, the tasks of each organizational unit, the measures taken for the fulfilment of the objectives, and the method for controlling and ensuring their fulfilment.

In the mid and late 1980s, ideological campaigns focused on the twin concepts of 'Democratic Centralism' and 'Workers' Self-Management and Autonomous Economic and Financial Administration and Management' proclaimed as the bases for a new economic policy. According to the former principle, there were supposed to be two-way relationships among enterprises, 'centrale', ministries, and the State Planning Committee (CSP). The first direction of the relationships, referred to as the principle of 'Establishment of a Draft Plan from Bottom Up', began with enterprises submitting proposals concerning their production plans on the basis of 'orientative levels and plan normatives'. The former included minimum levels of output and exports and maximum levels of investment and imports; the latter set ceilings on various 'efficiency indicators', such as production costs, fuel inventories, and energy consumption, and floors for profits, labor productivity, net production, the profit rate, etc.

These 'draft plans' were submitted to the intermediate levels of authority, the 'centrale', which 'centralized' the proposals of all the enterprises within a branch of activity and geographic region.[3] But even these proposals, constrained as they were, in practice were almost meaningless, as the revised versions of the proposals, aggregated and further conveyed by the centrale to the relevant ministries and thence to the CSP, could differ significantly. Although enterprise directors often bargained over the parameters of their plans with the bureaucrats of the 'centrale', the latter usually won the disputes.

The other direction of 'Democratic Centralism', the one that really did function, began with the design by the CSP of five-year 'sole national plans for economic and social development', which were then disaggregated into one-year plans. After analysis by the Council of Ministers, the plans were submitted to the Central Committee of the Communist Party and the Supreme Council for Economic and Social Development, and then enacted into law by the Grand National Assembly. These extremely detailed plans were disaggregated over the ministry, central, and enterprise levels and were compulsory for each of them. This was the so-called principle of 'Correlation of Tasks from Top Down'.

From this discussion, it should already be apparent that the 'Workers' Self-Management and Autonomous Economic and Financial Administration and Management' of enterprises, the second of the ideological concepts, was essentially non-existent. Workers were supposed to administer jointly the use of the means of production, to participate directly in the management of their enterprise, and to be responsible for 'the assets entrusted to them by society'. In fact, the enterprises could make decisions neither on their production nor on their suppliers, the contracts between suppliers and producers being determined by their 'centrale'. They had, moreover, little freedom in the use of their profits, which had to be distributed among a set of special purpose funds in a prescribed fashion. The 'Workers' Self-Management' concept was mostly interpreted in practice as the responsibility of enterprises to cover their costs from revenues and to obtain a certain profit (the profitability rate was supposed to remain within a specific percentage range). The enterprises, however, usually failed to comply with this policy, being unable to meet the unrealistic plans set by the superior authorities, even when they overstated their results. The state subsidized the loss-making enterprises or escaped through the mechanism of inter-enterprise debts.

Central planning was facilitated by a size distribution of enterprises highly skewed toward larger concerns. The Romanian economy was characterized by an enormous degree of horizontal as well as vertical integration, and perhaps the largest average enterprise size in Eastern Europe. Table 7.1 expresses the 1990 size distribution for industrial enterprises in terms of ranges of the number of employees, showing the number of enterprises and their percentage share, the number of employees and percentage share, and the percentage share of industrial production for each size category. The dominance of larger enterprises is remarkable: enterprises with more than 2,000 employees accounted for nearly two-thirds of the total number of employees and two-thirds of total industrial production. Less than 1 percent of workers were employed by enterprises with fewer than 200 employees.

Table 7.1 Size distribution of industrial enterprises in Romania, 1990

	Enterprises		Employees		Production
Size of enterprises by number of employees	Number	% share	Number	% share	% share
less than 200	169	7.6	24,288	0.7	1.9
201–500	456	20.3	162,505	4.4	5.2
501–1,000	538	24.0	391,386	10.6	10.7
1,001–2,000	515	23.0	723,116	19.5	18.9
2,001–3,000	245	10.9	592,538	16.0	14.3
3,001–5,000	197	8.8	768,760	20.8	20.6
over 5,000	121	5.4	1,039,263	28.0	28.4
Total	2,241	100.0	3,701,856	100.0	100.0

Source: Comisia Nationala pentru Statistica, 1991

The general infatuation of the socialist countries with industrialization was still more pronounced in Romania, particularly after Ceausescu's accession to power in 1965. From a predominantly agrarian economy, Romania was supposed to become 'an industrial-agricultural country in full development'. The percentage of fixed assets in industry rose two and a half times, from 19.5 in 1950 to 47.5 in 1989, while that in services fell by half, from 34.6 to 17.1.

The evolution of the branch structure of employment from 1950 to 1989 is presented in Table 7.2. The proportion of employment in industry rose from 12 to 38.1 percent over this whole period; the steepest years of increase were from the late 1960s through the 1970s. Meanwhile, employment in agriculture greatly contracted and trade and services experienced modest growth.

Table 7.2 Branch structure of employment in Romania, 1950–89

Percent of total employment by branch	1950	1960	1970	1980	1989
Industry	12.0	15.1	23.0	37.1	38.1
Construction	2.2	4.9	7.8	7.4	7.0
Agriculture and Forestry	74.3	65.6	49.3	28.9	27.9
Transport and Communications	2.2	2.8	4.2	6.8	6.9
Trade	2.5	3.4	4.3	5.8	5.9
Services and Other	6.8	8.2	11.4	14.0	14.2
Total	100.0	100.0	100.0	100.0	100.0

Source: Comisia Nationala pentru Statistica, 1991

The industrial bias towards heavy industry was still more pronounced, as reflected in the growth of this sector in Table 7.3. The proportion of industrial production accounted for by fuel, metallurgy, metal working, engineering, chemicals, and mining grew from about 35 percent in 1950 to 60 percent in the late 1980s. The biggest increase was in engineering (machine building), from 6.3 percent of industrial production in 1950 to 23.4 percent in 1980, although it declined thereafter.[4]

Table 7.3 Sub-branch structure of industrial production in Romania, 1938–89

Percent of industrial production by sub-branch group	1938	1950	1960	1970	1980	1985	1989
Electric and thermic power	1.1	1.9	2.5	3.2	1.8	3.5	3.9
'Heavy industry'[a]	36.5	35.3	47.9	52.4	59.3	60.7	59.3
'Materials'[b]	11.9	13.6	11.7	11.2	8.9	8.4	8.7
'Light industry'[c]	50.5	49.2	37.9	33.2	30.0	27.4	28.1
Total	100	100	100	100	100	100	100

a The designations and groupings are the authors'. 'Heavy industry' includes fuels, ferrous and non-ferrous metallurgy, machine building, chemicals, and mining of non-metaliferrous ores and abrasive products
b 'Materials' includes building materials, forestry and woodworking, and pulp and paper
c 'Light industry' denotes glass, china and faience, textiles, ready-made clothing, leather goods, furs and footwear, foods, soaps and cosmetics, 'polygraphy' (printing) and other branches

Source: Comisia Nationala pentru Statistica, 1991

The low and declining proportion of output in light industry during the communist period reflects the bottom priority assigned to consumption. The consumer market in Romania was dominated, as in the other countries, by black market transactions, although the magnitudes are naturally unmeasurable. But the extreme scarcity of nearly all consumer goods, even compared to the other socialist countries, meant that even the concept of consumer choice was ludicrous. The devaluation of consumption relative to investment is also apparent from their relative shares in GDP: for instance, 56 percent and 34 percent in 1983, respectively.[5]

Romania followed a policy of self-sufficiency virtually to the point of autarky, despite the ostensible intent of 'cooperation with all countries, irrespective of their social and political system'. In the second half of the 1980s, exports were promoted at all costs, with incentives offered to enterprises fulfilling the export plan, even at the expense of supply to the domestic market. Imports were systematically diminished such that, by the late 1980s, almost no consumer goods entered the Romanian market, and, according to Montias, enterprises were 'starved' for essential inputs. The state, even the entire nation and complete economic apparatus, was so closely identified with the person of Ceausescu that consumption and living standards were sacrificed to repay foreign debts before they were due: to such a degree did the personal pride of this person-state come before the interests of the people.

The labor market was subject to a bewildering variety of constraints, such as the strict regulation of migration by the Ministry of Interior, including the virtual prohibition on migration to the ten or so largest cities (the group of so-called 'closed cities') and the requirement that university graduates of the better quality 'day courses' work for at least three years in the countryside (the so-called 'apprenticeship period'), even after which it was difficult to return to a 'closed city'. Jobs for graduates were centrally allocated, although the best students were given some choice of position. Wage-setting was completely centralized, with each enterprise obeying a standard set of procedures: given a branch (industry), occupation, and length of service (tenure), the wage was fully determined. This is in sharp contrast with some of the other East European countries, in which regulations greatly hampered wage flexibility, but did not completely specify them a priori.

The center also interfered with personnel decisions. A sine qua non for any kind of professional advancement in any field was membership of the Communist Party, which thus functioned as a personnel department for the whole economy even more than usual for the region. Although Ceaucescu attempted to micro-manage the entire economy, his fear of competition led to what many Romanians agree was a systematic, if inconsistent, promotion of incompetence.

In Romania's case, these policies, to some extent characteristic of all the socialist economies particularly in the initial decades of communist rule, were carried to an extreme extent. Moreover, unlike most of the other countries, Romania experienced no serious attempts at reform over the whole period. In the other countries, these reforms, which usually prominently included some decentralization of allocational decisions, were carried out with varying degrees of conviction and consistency, but they at least gave the peoples of their countries some taste of a different economic system, some experience of making real economic decisions, particularly as producers. They also created ambiguous structures of property rights that have greatly affected, in some cases arguably impeded, the ability of the new governments in those countries to organize ownership reforms.[6]

Also like the other centrally planned economies, but again to an even greater extent, the Romanian economy was already in severe recession in the late 1980s, before the communist downfall. After several years of essentially no growth, even according to the official statistics, GDP plummeted almost 7 percent in 1989 compared with 1988. Production in industry, construction, and municipal and banking services were already falling rapidly from 1987–88 peaks.

3. New institutions for privatization in Romania[7]

The centerpiece of the Romanian privatization policy, as set forth in the 'Privatization Law' of August 1991, is an immediate (although indirect) transfer to all adult Romanian citizens of 30 percent of the shares in all state-owned 'commercial companies', combined with a plan to sell the remaining 70 percent in the next seven years. The Privatization Law took as its point of departure the corporatization of state enterprises in July 1990: all of Romania's state-owned enterprises were transformed either into joint-stock or limited-liability companies ('commercial companies'), to be privatized subsequently, or into state-owned companies (*regies autonomes,* sometimes referred to as 'autonomous units' or 'self sufficient administrations'), to remain under state control.[8] The first important new institution, the National Agency for Privatization and the Development of Small and Medium Sized Enterprises, or 'National Agency for Privatization' (NAP), was also created at that time. The Privatization Law subsequently provided for the founding of five so-called 'Private Ownership Funds' (POFs) and one 'State Ownership Fund' (SOF), which divide the responsibilities amongst themselves for interim management of the commercial companies, and, together with the NAP, share the responsibilities for privatization.

At the level of state-created bodies, therefore, control of the process is spread over a number of new institutions. However, enterprises selected for the program are obliged to participate: managers do not initiate the process, as is usual in Hungary, and workers may not block it, as in Poland. Moreover, the methods of privatization are to be determined exclusively by the three types of state-created institutions. Local governments, branch ministries, and other government organs play only minor roles, and little initiative and influence are left to the enterprises: the program is thus quite centralized.[9]

These new central bodies, however, have a complicated set of tasks to perform, and the division of tasks among them is still more complicated. The rest of this section discusses each of the institutions in turn and offers some observations on their organizational design and on their often criss-crossing responsibilities.

The *National Agency for Privatization* (NAP) is the government body formally responsible for the coordination, guidance, and control of the privatization process. The NAP is under the supervision of the government, and the Prime Minister appoints the NAP President (sometimes called 'Secretary of State'). It is charged not only with implementing the program of privatization of state-owned commercial companies, but also with encouraging the creation and development of private small- and medium-sized enterprises. In addition, the NAP has responsibilities associated with the early privatization program, sales of assets, and leasing, contracting out and concession arrangements.

With regard to the free distribution and sales of shares program, the NAP has the following specific tasks:

a) to determine the method and coordinate the distribution of Certificates of Ownership;
b) to prepare draft statutes (bylaws) for the Private Ownership Funds and submit them to the government for approval;[10]
c) to submit draft methodologies concerning sales of shares and to approve, within thirty days, the sale of shares in a commercial company and its terms, in the event that the SOF loses its majority stake in the company through this sale;
d) to assist companies involved in the privatization process, including approving contracts of special assistance with foreign consulting firms;
e) to prepare a draft statute for the establishment and operation of the State Ownership Fund;
g) to conduct evaluations and feasibility studies, to undertake consulting and brokering, and to charge for these services.

The NAP was thus supposed to be no longer directly involved in privatization once the SOF and POFs had been set up. According to this original plan, the role of the NAP was to create the legal and institutional framework for privatization, while leaving the task of implementation to the new institutions, the SOF and POFs. In the Summer of 1992, however, the 'Shareholder's Agreement,' the annex to the statute setting up the Private Ownership Funds, gave the NAP an additional responsibility:

h) through its local branches, to organize the privatization of small enterprises.

As is discussed at length below, the clarity of the allocation of responsibilities for privatization, and thus to some degree the transparency of the whole process, has thus been superseded by a division of labor that is at least somewhat more nebulous.

The internal organization of the NAP, particularly after its re-organization in early 1992, could also be more transparent. For instance, the rationale allocation of responsibilities among particular divisions is unclear. The concessioning program and Certificates of Ownership are together in a single division, and Personnel and Private Sector Protection are together in another.

The *State Ownership Fund* (SOF), established in July 1992, is a public institution charged with transferring to private ownership the shares in commercial companies under its administration, initially 70 percent of the shares in each company. According to the Privatization Law, its tasks are as follows:

a) to draw up and execute an annual program of privatization, such that 10 percent of all shares are sold each year, thereby liquidating the state's holding by the end of a seven-year period;
b) to define minimum performance criteria for the commercial companies, including dividend policy;
c) to restructure or liquidate commercial companies;
d) to cooperate with the Private Ownership Funds in accelerating the privatization process;
e) to carry out the customary tasks required of shareholders at general meeting.[11]

As mentioned above, this original policy, as expressed in the Law, was modified through the 'Shareholder's Agreement', whereby the SOF retained responsibility for the restructuring and privatization of the large enterprises only. The NAP acquired the responsibility for privatizing small firms, and the POFs the responsibility for medium-sized firms, as discussed further below.

The SOF is supposed to finance its privatization and restructuring activities from the revenue from privatization sales. According to the Privatization Law's unpublished preamble, the budget of the SOF is to be completely separate from that of the state. The SOF is exempt from the profit tax, and in fact forbidden from making any payment to the state or local budgets. This separation is an important step in increasing the independence of enterprises from their founders (typically branch ministries) and thus in the overall privatization process.[12] The matter is, however, somewhat confused in that the Law also states that any remaining obligations of the SOF upon its liquidation are assumed by the state budget.[13] Among permitted uses of revenue, the SOF may make loans to Romanian natural or legal persons purchasing shares or assets in the privatization of commercial companies. The question of how hard the budget constraints will become thus arises.

It is interesting to note that all of the SOF's 'tasks' are framed as commands to be executed. This is natural if the SOF is conceived as a state institution, but, according to the Privatization Law, it is supposed to 'operate according to commercial principles'. This seems to confuse the SOF's proper role: is it state or is it private? Revenue maximization is not supposed to be an important objective in privatization sales, but the SOF is nevertheless supposed to be self-financing and 'commercial'.

The task of defining 'minimum performance criteria' for the commercial companies seems to represent a lack of clear division between the role of a real owner, who would exercise 'voice' and restructure the company or exercise 'exit' and invest elsewhere, and the role of the state, which has particular public policy goals to fulfil. The task of carrying out 'the customary tasks required of shareholders at general meeting' also seems to imply a similar misunderstanding that, in a market economy, shareholders do whatever they choose to do voluntarily: shareholders have no duties or tasks.

Concerning governance, the SOF is supervised by a Council of Administration (Board of Directors) consisting of seventeen directors, including the State Secretary for Privatization, five directors appointed by the President of Romania and supposed to be 'chosen among persons trained and experienced in commercial, industrial, financial and legal matters', three appointed by the permanent Bureau of Senate and three by the permanent Bureau of the National Assembly, and five chosen among the leading staff of the central public administration and appointed by the Prime Minister. The appointments may also be revoked by the appointers. In other words, the Council is comprised of political appointees coming from various groups; the design seems aimed more at balancing political coalitions than at achieving skilled governance.

The Council elects a President and Vice-President, neither of whom may be the NAP President, and appoints a General Executive Manager to carry out the Board's and President's decisions. The Annex to the Statute of the SOF states that the staff of the SOF are to receive 'a wage or compensation system with specific incentives', presumably tied to the amount of privatization accomplished, but how this will be implemented is unclear. The Statute itself says that the directors' compensation will have 'fixed and variable parts', but what the variable part is supposed to depend upon is not specified. This combination of public appointment with market-type incentives seems again to blur the boundary between what is presumably appropriate for the state and what is appropriate for the private sector.

The *Private Ownership Funds* (POFs), established in August 1992 and expected to begin operation in November 1992 after a two-month training period, are organized as joint-stock companies, also supposed to operate on 'commercial principles'. As described further in the analysis of the program in Section 4 below, they receive 30 percent stakes in a set of commercial companies allocated to them by the NAP. Each POF is in turn owned by all adult Romanian citizens through their Certificates of Ownership (vouchers). The Privatization Law stipulates the following objectives:

a) to seek to maximize profits accruing to their owners, the holders of Certificates of Ownership (vouchers), and to maximize the value of those Certificates through investment and portfolio management;
b) to provide brokerage services for the exchange of Certificates for direct shares in commercial companies;
c) to accelerate the privatization of the shares held by the SOF in the commercial companies allocated to them.

Although the Privatization Law stipulates these as 'objectives', it may be revealing that the 'Overview of the Privatization Law', published together with the Law in a single booklet, states, 'The

POFs are *obliged* to manage the shares allocated to them so as to maximize the value of the Certificates of Ownership.' (National Agency for Privatization, emphasis added.) But if these institutions are truly private, as their name claims, it seems odd to specify obligations as opposed to incentives. Again, this may indicate a lack of understanding of the proper boundary between state and private.

As discussed above, the objective (c) has been amplified through the 'Shareholder's Agreement', which divides privatization responsibilities among the POFs, SOF, and NAP, and is supposed to be signed by the SOF with each POF. With regard to the medium-sized companies in their portfolios, the POFs are given specific responsibility for privatizing the SOF holding; this is supposed to be accomplished within five years. But why should 'private' institutions be ordered to sign any so-called 'agreements'? What is supposed to be their interest in selling the shares of another shareholder? Privatization transactions are extremely costly, and no private, for-profit institution would undertake them without appropriate compensation, but that is precisely what the POFs are 'agreeing' to do.

The statutes of the POFs also require them to announce periodically both the 'market' value and the 'nominal' (book) value of their Certificates. The purpose of this is by no means clear. The market value depends, first of all, on the existence of a secondary market for the Certificates, as will be discussed later, but why should the POF be *required* to 'announce' it? The announcement of the nominal value may be intended only to provide information to 'guide' the market, but book value is hardly a reliable indicator of anything. It seems clear that as long as this nominal value is followed, the critical acquisition of information about the market value of productive assets will be discouraged, the development of the economy distorted, and growth and efficiency reduced.

The Privatization Law stipulates that the POFs may distribute their profits as dividends, deposit them in interest-bearing accounts, or use them to finance 'other commercial activities within [their] scope of activities'. However, the draft statutes require that profits are capitalized and not distributed as dividends during the first three years. But this is, once again, a constraint on the ability of the POFs to behave like a private institution; it is a further attenuation of private property rights.

The design of the POFs, as is generally true of intermediaries in a voucher privatization program,[14] may have important implications for the shape of the future financial system. For instance, if allowed to conduct banking-type functions, the intermediaries may evolve into German type universal banks; if the funds are more restricted, an Anglo-American type financial system could emerge. After five years, the Romanian POFs are supposed to become 'ordinary mutual funds, in the Western sense' (and remaining Certificates of Ownership become ordinary mutual fund shares), but in terms of behavior, governance, and activities, it is not clear what that means. The precise scope of activities permitted the POFs has yet to be determined.

With respect to governance, each POF is supervised by a seven-member Council of Administration, nominated and revocable by the government and approved, separately, by the National Assembly and the Senate. As with the members of the Council of Administration of the SOF, there is a danger that political considerations will dominate the POF Council members' selection, although they are supposed to be 'chosen from persons with commercial, financial, industrial, or legal experience'. (Agentia Nationala pentru Privatizare, 1991, p. 7.) They elect a POF President and a Vice-President from their number.

Although no shareholders meetings will be held during the first five years of operation (under the rationale that meetings with 16.5 mln shareholders are infeasible), the Certificate holders are nonetheless given certain rights to intervene in the fund management, including procedures to request a financial audit or to replace a member of the Council of Administration. The action must be supported by at least 100 persons holding at least 10,000 Certificates in the fund in question. The National Agency for Privatization is the ultimate adjudicator of such actions. How effective such control will be is difficult to predict in advance, which heightens the importance of governance from other sources.

Because the normal methods of governance (by supervisory boards or shareholders) and the forces of competition are likely to be weak in the case of privatization intermediaries, the use of incentive pay to improve the intermediaries' performance takes on added importance. Even though the intermediaries are private, it seems arguable that the state should design them to function as well as possible, and therefore set up such incentives initially. Simply labelling these funds 'private' does not, of course, make them behave so, and even if they should try, the weakness of the market environment implies that their learning could be rather slow.

In Romania, however, while the use of some kind of incentive pay is under consideration for the POF managers, it is not part of their Statutes and essentially left to the discretion of their Councils of Administration. Compared to the state-mandated incentive pay for the SOF, however, this omission is somewhat puzzling, since the POFs are the putative private owners, for whom such incentives are presumably more appropriate. The results of relying on the Councils to establish appropriate incentives will depend on just how effective a control and governance structure those Councils are able to provide.

It should also be pointed out that the design of such a compensation scheme is an enormously difficult problem due to the variety and complexity of the tasks that the POFs are supposed to fulfil: fund management, active governance of companies, brokerage services, and privatization. Since some of these activities are supposed to be undertaken without attention to their impact on profits, there are no clear, comparable units of measurement for their accomplishment.

Moreover, any compensation scheme which neglects or places too low a weight on a particular objective will result in sub-optimal or even no effort being devoted to that activity. This highlights the importance of setting these incentives as well as possible initially.[15]

Thus, the POFs are an odd mixture of state and private elements. They are indeed owned by private individuals, but a single individual out of 16.5 mln citizens has at least initially no possibility and no incentives to influence the POF in which he/she is supposedly an owner: in other words, there is a classic governance problem. Moreover, since the state has established these funds, there is a danger that the fund managers may behave like their predecessor bureaucratic rent-seekers rather than competitive profit-maximizers.[16] The next section presents a more detailed analysis of the program itself, and thereby raises more questions about the appropriate functions and governance of the POFs.

4. The large privatization program in Romania

In theory, the free distribution of 30 percent of company shares to the Private Ownership Funds could be analyzed separately from the subsequent sale of the remaining 70 percent held by the State Ownership Fund, because the two processes are conceptually and temporally distinct, although they apply to the same set of assets. But both the methods and the institutions overlap across the two aspects to such a degree, that it may be clearer and more convenient to consider them simultaneously, as if they were a single program.[17]

This 'large privatization program' covers all the state-owned commercial companies, which were the product of corporatization, the first step in the privatization process whereby former state-owned enterprises were converted into either state-owned commercial companies or *regies autonomes*. The state-owned commercial companies are joint-stock or limited-liability companies with a share-based ownership structure, so that the problem of divesting the state's sole ownership can then be addressed. The division of enterprises between the two categories of *regies autonomes* and commercial companies was made by the branch ministries and local government, for the enterprises subordinated respectively to each. Fields considered strategic for the economy, such as the arms industry, energy, mining and natural gas exploitation, transport and telecommunications, were reserved for the *regies autonomes*, which are supposed to remain indefinitely under state ownership, although some of their subunits are being sold through the 'sale of assets' program.

About 2,000 large state-owned enterprises were subject to corporatization and simultaneously split into smaller units, so that by the end of 1991, about 5,800 commercial companies with state capital were registered.[18] Table 7.4 shows the distribution of the number of

Table 7.4 Sectoral distribution of state-owned commercial companies as of June 1992

Sector	Commercial companies		Registered capital		Employees	
	Number of units	% share	Value (bln Lei)	% share	No. of persons	% share
Industry	1425	24.0	731.5	52.6	2294953	54.1
Agriculture and food ind.	1872	31.6	301.2	21.7	797027	18.8
Domestic trade	621	10.5	66.5	4.8	237393	5.6
Construction	463	7.8	61.8	4.4	366033	8.6
Transportation	512	8.6	87.8	6.3	181485	4.3
Tourism	202	3.4	29.2	2.1	78402	1.9
Other	836	14.1	111.9	8.1	283674	6.7
Total	5931	100.0	1389.9	100.0	4238867	100.0

Source: Unpublished data from the National Agency for Privatization. Information on about 200 commercial companies was unavailable

companies and their employment and book capital across branches of activity (sectors or industries); by all three indicators, this part of the state sector of the Romanian economy remains clearly dominated by industry and agriculture. Table 7.5 contains information on the size distribution of the commercial companies according to employment and registered capital. By contrast with the private sector, state-owned commercial companies are still mostly very large: only 0.3 percent of employees work for companies with fewer than 50 employees, 4.8 percent for companies with fewer than 200, and 17.8 percent for companies with fewer than 500. On the other end of the distribution, companies with more than 1,500 employees account for 53.7 percent of total employment. Thus, this sector is still quite concentrated, despite the splitting up of approximately 2,000 former state enterprises to form the approximate 6,000 commercial companies. Together, Tables 7.4 and 7.5 illustrate the hypercentralized and hyperdistorted character of the part of the Romanian state sector that is slated for privatization and likely (hopefully) to undergo drastic restructuring.[19]

The program fixes the proportion of each company's shares in the 'free distribution' at 30 percent. This 30 percent share has been administratively allocated to one of the five POFs, and the remaining 70 percent is held by the SOF. The 'Certificates of Ownership' received by each citizen are actually shares in each of the POFs. These funds are established by the state, and they alone receive company shares. The entry and functioning of other intermediaries is not yet regulated by law.

The method by which companies are allocated to intermediary funds is an important issue more generally in the design of mass

Table 7.5 Size distribution by employment and capital of state-owned commercial companies as of June 1992

Indicator	Number	% share
Number of employees		
less than 50 employees	428	7.4
	(10,986)[a]	(0.3)[b]
51–200 employees	1,484	25.8
	(189,513)	(4.5)
201–500 employees	1,724	29.9
	(553,464)	(13.0)
501–1,000 employees	1,023	17.8
	(723,271)	(17.1)
1,001–1,500 employees	388	6.9
	(483,468)	(11.4)
1,501–2,000 employees	254	4.4
	(441,773)	(10.4)
over 2,000 employees	450	7.8
	(1,836,502)	(43.3)
Registered capital		
less than 100 mln Lei	2,537	59.6
100–500 mln Lei	1,926	32.5
over 500 mln Lei	468	7.9

a. Numbers in brackets represent total number of employees working at firms with employment size of the given range
b. Numbers in brackets represent the share of the number of employees within each range in the total number of employees

Source: Unpublished data from the National Agency for Privatization

privatization and voucher programs. In Czechoslovakia, the funds compete together with individuals for shares in the companies; in Poland, a number of schemes are under discussion, including choosing in random order from a list. In Romania, the allocation is purely administrative, according to the following principles. The funds are similar in size, measured by profits, capital, or employment. With regard to 2,500 small enterprises (roughly defined as those with capital of book value less than 50 mln Lei), the funds are specialized geographically; having head offices in various cities throughout the country is also supposed to make trading more accessible to the population outside of Bucharest. With regard to medium and large enterprises, special attention is paid to 'critical' or 'strategic' sectors, which include both those in difficult financial circumstances and those that are 'vitally important and have a great impact on the development of other activities'. Enterprises within each of the critical sectors of metallurgy, machinery, chemical and petrochemical, agriculture, banking and finance, commerce, and transportation are supposed to be distributed across funds, while funds specialize in the non-critical, 'color' sectors.

Beyond the 30 percent privatization through this distribution to the five POFs, the Privatization Law stipulates that the remaining 70 percent be sold by the SOF within a seven year period. As described above, the program has recently been changed, in that although the SOF retains its role as (temporary) owner, the responsibilities for privatization have now been divided among the NAP, SOF, and POFs. For instance, in addition to taking an active ownership role as the core if not majority investor, the POFs are supposed to privatize within five years the remaining 70 percent share in the SOF for approximately 2,000 medium-sized companies (the definition is still not precisely determined, but roughly includes companies with book value between 50 and 500 mln Lei and number of employees between 200 and 500). These companies are thought not to require significant restructuring, although the basis for this assessment is unclear. More importantly, the POFs have no explicit interest in this privatization; as supposedly 'private' institutions, why should they be involved in what should arguably be a state role? As discussed above, why should they have made this 'agreement' in the first place?

Small enterprises are intended to be fully privatized (including the POF shares), mainly through management and employee buy-outs; this is supposed to be organized by the branch offices of the NAP together with representatives from all the POFs, which also divide the sales revenue among them. Price is, however, not considered an important criterion for these transactions: obviously the precise role and incentives of the POFs have thus not been fully worked out. Why should a supposedly private POF have any interest in these sales if price is no object? And why should all POFs share in the sales revenue if only one POF is the official 'owner'? In any event, it is interesting to note that voucher privatization will thus turn out to be merely a step on the road to insider privatization for these small enterprises.

The SOF retains the responsibility of restructuring and privatizing between 800 and 1,000 large enterprises, with no involvement from the POFs. The sale of shares may take any of the following methods: public offering, open auction or an auction limited to preselected bidders, sale of shares through direct negotiations, or any combination of the above. An exception is provided by the Privatization Law in the event that a potential purchaser wishes to acquire 100 percent of the shares; the SOF is then supposed to delegate to the POF the power to negotiate the sale.

It is, of course, one of the big issues in privatization whether restructuring should precede or follow the transfer of ownership. Why the Romanian state, as represented by the SOF, should be in a particularly advantageous position to execute this is uncertain. Given the absence of fairly distributed domestic capital (because most savings are believed to be 'dirty money' of the nomenklatura and black marketeers), the unacceptability of extensive foreign ownership (as well as insufficient foreign interest), and the lack of skilled personnel in Romania, it is doubtful that the success of the German *Treuhandanstalt* in privatizing through individual sales can be repeated.

Furthermore, the accomplishment of this complicated division of labor between funds is uncertain, not least because it seems to depend on a number of factors that are not yet determined. For instance, the Privatization Law (passed in Parliament in August 1991) mandates that the SOF privatize one-seventh of its holdings annually, so that privatization of these enterprises should be finished in seven years, but granting the initiative to the POFs to privatize medium-sized enterprises seems to put this goal beyond the power of the SOF to enforce. The members of the Council of Administration (functioning like a Supervisory Board) of a Commercial Company, moreover, are appointed at least initially by the SOF and POFs, 70 percent from the former and 30 percent from the latter. Under these circumstances, it may be difficult for the POF to take the initiative in privatizing the medium size companies. Finally, as discussed in the previous section, it is unclear what incentives the POF managers will be given to accomplish the diverse objectives specified by the Privatization Law.

Turning to the individual participants, the 'new owners', all citizens over eighteen on December 31, 1990, 16.5 mln people, are eligible during the period June to November 27, 1992 to receive Certificates of Ownership (one for each POF). The Certificates are issued in bearer form for a fee of 100 Lei, less than 1 percent of the average gross monthly wage, meant to cover the distribution cost. In some other countries, a more substantial price is set for participation in the program, for instance, a quarter of the monthly wage in Czechoslovakia; it can be argued that a non-trivial cost of participation is helpful psychologically and raises the issue of choice already in the minds of the participants.

Like the Polish Mass Privatization Program, the Romanian program allows no choice initially: a Certificate is merely an equal share in all the privatization intermediaries. In this sense, neither the Polish nor the Romanian are really voucher programs, although they are in the sense that they use the artificial capital of vouchers to transfer ownership. Unlike the Polish program, however, which plans to postpone the distribution of fund shares for at least one year, the Romanian Certificates have already been distributed, in advance even of the establishment of the POFs. The Certificates are legally tradable, with the exception that they may not be sold to foreigners. Thus, instead of providing choice directly, the Romanian program relies on the operation of secondary markets to provide the possibilities for exit and entry and for market signals. The Certificates are already trading through the Foreign Trade Bank, through newspaper advertisements, and on the street.[20] A stock market is supposed to be established on December 31, 1992; only foreigners are excluded.[21]

In addition, however, the Certificates also have uses on the sales side of the privatization program. In this sense, choice is allowed, and the Certificates do represent a kind of voucher. For instance, the Certificates pertaining to a particular fund may be used to purchase company shares from the POF that owns the 30 percent stake, whereupon the fund annuls those Certificates.[22] This remains only a theoretical possibility because it is unclear how the price (number of shares per Certificate) will be determined or even if this is at all a meaningful provision.

The official version is that the price should be the 'market price', but no market yet exists, and it is doubtful that the stock market will be functioning adequately enough to provide some guidance. As noted above, the Certificates are already trading for cash, but unless the SOF has managed to sell some shares, there will be no shares to trade and therefore no market. On the other hand, if there should happen to be shares trading on the stock market, then the possibility of acquiring them from the POFs seems redundant. If a buyer wishes to acquire a large stake, would the POFs be forced to sell at the stock market price? The rationale for this use of the Certificates remains nebulous. What does emerge clearly from this analysis, however, is that the type of giveaway in the Romanian program, where intermediaries alone receive the initial allocation of shares, certainly does not encourage the possibility of active individual owners; nor does this possibility of acquiring the shares from the POFs in exchange for Certificates seem to enhance it much.

In any case, small companies are not intended to be sold in this way. Another use of Certificates, however, is that employees of those small companies may use them to buy shares from the POF in the case of an employee buy-out. In this event, the employee may use his or her Certificates from all the funds. As already noted, this is an interesting case where voucher privatization will have merely served to facilitate insider privatization.

Finally, the Certificates pertaining to a particular POF may be presented to the SOF, when the latter is engaged in the sale of shares in a company belonging 30 percent to that POF, in order to receive a 10 percent discount on the public offering price. The reason offered why only Certificates pertaining to that particular POF may be used is to stimulate trading among Certificates for different funds. Restrictions on this use include the provisions that one person may use no more than ten Certificates for purchasing shares in a particular company, that each Certificate may be used only once for the shares in that company, and that the total value of the discount can be no more than the 'market value' of the Certificates. There seems again to be a difficulty here that the value of the Certificates is somehow circular: its value in a particular use depends on its market value, which depends on its value in various uses, etc.

Despite the appearance of openness (if not transparency) and lack of special rights for insiders in the Romanian process, there are, in fact, some specific provisions for employee preferences. In any public share offer, the employees/management are supposed to receive the right, during a limited time period prior to the commencement of the public offering, to purchase up to 10 percent of all the shares at a discount of 10 percent off the public offering price. In an auction, their bid wins if they offer no less than 10 percent less than the highest bid, and agree to all other conditions of the offer. In connection with a negotiated sale, all terms being equal, the sale is supposed to be awarded to an employee or management offer. Employees or management wishing to purchase shares may also receive financing assistance from the SOF, the POFs, and commercial companies, in the form of credits, deferred payment arrangements, or payment by instalments. Thus, despite the fact that the Romanian program contains elements of both voucher and mass privatization, other methods involving insider preferences and individual sales are quite prevalent.

5. Conclusion

This chapter has presented a detailed analysis of the Romanian large privatization program, the free distribution and subsequent sale of shares in commercial companies. Emerging from this analysis are several broader conclusions about the transition process in Eastern Europe as a whole. First, the preconditions of the process are crucial determinants of the feasible set of policies, and not for purely political reasons. The clarity of property rights arrangements was much greater under those regimes with the most centralized, strongest states. What information regarding the quality of assets exists, and whatever incentives exist to privatize, exist at the center, and is much less dispersed and decentralized. Given that property rights are clearer at the starting point of the process, it is now much easier for the state to alter them.

Second, although these considerations suggest that it is precisely those East European countries with least experience of the market that may be able to effect the most rapid transition, this 'advantage of backwardness' may be frittered away and not exploited. For instance, the unclear divisions of labor among the new institutions responsible for implementing the privatization of the Romanian commercial companies may muddy implicit property rights that before were clear. Furthermore, the relative lack of power of insiders may make the process more egalitarian, but it does not imply that competitive rather than administrative mechanisms will be used.

Third, the critical issue in large, state-directed, 'mass' privatization programs, such as the Romanian, is ensuring that the state does in fact dissolve rather than perpetuate itself. As of October 1992, the 30 percent free distribution to the POFs had taken place, and the Certificates of Ownership in the POFs were distributed among the population, but 70 percent of the shares in the state-owned commercial companies still remained to be privatized through individual sales. Despite the legal provision for complete divestment within seven years, it was not clear how this was supposed to be accomplished or even when precisely this seven-year period was supposed to begin.

Finally, the fact that so little use is made of competitive, market-like mechanisms seems to make the successful completion of the Romanian program difficult to achieve. The use of such mechanisms may contribute to what Frydman and Rapaczynski (1991) have called 'successful institutional innovation', a process that both reveals information to allow for corrections to be made and that also functions to correct itself, thus making it easier to ensure that the privatization program is actually concluded, and that markets do, in fact, take over from state control of the economy. In this light, much of the success of the Romanian program, as with many other privatization programs in Eastern Europe, clearly depends on the specific design of the institutions implementing the process and on how well those institutions actually function.

Notes

1. The ideas in this chapter have been considerably influenced by the more general work on East European privatization of Roman Frydman and Andrzej Rapaczynski, to whom we owe a large intellectual debt. Members of the Privatization Project country team in Romania, Ion Andrei, Luoana Dulgheru, Elena Gheorghiu, Costea Munteanu, and Ladislau Randjak, provided valuable assistance with data collection. All errors and all interpretations, however, are the sole responsibility of the authors and should not be attributed to any of these individuals or their institutional affiliations.
2. Originally due to Alexander Gerschenkron, it was Roman Frydman and Andrzej Rapaczynski who were the first, to our knowledge, to apply this phrase to Eastern Europe, in particular Czechoslovakia.
3. Oddly, these regions corresponded with neither existing administrative divisions nor areas with some clear economic meaning; they rather seemed to have been somewhat arbitrarily determined, although there was a concern that centrale within a given branch of industry be of roughly equal size.
4. The fuel and raw material intensity of Romanian production also increased enormously. One measure is the use of electricity per worker: in industry as a whole, the number of kilowatt hours increased by a factor of almost four from 1960 to 1989 (Comisia Nationala pentru Statistica).
5. I. Lacatus points out a number of interesting inconsistencies and implausibilities in the official consumption statistics, simulates the movement of consumption and other variables under alternative assumptions, and concludes that the actual share of consumption in GDP may have been as low as 32 percent.
6. The legal devolution of property rights in Hungary to enterprises, and especially to managers, is thoroughly analyzed in L. Szakadat (1993). M. Mejstrik and J. Hlavacek (1993) argue that managers in Czechoslovakia acquired implicit property rights through their bargaining power vis-a-vis

the center. And J. Szomburg depicts the rights granted to workers' councils in Poland as perhaps the most important precondition for the nature of the Polish privatization process.

7. This section, and the one following, draw heavily on our joint research with Roman Frydman, Andrzej Rapaczynski, and the Romanian Privatization Project country team.
8. The *regie autonomes* may, however, be transformed later in whole or in part into commercial companies, which would allow them to enter the privatization process at a later date. More information about these legal forms, the corporatization process, and the program for the 'Sale of Assets' (under which assets of both the commercial companies and the *regies* may be privatized separately) can be found in Frydman, Rapaczynski, Earle, Sapatoru *et al.* (1992).
9. There are also some elements of decentralization in the overall privatization process. In the process of corporatization, the management and employees often initiated splitting the former enterprise into smaller units. In the so-called 'early privatization', the sale of shares in whole business entities is initiated by the enterprises themselves, and the sale of assets may be proposed by the enterprises as well as by an interested buyer, although the NAP has the ultimate decision-making authority in both cases. The Privatization Law allows the possibility that the SOF may contract out some of the privatization transactions to investment management companies. Finally, managers and workers may make proposals for employee buy-outs, particularly of the smaller enterprises.
10. According to the Law, the statutes are then supposed to be submitted to Parliament for final approval. In fact, the draft statutes were submitted in Spring 1992 to Parliament, which went into recess, however, without voting on them. The basic statutes were enacted by government decree in the interim.
11. The SOF has also been given the right to contract out its activities to consulting firms.
12. Nonetheless, this budgetary separation does not itself necessarily imply, nor does corporatization, the end to subsidies. In 1991, subsidies to cover losses at all state-owned commercial companies and *regies autonomes* consumed 37 billion Lei, or about 7 percent of state budget expenditures. An addition 63 billion Lei, almost 12 percent of the budget, were spent subsidizing prices. But Romania is hardly alone in this respect.
13. The Law stipulates that the SOF will be liquidated when the complete (100 percent) privatization of the Commercial Companies is achieved. If this goal is not attained in seven years, and, as noted, nothing but the admonition of the law exists to enforce or encourage it, the Parliament will determine the future of the SOF and of the administration of the remaining state holdings.
14. Earle, Frydman, and Rapaczynski (1993a) contains a discussion of this issue in a wider context.
15. B. Holmstrom and P. Milgrom examine multi-task principal-agent problems generally, and Earle and Sapatoru (1992) analyze this problem in the particularly interesting and important case of POF manager compensation.
16. Frydman and Rapaczynski (1992) discuss this problem, particularly

motivated by the case of the intermediaries in the Polish mass privatization program.

17. This chapter is primarily concerned with this 'large privatization', but it should be pointed out that there are other privatization programs both in the planning stages and already underway. The NAP has begun implementing programs to sell, lease, or contract out the management of enterprise assets, mainly small retail outlets, and an 'early privatization' program to sell shares in a small number of selected state-owned companies. In addition to the privatization of business units, the return of land to private ownership is provided for under the legal framework of the Land Law, applicable to about 75 percent of Romania's agricultural land. State-owned apartments, except for those in buildings with complications in defining ownership rights due to the possibility of reprivatization, are also being sold. More information on these programs can be found in Frydman, Rapaczynski, Earle, Sapatoru *et al*. (1992).
18. The process of splitting up and reorganizing has continued, however, so that 7,783 state-owned commercial companies (accounting for about 4.5 percent of the total number of registered companies) were on the Commercial Register as of June 1992. However, this number includes about 1,300 branches or subsidiaries of companies which are listed as separate commercial companies, but do not submit a distinct balance sheet to the Ministry of Finance, as well as about 140 cooperative associations that are not subject to the provisions of the Commercial Companies Privatization Law, and 22 holding companies. There thus seem to be about 6,321 commercial companies, as far as anyone can tell, undergoing privatization through this program.
19. The centrale, described in section 2 above, were eliminated in early 1990, in an attempt at de-monopolization. Since then, however, new 'holding companies' have been created in certain sectors, especially oil, metallurgy, heavy industry and agriculture, and with a complicated cross-ownership structure. Their role is controversial: officially not a mere continuation of the former centrale, they are alleged rather to be 'voluntary' associations to help the companies in the sectors most affected by transition, especially with the supply of raw materials (which mostly came from the former CMEA countries and were centrally distributed) and with selling their products (which were also directed towards East European markets). The holding companies may also, however, be viewed as perpetuating the indirect control of the state and as a hindrance to privatization; certainly both the ownership structure of the companies in the holding and how the holdings will be treated in the privatization process remain unclear. See Frydman, Rapaczynski, Earle, Sapatoru *et al*. (1992) for further discussion.
20. Already in August 1992, the Romanian Foreign Trade Bank had begun a brokerage service for the sale and purchase of certificates. Those willing to purchase place an order stating how many vouchers they would like and the price they are willing to pay, and those interested in selling stipulate their desired quantity and price. Transactions are supposed to be concluded only when buy and sell orders have identical prices; there seems to be no explicit price adjustment mechanism, thus tradability could be hampered if the volume of orders is thin. As an example of the less formal transactions, which popular belief attributes mostly to Gypsies, the authors of this chapter received such an offer on a Bucharest

street in July 1992, with an 'initial asking price' of 2,000 Lei.

21. To prevent speculative swings in the price of the certificates, for instance to keep the value from falling precipitously on the opening of the stock market, the POFs are allowed to engage in trading their own certificates. But it is not always clear from discussions with government officials whether it is only that the POFs are permitted this activity, or that they are expected to undertake it, which would again seem to overstep the proper boundary of state and private sectors. As with any attempt to set or influence prices, this could also be a dangerous, or at least an expensive, activity, particularly since the POFs are unlikely to have much cash reserves or liquidity.
22. The law sets no limits on the number of certificates that any individual can use in this way, but the POF's Council of Administration may set such a limit.

References

Agentia Nationala pentru Privatizare, *Information Bulletin: Commercial Companies Privatization Law*, Bucharest, 1991.

Comisia Nationala pentru Statistica, *Statistical Yearbook of Romania, 1990*, Bucharest, 1991.

Earle, J. and D. Sapatoru, 'Executive Compensation and the Governance of Privatization Intermediaries in Romania', Central European University Privatization Project, working paper, 1992.

Earle, J., R. Frydman, and A. Rapaczynski, 'A Comparative Analysis of Voucher Privatization Programs in Eastern Europe', forthcoming in *The New Europe: Evolving Economic and Financial Systems in East and West*, Kluwer, 1993.

Frydman, R. and Rapaczynski, A. 'Evolution and Design in the East European Transition', Central European University Privatization Project, working paper, 1991.

Frydman, R. and Rapaczynski, A. 'Privatization and Corporate Governance in Eastern Europe. Can Markets be Designed?' in G.Winckler (ed.) *Central and Eastern Europe: Roads to Growth*, International Monetary Fund, 1992.

Frydman, R., A. Rapaczynski, J. Earle, D. Sapatoru *et al.*, *The Privatization Process*, CEU Privatization Reports, Vol. 1, CEU Press, London, 1992.

Holmstrom, B. and Milgrom, P., 'Multi-Task Principal-Agent Analyses: Incentive Contracts, Asset Ownership and Job Design', Technical Report No. 6 of the Stanford Institute for Theoretical Economics, July 1990.

Lacatus, I., 'Levels and Patterns of Consumption in Romania', unpublished paper of the Central European University Economics Program, 1992.

Mejstrik, M. and Hlavacek, J., 'Preconditions for Privatization in Czechoslovakia in 1991/92', in this volume.

Montias, J.M., 'The Romanian Economy: A Survey of Current Problems' in *European Economy*, Special Edition No. 2, 1991, pp. 177–198.

Szakadat, L., 'Property Rights in a Socialist Economy: the Hungarian Case', in this volume.

Szomburg, J., 'The Decision-Making Structure of Polish Privatization', in this volume.

8

Small privatization in Poland: an inside view

Piotr Tamowicz

Forty years of a command economy have left Poland with highly inefficient trade. Communism meant administrative division of markets and branches among the state-sector and cooperative industries and the restriction of the development of private entrepreneurship.

After the collapse of the communist regime in Poland in 1989, the new government realized that without radical changes in the ownership structure, economic progress would not be possible. Small privatization, which began in 1990, was the first visible step in restructuring ownership relations and building up a new market order in Poland's economy. The purpose of this chapter is to present the concept of this process and its goals, participants, results, and problems.

The chapter is divided into five sections. The first presents a definition of small privatization, which seems necessary because these words are often used in a misleading way. This section states what the goals of small privatization theoretically should be. Section 2 describes the legal framework of small privatization that allowed this process to emerge. Section 3 presents the techniques of asset allocation (employed by municipal authorities), the participants of the process, and the conflicts that emerged. The techniques of allocation were based on two opposite approaches to small privatization. The first allocated assets according to administrative criteria. The other, market-oriented technique of asset allocation was based on auctions. The techniques employed determined who would benefit from this process and who would lose. This led to conflicts among groups participating in small privatization: insiders (employees), outsiders (private entrepreneurs wishing to rent business premises), and municipal authorities. These conflicts often resulted in the slowing down or blocking of small privatization and to reducing the extent of market-oriented solutions. Section 4 discusses basic barriers to the process, that is, inventory evaluation, lack of human capital, and an unclear legal status of municipal real estate. Finally, Section 5 proposes some conclusions concerning small privatization.

1. Defining small privatization: the goals and dynamics of this process

1.1 The problem of definition

Small privatization can be defined as the efforts undertaken by municipal authorities to transfer to individual persons or private enterprises the right to use (rent) municipal assets that facilitate economic activity, access to which for private entrepreneurs had been restricted or simply impossible.

This definition is bound to raise many doubts about what is covered by small privatization, but it allows us to distinguish two key elements of this process. First, small privatization refers to municipal assets to which so far the private sector's access has been limited. It is local (municipal) and not central authority that initiates and carries out the process, although there may be involvement by the center in the form of advisory assistance, and it is an individual person or a partnership that is the beneficiary of the process.

Second, the adjective 'small' preceding the word 'privatization' refers both to the scale of the process, that is to its local dimension, and above all to the transfer of an incomplete set of property rights (for rent and not sale). This may result not only from the owner's (municipality) reluctance to alienate certain items of its property, but also from objective obstacles making such a sale impossible. This definition emphasizes the renting of municipal assets. Sale is not excluded, nor is it to be regarded as a wrong step on the privatization path, but it has only rarely occurred.

In the case of business premises, renting seems to be easier because it does not require large sums of capital, especially for small partnerships. However, when the owner is a municipality there can be some problems with rental arrangements due to the fact that a municipality is more bureaucratic than an economic institution. Instead of charging market rental fees, a municipal official may quote lower or higher fees in order to achieve certain social, political, or personal goals, that is, giving away privileges according to non-economic criteria.

1.2 The goals of small privatization

Small privatization should aim to contribute to the development of both resource and product markets. Resource markets would be developed through the creation of a free market for the business premises owned by the municipalities not subject to price or rent regulation, and not giving special treatment to any group such as employees. Product markets would be developed through the creation of economic units with a strong financial basis and incentives to invest and expand.

The two types of market development are interrelated and require brief explanation. In Poland, companies willing to enter the market for municipal business premises face two problems. First, it is the under-development of the financial market that together with high interest rates limits access to credit, especially for newly established companies. Therefore entrepreneurs must rely on their own savings, which are rather modest (and reduced by inflation), and on loans from relatives. Second, the supply of municipal business premises is small and inelastic.

These two facts lead to the conclusion that certain participants interested in rental contracts will demand special treatment (that is, low rental fees and easy access to loans) to balance their weak financial position. To gain these privileges, they will lobby and organize political pressure. If they are successful, and the municipal authorities award them the rental contracts, the market may become dominated by companies with small financial resources. The privileges will guarantee their existence in the market and reduce incentives to invest and expand.

Incentives to invest may be especially lacking when the business premises are taken over by employee-owned companies (employees of the shops when they were run by state-owned enterprises). These people often lack management skills and instead of thinking how to cut costs and increase output, may demand from municipal authorities additional privileges in the form of lowering rental fees. The over-development of the wholesale market with many private companies offering goods on soft credit terms constitutes another element which will support financially weak companies in the market.

1.3 Assets subject to small privatization

Small privatization covers municipal business premises. Because so far most of the information available, both in quantity and quality, refers to shops, we will put greater emphasis on them in the present work.

In December 1989, there were about 151,000 shops in Poland. About 124,000 of them were operated within the network of state and cooperative retail shops. The rest, that is, 27,000, were operated by the private sector. If we look at the area, the position of the public sector appears to have been still stronger. At that time, the total area of shops amounted to about 15 million square meters, of which the state sector controlled 95 percent of this area, while the private controlled only 5 percent. Within the state sector, 71 percent was used by the cooperative industry.

No information on the ownership of those facilities is available. This is due to the fact that under the communist regime ownership did not matter and no-one was interested in keeping records. Now the process of inventory taking is underway, but because there are more than 2,000 municipalities in Poland this data is dispersed and hard to obtain.

The process of renting business premises to private units is presented in Table 8.1.

Table 8.1 Renting businesses to private units

	Number of communal shops that have been rented
1990 first half	10,241
1990 III quarter	5,042
1990 IV quarter	7,853
1991 I quarter	5,139
1991 II quarter	2,169
1991 III quarter	1,768
1991 IV quarter	1,574
Total	33,786

From among 10,241 shops transferred to private units in the first half of 1990, only 961 shops (9.3 percent) were allocated by auctions. In the first half of 1990, no auction was organized in 14 of the total 49 voivodeships (districts) existing in Poland.

Small privatization accelerated month by month. In the third quarter of 1990, no shops were newly rented in five voivodeships, and in the fourth quarter of 1990 this number was reduced to two voivodeships. By the first quarter of 1991, there were no voivodeships where no transfer of shops had taken place.

2. The legal framework of small privatization

The ownership transformation within small privatization, as opposed to other processes reforming property rights, has taken place without any special regulations because of the specific character of the assets, which were possible to privatize based on the already existing legal regulations.

Three acts from among many regulations important to small privatization were especially important: the Economic Activity Act, the Local Self-Government Act, and the Housing Regulations Act. All these acts were passed separately without referring to small privatization, but they nonetheless constituted the legal framework of small privatization.

Until 1989, the undertaking of economic activity by private entities was subject to strict state control and regulation through the necessity to obtain permits. Such procedures were extremely time-consuming and discouraging. The administration was not very much inclined to issue such permits. The Economic Activity Act, passed in December 1989, broke with this philosophy. Currently, any person by virtue of law has the right to undertake any economic activity within the legislation in force. Removing administrative barriers facilitated the quantitative expansions of the private sector. In 1985, there existed about 418,000 private, unincorporated firms. In December 1988, this increased up to about 660,000 private units employing in total 1,181,000 people. In December 1990, this number had increased up to 1,135,000 business units, employing 1,915,000 people. By the end of 1991, the number had increased to 1,420,000.

This, although seemingly not connected with small privatization, facilitated the emergence of a group of potential participants and beneficiaries of small privatization. This meant that a constituency was formed of people most concerned that this process should progress. We believe that it is likely that if this Act had not been passed it would have been very difficult to find groups other than insiders (employees), as participants of small privatization.

The Local Self-Government Act, brought into force in May 1990, was another legal regulation of high importance for small privatization. This Act created a new structure of local government in which municipalities ('communes') enjoy the status of legal persons. Among the municipalities' duties, we can count dealing with such matters as land management, environmental protection, street cleaning, water supply, etc. Municipalities finance their activities from taxes and subsidies.[1] The Municipal Council, elected by the citizens for a term of four years, is the municipality's legislative body. The functions of the executive body are performed by the Municipal Board consisting of up to seven members. The Board is elected from among the members of the Municipal Council. Besides the new structure of municipal authorities, the Local Self-Government Act granted the municipalities property rights to certain groups of national property. The importance of this operation (called communalization) for small privatization is that it created a clear owner who could supervise property effectively and therefore initiate small privatization.

The housing regulations in force since 1974 have constituted the legal framework for the privatization of shops. Until June 1990, the regulations were more a barrier than a stimulating force. This was the result of the existing 'special renting mode' and administrative fee setting. The 'special renting mode' introduced by the communists after the war was a form of restricting property rights to which the legal owner was entitled: the owner could not freely dispose of his/her property. The 'special renting mode' was valid only in the case of private property. In the case of municipal premises, the administrative setting of rental fees on a very low level by the Council of Ministers was a much more important barrier in privatization. This low level of rental fees was a form of protection for insiders, because it made it impossible to use auctions to allocate business premises. The June 1990 amendment to the Housing Regulations Act abolished the 'special renting mode' and gave the municipalities the power to determine rental fees in the case of business.

These three laws established the legal foundations enabling and facilitating the course of small privatization. They facilitated the emergence of the new group of recipients of small privatization. The Local Self-Government Act created – at the local level – a real owner who was able to run small privatization. As a result, small privatization was also decentralized. The abolition of restrictions levied by the Housing Regulations Act untied the hands of the owner and allowed him/her to execute property rights.

3. Techniques, main participants and conflicts under small privatization

The lack of legal regulations precisely defining and imposing modes of asset allocation within the process of small privatization forced municipal decision-makers to work out individual procedures. Municipal authorities could choose from a set of techniques lying between two extreme options reflected by different attitudes to asset allocation.

The first, called below the administrative option, was a slight modification of the mechanism existing in the planned economy. The right to use municipal assets was transformed on the basis of an administrative decision and procedure.

At the other extreme was an allocation on the basis of market forces – the interaction of demand for and the supply of business premises. In that case a person who offered the highest price (rental fee) in an auction was awarded the rental contract.

3.1 The basic participants

Before the techniques of asset allocation are described, it is necessary to present the basic participants of small privatization.

We can distinguish three basic groups. First, we have the group of insiders, which includes people employed in shops rented and operated by state-owned enterprises, as well as private agents acting on behalf of state enterprises. In 1989, about 452,000 people were employed in the network of state-run shops. Insiders also include a group of private entrepreneurs who very often succeeded in acquiring the rental contracts only due to informal contracts with the local officials. In December 1989, 88,000 people were employed in private retail commerce.

It can be assumed that the behavior of insiders under small privatization was determined by two factors. The first is that small privatization and the abolition of the special renting mode created a situation where rental contracts with state-owned enterprises could be dissolved and as a result the insiders could lose their jobs.[2] The second is that small privatization created a chance for individuals to start their own business. These two factors together with the underdevelopment of the financial market led insiders to demand special privileges in the form of access to rental contracts. In the case of private entrepreneurs who had already obtained rental contracts, their behavior under small privatization was shaped by their effort to retain rental contracts.

The group of insiders enjoyed some elements of internal organization which resulted from the character of their employment: organizational ties within the structures of state-run enterprises. This enabled them to undertake and coordinate joint actions against other parties in a situation of conflict.

The outsiders consist of private entrepreneurs, already in a market and interested in renting premises to expand activity, as well as people wishing to rent premises in order to start economic activity. The outsiders' prospects of undertaking relatively unrestricted economic activity improved after December 1989 when the Act on Economic Activity was passed. However, for business entities access to such resources as municipal premises was limited until 1990 due to the monopolization of commerce (both retail and wholesale) by the state and cooperative enterprises. It is hard to estimate how large the group of outsiders is, but information on the number of participants in the auctions may cast some light. For instance, in Warsaw, 225 persons bid for 20 shops at one auction; at another 200 persons bid for 30 shops. In Lodz, 397 persons bid for 60 shops. Those numbers show that this group is not of marginal importance.

Municipal authorities constitute the third group of participants. Their role in the process results from the fact that they were both the owner of the assets and the decision-makers. The local elections held on 27 May 1990 were a turning point in the principles according to which local self-governments operated. Until then local self-governments were dominated by people with close connections to the ruling establishment, but these elections resulted in the replacement of the majority of local-level decision-makers.

3.2 Techniques

Because the decision about who is granted the right to rent the shop was derived from the mode of determining the rent, it is necessary to present both options from that point of view.

Administrative setting of rental fees for municipal business premises was on the basis of an analysis of maintenance costs and the expected solvency of the future user. The fact that auctions resulted in much higher fees is evidence of just how off-the-mark those fees were when set administratively. For instance, in the Warsaw district of Mokotow, rental fees set administratively amounted from 5,000 to 25,000 zloty per square meter, while at an auction, rents reached as much as 1,560,000 zloty per square meter. In another Warsaw district, they reached 200,000 zloty. In Opole, rental fees set administratively were 5,000 to 60,000 zloty, while at auction they reached 500,000 zloty per square meter. Rental fees varied according to the location and type of branches.

Market determination of rental fees by auction was a completely different mechanism. Participants of auctions bid for the right to rent business premises; the winner was the person who offered the highest rental fee. Participants of the auction were usually restricted to private people or firms, with a deposit of up to several thousand zloty to take part.

Pressure put on the municipal authorities by insiders who insisted on having priority in access to municipal assets, together with the skeptical attitude of some members of the municipal decision-making bodies to market solutions, often led to limiting the market allocation.

To what extent market allocation was at a disadvantage may be demonstrated by the fact that in the first half of 1990 only 961 out of 10,474 (that is 9.3 percent) municipally owned shops rented to private users were allocated by auctions. Moreover, even when auction was chosen as the main allocation method, insiders frequently enjoyed special privileges, for instance, in the form of partial rental 'givebacks' or the restricting of participation to current employees.

The existence of such an administrative market for municipal properties may also have an effect on the non-municipal as well as the municipal market due to the different extent of regulation existing in each. Setting rental fees in the municipal market below equilibrium will lead to excess demand. The unsatisfied demand will be shifted to the non-municipal market, which in the situation of insufficient supply of premises will force rents up above the level of prices on the municipal market. The difference between those two levels of rental fees constitutes the cost that someone would be willing to pay in order to rent a shop on the administrative market. The parallel existence of regulated and non-regulated markets thus creates a potential source of corruption.

The difference between administrative and market rental fees will also reflect the level of losses for the municipal budget in the form of non-earned rent. In other words, it will reflect the amount of subsidies the municipality paid to users of municipal premises. Moreover, the current owners of the non-municipal market will attempt to limit investments on the municipal market to keep the supply of premises low (and force demand to switch to the non-municipal market). They will endeavor to limit the inflow of investment capital into the non-municipal market to keep rental fees at a high level, which will mean extra profits for the owners dealing with the rental business. These observations suggest that the creation of an administratively regulated market of municipal shops, planned to serve the citizens, could eventually become the source of a vast number of problems of an economic and social nature.

3.3 The dynamics of the conflicts

Small privatization is bringing about changes which disturb the existing status quo and lead to conflict between the main participants of the process. Those conflicts, even though they never spread beyond the local level or caused violent eruptions of social unrest, exerted a definite influence on the pace and direction of the course of small privatization. Conflicts occurring under small privatization were caused by threats to the interests of the participants.

We can study the course and the results of the conflicts by examining the example of Krakow in 1990. Until the local election, the allocation of business premises had been arranged on an administrative basis, visibly favoring insiders. Because in this situation, the threat to the interests of this group was very weak, no greater tensions occurred. By June 1990, 481 shops had been rented to private entities, compared with a total number of 3,189 shops utilized by state enterprises at that time. As none of the rented premises was allocated by auction, it is reasonable to suppose that insiders were the main beneficiaries of the process. After the local election (27 May 1990) the problem of how to cope with small privatization became so controversial that it caused a split within the city authorities into two camps. The City Board favored the administrative approach, while the City Council proclaimed itself in favor of auctions.

Insiders preferred administrative allocation and several hundred people picketed the town hall when there was a session on small privatization. Their position gained the trade unions' support. But the City Board's actions were blocked by the City Council, freezing any privatization steps. The situation was again at a deadlock when the City Council passed a regulation (22 February 1991) requiring auctions in small privatization. The insiders then lodged a protest to the Krakow Voivode (President of Voivodeship) stating that excluding state-run enterprises from administrative allocation was not in conformity with the law. This action was intended to maintain the status quo, but did not produce the expected results. The struggle of interests and goals seriously slowed down the whole process so that no municipal shops were transferred to private entities, even to insiders, in the second half of 1990, while in the first quarter of 1991 only 23 shops were rented to private entities. This several month long deadlock was the price that had to be paid to get closer to the market option.

In Wroclaw, pressure exerted by insiders in the form of a short strike resulted in their being granted preferential treatment when participating in auctions.

We cannot easily generalize from these cases. Nevertheless, they show that the conflicts arising around small privatization focused on the insiders' attempts to assume a privileged position, giving them advantage over the other participants of the process. The passive reaction of the outsiders, coupled with a frequent lack of a clear-cut stance on the part of the municipal authorities, conspired even more to create solutions of an administrative character and an imbalance favoring insiders.

To conclude it is worthwhile to recite the arguments put forward for each option.

In favor of the administrative option it was claimed, first, that deregulation of rental fees would bring about an increase in prices of commodities traded in those shops. Second, allocation by auctions could result in a sudden increase in unemployment among employees in those premises, because they lack sufficient funds to finance market rental fees (in 1990 the average pay in the trade sector amounted to 83 percent of the average pay in five main sectors of the economy). Third, the branches and products characterized by low profitability and thus unable to pay a market rental fee, but which are 'indispensable' for citizens, will disappear.

In favor of the option of market allocation were cited the need to create competition among firms and the opportunity to increase budget revenues. According to statistical data published in *Gazeta Samorzadowa* (Self-Government Gazette), early in January 1991, 66 towns covered their expenditures from their own income by less than 50 percent, 139 town-communes by less than 40 percent, and 335 communes in the country were able to finance less than 25 percent of their expenditures. Eighty-nine communes in rural areas spent 100,000 zloty at most (about 10.5 USD) per capita annually. Nonetheless, this argument seems not to have been very successful in promoting market solutions.

4. Barriers to small privatization

Two elements seem to be the most visible and hard-to-overcome barriers to small privatization.

The shortage of skills appropriate for a market economy must be recognized as the most important barrier. Direct consequences of this shortage include the problems that the local authorities had in formulating clear rules of asset allocation and in preparing inventories. Because salaries in local administration are very low (lower than the national average), it is difficult to attract high-quality workers. The barrier of human capital also appeared in the form of weak consulting and scientific markets that were unable to supply decision-makers with adequate conceptual support.

The second barrier slowing down the process was the unclear legal status of municipal property. The central government expected municipalities to complete this operation within three months, but this was unrealistic. As was mentioned before, property rights under communism did not matter, and now it appears that many properties have two notary registries. In that situation it is a real problem to find out who is the owner. For example, in the city of Lodz out of 175,000 properties expected to be municipal property, only 20 percent enjoy clear property rights. This means that in about 140,000 cases the court will have to decide who is the proper owner: the municipality or someone else. The unclear legal status has allowed a situation to develop that has discouraged the sale of business premises.

5. Conclusions

Two fundamental objectives were mentioned in the case of small privatization: first, as the process supporting the creation of a product market which can be understood as creating business units with a strong financial basis, and second, as the process initiating the mechanism of market allocation of resources. The degree to which the first objective has been realized can be partially estimated on the basis of the increase in the number of private business entities. These data were cited above. It is difficult to specify to what extent small privatization contributed to accelerating the process of creating such entities, just as it is difficult to specify which of those entities are well equipped with capital and which are weak. We can assume that employee-owned companies renting municipal shops in many cases are financially weaker than companies formed by outsiders (especially for those who were dealing with economic activity, and because of that have more savings than others). However, in the situation when the market is not yet fully developed, and in some sections competition is still weak, development of the commodity market may be slowed down because of the existence of many financially weak entities there. This pace may be reduced further by administering rental fees which are a form of subsidy keeping insiders in the market, instead of forcing them to undertake appropriate adjustments. We can present, in a similar mode, how advanced we are in achieving our second objective. Although we do not have sufficient data concerning the whole process, the proportion of shops allocated to business units by auctions against the total number of allocated shops in the early half of 1990 (9.3 percent) can show the delay in finding solutions aimed at creating a resource market.

It is difficult to determine whether the number of business premises rented to private entities increased in the latter half of 1990 – that is after the local elections – as compared with the number in the early half of 1990. It could have been a result of the fact that new people assumed offices in the municipal authorities or, on the other hand, the natural acceleration of the process that started in the early half of 1990. Definitely the number of voivodeships where no shops were rented to private entities (in the early half of 1990 – before the local elections – such 'dead voivodeships' did not exist) was systematically falling.

Conflicts that erupted as the result of conditions of allocation slowed down privatization from place to place. However, it is difficult to say how strong the influence of this factor was in general terms. The question as to whether those conflicts could have been avoided seems to be pointless. It is beyond argument that the changes, not just modifying but destroying the past order and structure of interests must produce negative reactions, especially among those who were beneficiaries of this structure until now. What is more important is the search for methods of neutralizing attitudes hindering small privatization. That should undoubtedly happen through directing privatization both to insiders and outsiders. This would demand that local authorities assume a stronger position on the matter and provide some encouragement to outsiders to articulate their expectations as to access to municipal resources.

The local character and the mode of realization are the characteristics of small privatization. A debate about the degree of centralization or decentralization of the process would be in its nature a debate on the sense of self-governments' existence. The autonomy of local governments in Poland has strong political support and any move to centralize small privatization would even be interpreted as a threat to these self-governments. Moreover, placing the power to make decisions concerning small privatization with the local micro sphere is arguably better than having centralized steering of the process. It is, first of all, the result of shortening the channels of information flow and, second, the logistical possibility of steering the process effectively and relatively fast. The experiences gained from the implementation of administrative allocation of business premises may lead to attempts to limit municipal authorities' freedom in the matter. Definitely creating certain legal barriers restricting the possibility to employ administrative solutions would be beneficial. Nevertheless the introduction of this solution would mean breaking a very strong self-government lobby, which is not very likely.

The material presented above sheds some light on the course of small privatization. A more illuminating analysis will be possible when more reliable data are available. Observation of how municipal resource markets function when there are different levels of market regulations in place might be a very interesting supplement to the valuation of costs and benefits of small privatization.

Notes

1. The following constitute the commune's revenue: taxes and local fees (a tax on roads, a tax on dogs, a fair trading fee, a real property tax). Apart from that the municipal budget receives 5 percent of the income tax paid to the central budget by the legal entities situated within the municipality and 30 percent of tax on wages.
2. The danger of losing one's job was fueled by the constant increase in the number of unemployed and a substantial decrease in real earnings; according to the data of the Central Planning Office the purchasing power of salaries and wages dropped in 1990 by 15 percent as compared with the previous year. In January 1990 unemployment amounted to 54,000 and was rising by about 100,000 every month reaching 1,126,000 by the end of the year.

PART III

The Stock Market and foreign capital: some evidence from Hungary

9

Evolution of the Hungarian capital market: the Budapest Stock Exchange

Kálmán Mészáros

Introduction

In this study I shall offer a general overview of the evolutionary emergence of one of Europe's youngest stock markets, the Budapest Stock Exchange (BSE).

Going back to the roots of postwar securities trading in the early 1980s, I first dwell on institutional aspects culminating in the re-opening of the BSE in 1990 and then on its main organizational framework and operational mechanism. I then proceed to make the reader familiar with progress in the legal environment, detailing present regulations in securities trading.

Having presented institutional and legal structures, I next try to provide insight into actual happenings on the Hungarian capital market embedded in historical – and as such somewhat arbitrary – perspective.

Finally, this chapter summarizes and evaluates the BSE's first year and a half of functioning, highlighting major problems, trends, and domestic and international conditions affecting its performance, as well as future tendencies.

An attempt has been made throughout the chapter to point out privatization contexts wherever possible.

The Budapest Stock Exchange: historical review

The re-opening of the Budapest Stock Exchange was preceded by long and serious debate. Many doubted whether the establishment of a stock exchange was justified in an economy based primarily on state ownership, whether it was advisable to create a strict law regulating the public issues of securities and defining the interests of investors, and whether there was any point in creating a concentrated market at a time when only very few securities met the requirements of such a law. Referring to the experience of developed Anglo-Saxon countries, some claimed that the re-opening of the stock exchange as a new institution was absolutely unnecessary.

Despite all these doubts the BSE was established on 21 June 1990. It had been argued that, due to the lack of domestic private capital and institutional network, companies would be heavily undervalued setting false standards for large-scale privatization. To dispel such fears companies were quoted parallel on the Austrian and Hungarian stock markets with arbitrage possibility ruling out major price deviations.

The history of the re-opening after an interval of some forty-two years goes back to the beginning of the 1980s. At the end of 1982, new decrees were passed regulating the terms of the issue of bonds, and increasing the range of those who could utilize this form of financing. The bond market rapidly took off and reached a peak in 1987 when the total value of annual issues increased threefold over the previous year, exceeding 17 billion Hungarian forints (HUF). Within this, the volume of bonds issued exclusively for private persons was three times the number of bonds sold to legal entities. Bonds were purchased primarily by individuals and mainly issued by companies and financial institutions.

Despite the absence of a stock exchange, marketing of the bonds on the secondary market increased and, following the introduction of the two-tier banking system (separation of commercial banks from the central bank), a pilot market was created for the above activities. On 22 December 1987, twenty-two banks and financial institutions signed the Agreement on the Trade of Securities, the legal precursor of the BSE, addressing issues of the organization of the uniform secondary market. From then on, in the securities business regular meetings – Stock Exchange Days – were held once a week (later twice and from the end of 1989 three times a week) in the Budapest International Trade Center. These meetings facilitated the refining of the first rules, the usage of the open-outcry method of trading and the settlement system of the would-be stock exchange.

Beside these decrees regulating the issue of bonds, many additional laws played an important role in the revival of the securities market. In 1988, decrees allowing the insurance of Treasury Bills by the state and Certificates of Deposit (Cds) by financial institutions were passed. The issue of securities for the public was first permitted by Act No. VI of 1988 – Economic Associations – providing an organizational and legal basis for the establishment and operation of associations (that is, modern company forms). Act No. XXIII of 1989 – Transformation of Economic Organizations and Associations – regulates transformation without liquidation, so-called full-scale transformation, whereby the economic association becomes the universal legal successor of the transformed organization or state enterprise. Another important law concerning the securities market is Act No. XIV of 1988 on Investment by Foreigners in Hungary which among other provisions guarantees the repatriation of the capital invested by foreigners (and its proceeds) in the currency of investment.

The public issue and marketing of securities and the establishment of the stock exchange is regulated by Act No. VI of 1990. According to this law, a stock exchange can be established by at least 15 founding members (companies with broker-dealer licence); with a stock capital of at least 150 million HUF, announcing the fact of establishment, approving the statutes and simultaneously electing the officers. The foundation must be approved by the Council of Ministers. In Hungary, a stock exchange is not established by a law nor by the Hungarian government, but by the firms organized to trade securities. The law does not preclude the possibility of establishing several stock exchanges simultaneously.

Organizational set-up

The BSE was established with a stock capital of 211.6 million HUF. Each one of the 40 founding brokerage agencies contributed equally 3 million HUF to the establishment. The National Bank of Hungary offered in-kind contribution and cash up to a total value of 30 million HUF. The Hungarian government through the State Development Institute (though not a member of the BSE) provided the right of use of a 300-square-meter stock exchange hall and offices, in the value of 61.1 million HUF.

The BSE is a fully self-governing and self-regulating organization, making its own decisions, electing its bodies and officers. Stock-exchange autonomy can be limited solely by the authorities and proceedings stipulated in the provisions of the Act on Securities. The stock exchange is a non-profit organization which plans to finance its operations autonomously.

The organizational set-up of the BSE is rather similar to that of corporations. The main organ is the General Meeting (GM). Each member has one vote. The Stock Exchange Council, a central organ for strategic and controlling decisions, is elected by GM. At least half of its members are representatives of the member broker-dealer companies, while others represent the interests of the issuers and investors, respectively.

The main operative and executory body is the Stock Exchange Secretariat, which provides for the daily operations of trading and settlement as well as for the preparatory work of Council's decision-making. The members of the Ethical Committee, a forum to create rules of fair conduct for the whole range of participants are also elected by the GM. To decide on legal issues of securities trading a Court of Arbitration is also elected by the GM, from among legal experts in this field.

Operational mechanism

The trading system of the BSE differs from practices in Germany and Austria, and resembles mostly the Anglo-American system. In securities traded on the stock exchange, three types of transactions can be carried out: spot, futures, and option deals.

Brokers announce their offers out loud for securities which in turn can be reciprocated by counter-offers as well as bidding. On the stock exchange all prices and price quotations are formed in free trading between sellers and buyers. Trading is directed by the Speaker, who also decides in cases of dispute.

Brokers are obliged to accept and carry out orders for securities, listed on the BSE. Stocks in the traded category (that is, of lower investment grade) are not, however, subject to this rule. If conditions for business are the same, brokers with licences for commercial and brokerage activities are allowed to trade securities on their own account only after having attempted to carry out clients' orders.

Settlements of payments and stock transfers have to be effected within five business days reckoned from the day of the transactions.

The main problems in the present functioning of the system are twofold: first, due to low-grade banking infrastructure and computerization, remittance of payment (particularly for foreigners) may take a substantially longer period; second, short of a BSE central depository, physical transfer of securities is cumbersome and disorderly.

General regulation of securities trading

In this section attention is focused on the most salient aspects of relevant legal regulations.

It is very important to determine the scope of those who are qualified to obtain a licence for issuing and trading securities. The State Securities Supervisory Board established by the relevant law can grant such a licence only to those limited-liability companies or joint-stock companies – having only registered shares – which have a minimum stock capital of 50 million HUF, deal exclusively with the marketing and trading of securities, and meet all the material, technical and personal requirements specified by the Act on Securities.

If an association wishes to buy and sell securities for only clients' orders (broker services), the terms and conditions of operation differ only in the amount of the minimum capital requirement. Consequently, stock brokerage activities in securities can be pursued as the sole activity and in possession of an authorization by a company which has a stock capital of at least 10 million HUF if it is a joint-stock company. Brokerage commissions are not subject to any restrictions; their typical range is between 0.5–1.5 percent with a minimum handling fee of about 300 HUF.

The Act on Securities and the Statutes of the Stock Exchange also regulate the suspension and termination of membership, which may occur upon voluntary withdrawal or exclusion due to violation of certain provisions of the Act on Securities, or if the State Securities Supervisory Board withdraws the brokerage licence. As a result of termination of membership the assets of the stock exchange may not decrease in value.

The Act on Securities also regulates the informational terms of publicly issued securities as opposed to non-public, private issues. According to regulations the company issuing shares must disclose relevant information on both the company itself and the securities in question, that is based on data not older than six months. The company is obliged to supply information on main figures of operation and financial status on a regular basis, at least once a year.

The statutes of the stock exchange define two types of securities; traded but not listed on the stock exchange, and those which are listed. Both are to meet basic requirements of publicly issued and traded securities, as stated in the Act on Securities. Furthermore, their transfer during issue shall not be excluded or limited and must not be under liquidation or bound by any pre-emption clause.

Securities traded but not listed on the BSE are required to have a minimum nominal value of at least 10 million HUF. In the case of shares (as opposed to bonds) at least 10 percent of the stock capital or 200 million HUF must be issued to the public. In addition, the joint-stock company is required to have a stock capital of at least 100 million HUF and out of the securities in question at least 1,000 must be issued. The issuer is to supply continuously information pertaining to its transactions. The introduction is carried out by members of the stock exchange. Within fifteen days following introduction, members of the stock exchange must offer at least 3 percent of the nominal value of the shares for sale and at least 0.5 percent of them in the course of the first five days.

Listed securities have to meet further requirements: public nominal value must be at least 50 million HUF; in the case of shares, at least 25 percent of the stock capital or 500 million HUF must be publicly offered and a minimum stock capital of 200 million HUF is required. The company is to issue at least 5,000 of the securities in question. The company is to complete at least one full business year and must also have its balance sheets audited.

A fee of 100,000 HUF must be paid by the issuer for the introduction of the securities on the stock exchange. In the case of listed securities, the fee is 300,000 HUF. There is also a fee to be paid for the continuous trading of securities on the stock exchange. As a rule, issuers are charged between 3–6 percent of capital raised, covering roughly evenly lead-management, underwriting, and selling fees.

Transactions in securities conducted by an insider or his agent using information which could affect substantially the price and not available for the public, as on all stock markets, are also strictly prohibited in Hungary.

In order to limit insider trading, the Director of the Stock Exchange Secretariat has the authority to suspend for a maximum of three days the trading of certain securities on the stock exchange if in the opinion of the Director the price or the nature of transactions deflects widely from the fair market price.

The Stock Exchange Council or the State Securities Supervisory Board can suspend for an indefinite period the trading of any securities should they find that there is no guarantee that further sales would be performed in the spirit of fair trade on the stock exchange or the transactions would endanger legitimate interests of the investor as well as the balance of the market.

Licensing of activities on the securities market which involve transfers of foreign exchange is performed by the State Securities Supervisory Board and the National Bank of Hungary. In order to develop the domestic stock exchange, securities issued inside the country can be traded abroad if listed on the BSE.

During the first term of operation (up to June 1991) of the BSE ten stocks were introduced. In reference to the two categories of stock, unlisted but traded and listed, six stocks belong to the first group: Martfü, Müszi, Dunaholding, Nitroil, Skála-Coop and Novotrade, and four to the second category: IBUSZ, Konzum, Skála-Sztráda, and Fotex.

Description, valuation, and main figures of the companies traded or listed on the BSE

Novotrade

Though Novotrade is the last company to have its stock included among the traded stocks of the BSE up to June 1991, it was the first company to have its shares publicly traded since 1984 in Hungary and is also the first ever East European company to have its shares traded on a Western OTC capital market (since September 1989). The company was, for that purpose, an obvious choice from among 30–40 candidates in that its main profile (software) had substantial strength but also diversified investments, and that its shares had already been traded publicly in Hungary in a range between 130 and 180 percent of nominal value between 1984 and 1989. The new issue for international investors (to the tune of about 1 million USD) was also a test model to see how Hungarian legal regulations would allow for such transaction and how the international investment society would react. Pricing was done on a rather random basis, since no international standard consolidated financial figures had been available, taking the lower limit of the previously domestically recorded price range (that is, 130 percent) as a fair starting point. At that time this was equal to a P/E ratio of about 6. Lacking a classic issue prospectus a press conference was arranged in Vienna for potential prospective investors. Due to the small size and exotic nature of the deal it was oversubscribed by some forty times within hours and the share price doubled within a week after trading had commenced. Up to now share prices have been moving within a wide range of 200–920 percent of nominal value.

A brief summary of the company follows:

Share capital: 425 m HUF (10,000 HUF par value each)
Last new issue: May 1990; 200 m HUF at 240 percent
Business line: software–hardware, wholesale and retail trading, about 70 subsidiaries with a highly diversified portfolio
P/E range (last 12 months): 10–40.
1991 expected consolidated total sales: 3.7 bn HUF
1991 expected profit after tax: 80 m HUF
Ownership structure: foreign shareholding about 80 percent; controlling shareholders: US Georgetown Group.

IBUSZ

Novotrade's success demonstrated that the way was open for larger-sized IPOs of Hungarian corporations, especially in sectors that have inherent expansionary potential due to Hungarian-specific comparative advantages (mainly in 'brain-intensive' and traditional Hungarian branches). Dozens of such companies had been screened and interviewed, and finally, all things considered, IBUSZ was held by all parties concerned as an optimal candidate for this project. It was of specific importance that, although run as a state-owned company, the legal form of IBUSZ has always been a corporation.

Financial figures for the last three years having been converted to international standards and audited by a recognized Western auditor, the company was able to match listing criteria not only of the BSE, but also – first among Eastern European firms – of a Western (the Vienna) stock exchange. The double flotation was timed so as to give a boost to the just re-opened BSE. Thus far, this transaction is the only privatization to have gone public: the state's stake was reduced from 100 to 63 percent, though largely in a latent way (that is, a capital increase), as existing state shares sold were only some 3 percent.

Pricing of the stocks posed difficult problems, especially in view of the fact that no Hungarian standard had existed before and there were public fears of selling out Hungarian companies at far too low prices. The parties finally agreed that the higher edge of P/E of companies working in the same field in the West (that is, a P/E of 10) should be applied. The public offering was about 30 million USD, twenty-three times oversubscribed in the first days of the subscription period. Allocation favored Hungarian and foreign small investors.

Due to the technical overdemand, prices rose to more than twofold in the first days of trading, causing thus some political turmoil over alleged underpricing. This fact coupled with the not yet ready privatization concept of the government unfortunately slowed down this method of privatization for state-owned companies. The next candidates to follow suit came in June 1991 on the market.

A brief summary of the company follows:

Share capital: 1.2 bn HUF (1,000 HUF par value each)
Last new issue: June 1990; 440 m HUF at 490 percent (P/E of 10)
Business line: tourism, banking, financial services
P/E range (last 12 months): 10–37
1991 expected consolidated total sales: 10 bn HUF
1991 expected profit after tax: 400 m HUF
Ownership structure: state 63 percent; public 37 percent
Market share in BSE securities trading: 1990 55 percent, 1991 1st quarter 7 percent.

First Hungarian Coop-Brewery Ltd.

The huge and lasting success of the first Western-type public offering encouraged others (primarily firms in the cooperative and private sectors, owing to the above-mentioned circumstances) to follow the same route despite the rather unfavorable international investment climate for new issues. Out of four firms racing neck-and-neck, First Hungarian Coop-Brewery Ltd. came out first to the market offering to the public about 10 percent of its stock, thereby getting in the traded category on the BSE. The issue price was fairly extravagant, reflecting a P/E of 23. Valuation might have considered two significant factors: on the one hand, IBUSZ stock market price neared this ratio and this was the first stock to follow it; on the other hand, this company is a typical one for acquisition in the medium term, so even this price might be sooner or later justified. The issue was slightly oversubscribed, but prices fell back by 20 percent within a short time.

A brief summary of the company follows:

Share capital: 935.1 m HUF (1,000 HUF par value each)
Publicly offered in October 1990: 94 m HUF at 255 percent (P/E of 23)
Business line: beer and soft drink production bottling (3 percent market share in Hungary)
P/E range (last 12 months): 14–23
1991 expected total sales: 1.3 bn HUF
1991 expected profit after-tax: 150 m HUF
Ownership structure: major shareholders: Kobánya Brewery, OKHB (Commercial and Credit Bank), foreign investors 49.98 percent, public 10 percent

Market share in BSE trade: 1990 2 percent, 1991 1st quarter 3.5 percent.

Rumors of an acquisition by an Austrian industrial buyer have recently become widespread.

Konzum Trading Ltd.

A rapidly growing wholesale and retail trading company in southern Hungary of the cooperative sector, it had already had its shares traded for some weeks in the OTC market in Austria before the new issue. Upon such rumors in mid-October 1990 a speculative buying spree skyrocketed prices to some 1,200 percent, so even a modest 900 percent issue price reflected a P/E of 19.5. The issue was slightly oversubscribed, and was thereafter the second stock to be ranked in the listed category on the BSE. Of course, a market correction soon lowered the share price by some 50 percent, and the stock has ever since been traded around this benchmark.

Recently there has been news that this stock will be quoted on the OTC market in Germany as well, which has substantially increased turnover but with price remaining relatively stable.

A brief summary of the company follows:

Share capital: 460 m HUF (10,000 HUF par value each)
Last new issue: October 1990, 60.4 m HUF at 900 percent (P/E of 19.5)
Business lines: wholesale and retail trade in food products, clothing and industrial products, catering, tourism
P/E range (last 12 months): 7.5–22
Total net sales: 900 m HUF
1991 expected total sales: 2.9 bn HUF
1991 expected profit after tax: 290 m HUF
Ownership structure: major shareholders: cooperatives, foreign banks; public about 30 percent
Market share in BSE trade: 1990 8 percent, 1991 1st quarter 19 percent.

Fotex

Hungary's most dynamically growing partly private company with a natural appeal to small private investors was set to tap the capital market in late October 1990. To achieve the most widespread shareholding structure, stocks were broken down to an unprecedented 100 HUF par value. Stocks were priced at 199 percent, reflecting a P/E of 14. The issue price was thus far perhaps the biggest success in Hungary: at the time of the stock-exchange crash in the West and the cab drivers' blockade in Hungary, thousands of people camped in front of the selling agents' offices one day before the subscription period to be able to subscribe for the 500 m HUF new issue. Subscription closed after two days; small Hungarian investors were favored in the allocation. Simultaneously, infrastructural weaknesses in retail investment banking became highly apparent as well as regulatory problems of share distribution. Fotex stocks were initially only in the traded category on the BSE, but this March – having fulfilled the more stringent requirements – they were promoted to the listed category. Since the commencement of trading, share prices have been moving at 10–20 percent above the issue price, though early spring prices were buoyed by the news of a new mega issue (1.37 bn HUF par value equal to about 52 m USD market value) to 270 percent, that is, 35 percent above last October's issue price. Volume in trading also increased dramatically during March and April 1991 while this deal was in progress. Fotex now has the highest market capitalization on the BSE: its market value has grown from 11 m HUF in 1984 to about 10 bn HUF in 1991!

A brief summary of the company follows:

Share capital: 4.47 bn HUF (100 HUF par value each)
New issue in October 1990: 500 m HUF at 199 percent (P/E of 14)
Business line: photo and optical services, glassware manufacture, wholesale and retail trade
P/E range (last 12 months): 14–22
1991 expected consolidated total sales: 4 bn HUF
1991 expected consolidated profit after tax: 712 m HUF
Ownership structure: main shareholders: Blackburn International (US), Skála World Trade, International Institutional Investors; public 15–20 percent
Market share in BSE trade: 1990 10 percent, 1991 1st quarter 60 percent.

Dunaholding

Dunaholding is a two-year-old company in an entirely new business. To secure the success of the new issue and to make the company known, a very aggressive PR campaign preceded the November 1990 subscription period. The issue price was fixed at 380 percent, tantamount to a P/E of 24 with unlimited new issue volume foreboding a price collapse once trading starts. The strength of the company lies mainly in the innovative and professional management and staff. However, it still remains highly speculative and risky. The stock was accepted by the BSE in the traded category. Prices, as a rule fell back by 30–40 percent, to reach the issue level only in recent weeks upon rumors of negotiations of a major partner taking a major stake in the company.

A brief summary of the company follows:

Share capital: 1.7 bn HUF (10,000 HUF par value each)
Last new issue: November 1990, unlimited HUF at 380 percent (P/E of 24)
Business line: financial and investment advisory services, portfolio management ('inherited' main holding is the biggest and controversial Hungarian stationery retail company 'APISZ')
P/E range (last 12 months): 17–28
1991 expected consolidated total sales: 4 bn HUF
1991 expected consolidated profit after tax: 400 m HUF
Ownership structure: main shareholders: Hungarian banks, IBUSZ and 30 companies; about 2,500 private shareholders
Market share in BSE trade: 1990 6 percent, 1991 1st quarter 1 percent.

Müszi

The next stock in the traded category on the BSE was Müszi, a 22-year-old company engaged in agricultural management control services and well known among the public thanks to a highly effective TV commercial in the mid-1980s. The trading in shares started in early December following a successful new issue of 80 m HUF at 180 percent (a P/E of 15.6) the previous month.

A brief summary of the company follows:

Share capital: 330 m HUF (10,000 HUF par value each)
Last new issue: November 1990; 80 m HUF at 180 percent (P/E of 15.6)
Business line: management, control computer and information services and software development for agriculture
P/E range (last 12 months) 11–13
1991 expected total sales: 1.4 bn HUF
1991 expected profit after tax: 44 m HUF
Ownership structure: 21 cooperatives as main shareholders, public about 30 percent
Market share in BSE trade: 1990 1 percent, 1991 1st quarter 1.5 percent.

Nitroil

There are speculations on the hidden motives that spurred this relatively little known and small company to go public in January 1991 and to have its stock quoted in the traded category of the BSE. Issue price was set to 150 percent (P/E of 12.6) to be followed by price improvement, although trends can hardly be asserted in view of sporadic trading.

A brief summary of the company follows:

Share capital: 274.9 m HUF (10,000 HUF par value each)
Last new issue: January 1991; 50 m HUF at 150 percent (P/E of 7 percent)
Business line: production of pesticides and chemicals for the pharmaceutical and plastic industry
P/E range (in 1991 1st quarter): 7–8
1991 expected total sales: 900 m HUF
1991 expected profit after tax: 58 m HUF
Ownership structure: main shareholders: DKV (oil refinery); Péti Nitrogen Works; SZKFI (hydrocarbon research institute)
Market share in BSE trade: 1991 1st quarter 0.05 percent.

Skála-Sztráda Ltd.

Like Fotex, this trading company has grown out of the Skála empire with Skála-Coop having retained majority control. Skála-Sztráda Ltd., located in a prospective growth area between Vienna and Budapest and with a business profile very similar to that of Konzum Trading Ltd., had its shares listed on the BSE in January 1991. The last new issue in August last year of 70 m HUF at a modest 146 percent (P/E of 3) was heavily oversubscribed and the stock price showed good gains thereafter, peaking out at 450 percent. Trade in these stocks is continuous and balanced on the BSE.

A brief summary of the company follows:

Share capital: 292.5 m HUF (10,000 HUF par value each)
Last new issue: August 1990; 70 m HUF at 146 percent (P/E of 3)
Business line: wholesale and retail trade in food, clothing, and industrial products, catering in northwestern region of Hungary.
P/E range (last 12 months): 4–9
1991 expected total sales: 3.3 bn HUF
1991 expected total net sales: 700 m HUF
1991 expected profit after tax: 150 m HUF
Ownership structure: majority shareholder: Skála-Coop Ltd.
Market share in BSE trade: 1991 1st quarter 1.2 percent.

Skála-Coop Ltd.

Skála-Coop Ltd., primarily a trading house and a conglomerate of companies (of which among others Fotex and Skála-Sztráda emerged), was the second Hungarian company to have its stocks traded in the Austrian OTC market in the wake of Novotrade. But partly due to its rather intricate internal and shareholding structure it was the last company up to now to have about 30 percent of its shares qualified in the traded category on the BSE. Ever since its foundation in 1976 as a company of the cooperative sector, it has won public acclaim through its incessant innovative and expansionary efforts. It created a new image in domestic trade pioneering into emerging and diversified ventures. During the last few years it has been doing its best to digest the far too rapid expansion and to streamline its business profile and company organization towards a holding-like structure.

A brief summary of the company follows:

Share capital: 3.261 bn HUF (10,000 HUF par value each)
Last new issue: August 1989; 500 m HUF at 130 percent (P/E of 7.7)
Publicly traded shares: 1.112 bn HUF maximal value
Business line: holding-like company engaged primarily in trading, manufacturing, and services – focus on wholesale and retail trading
P/E range (last 12 months): 8–22
1991 expected consolidated total sales: 32.6 bn HUF (net sales figures are not available)
1991 expected consolidated profit after tax: 880 m HUF
Ownership structure: main shareholders: domestic cooperatives, corporate and private investors 80 percent, foreign investors 20 percent (Tengelmann Group, banks) (Tengelmann Group has an option until 1995 to acquire majority control)
Market share in BSE trade: 1991 1st quarter 7.4 percent.

A brief report on the first year and a half at the BSE

As mentioned in the first section, due to direct linkage to the Austrian capital market, the BSE started its operation with a real boost with foreign investors playing prime roles. This linkage also made apparent the BSE's infrastructural deficiencies, owing to which 70–80 percent of trade in Hungarian stocks has been and is still transacted outside the country.

However, as compared with the preceding six months, trade volume on the BSE rose sixfold after its foundation on 21 June 1990, reaching a total volume of 7 bn HUF in 1990 (0.9 bn HUF until 21 June). Trade volume in the first quarter of 1991 followed this pace totalling about 2.5 bn HUF. About 90 percent of trade is done in stocks and 10 percent in bonds, a dramatic change compared with the pre-BSE period when this ratio was just the opposite. Major investors are foreign institutions and private persons, though Hungarian private investors are becoming more active with their number nearing 100,000 (1 percent of population).

Of the current 42 BSE members, those with full licence (74 percent) transact 90 percent of total trade, those with only brokerage licence (26 percent) only 10 percent. About 80 percent of total trade is concentrated among eight members.

A stock-exchange index was introduced in 1991 based on the market value of the eight most actively traded stocks. The index started at 1,000 based on the stance on 1 January 1991, and stood at 1,140 in mid-May.

As discussed earlier, trade on the BSE commenced with a boost of the first – and up to now only – privatization-like IBUSZ issue setting rather high standards for the following transactions. An unfavorable international investment climate coupled with recessionary signs and revised profit forecasts within the Hungarian economy led to a general downward trend in share prices in the second half of last year. In 1990 it was the Gulf Crisis, in 1991 the Gulf War, the collapse of the East European market, disturbances in the Soviet Union and recession in the domestic market that – more or less, directly or indirectly – affected all the stocks quoted on the BSE and national and international demand. Several new issues had to be postponed and prices were driven down to unforeseen bottoms. This is well demonstrated in Charts 9.1 to 9.3.

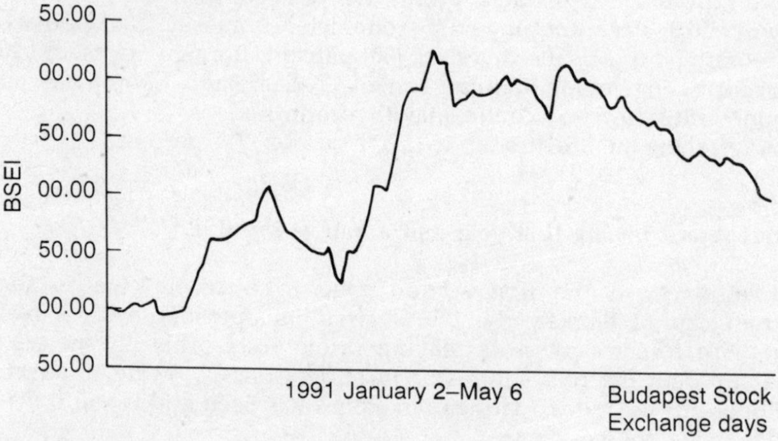

Chart 9.1 Budapest Stock Exchange

Chart 9.1 shows the BSE Index evolution: the high stand in March–April can be attributed to a high-priced Fotex mega new issue, since Fotex has a dominant weight in the index.

Chart 9.2 traces back IBUSZ stock prices in Vienna and Budapest: price differences can be attributed to the cost of arbitrage through a special share transfer mechanism (totalling about 5 percent).

Chart 9.3 compares the BSE Index and the VSE (Vienna) Index formation: they show a roughly similar pattern with two exceptions. In March–April, the BSE Index was artificially high due to the already-mentioned Fotex issue, and recoveries from price slumps were less

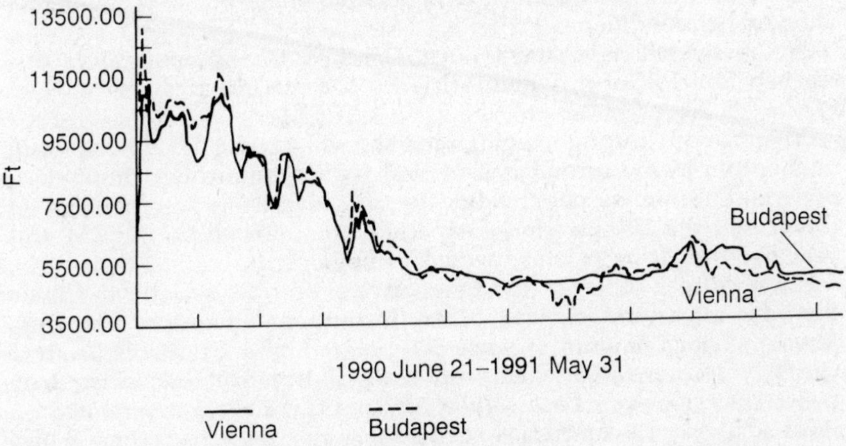

Chart 9.2 IBUSZ stock prices – Vienna–Budapest

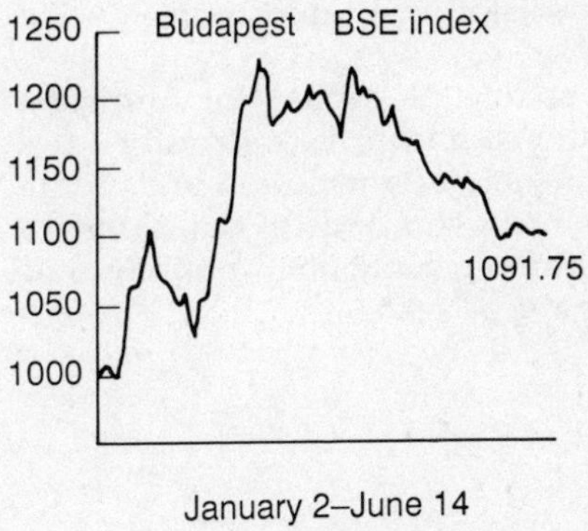

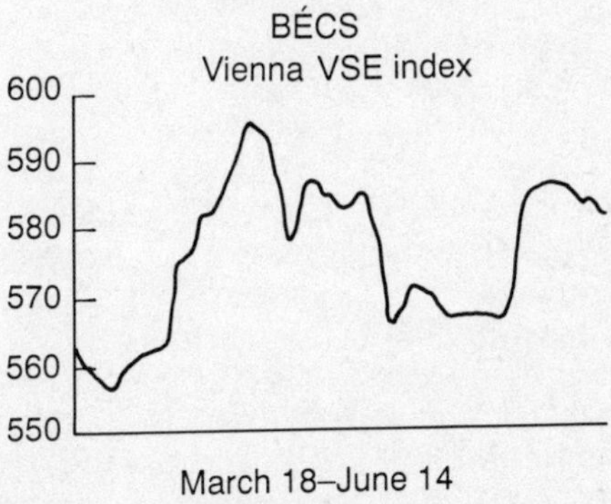

Chart 9.3 Budapest and Vienna Stock Exchange index

marked on the BSE due to the cumulative effect of external–internal unfavorable conditions.

On an overall assessment it can be said that support level was reached at a P/E of 5, while resistance became effective at a level of P/E of 15–20.

Privatization through going public will in all likelihood gain momentum in the second half of 1991 with presumably Pannonplast, Styl, and Danubius coming first on the market in the footsteps of IBUSZ. Of the 20 new stocks expected to be floated on the BSE this year 5–6 are to be of state-owned companies.

For a couple of years to come private persons will be the main domestic investors for lack of an institutional investors' network. Private savings amount to some 370 bn HUF and 2 bn USD (in hard currency accounts), of which realistically 5–10 percent could be channelled into stock purchase. While private firms have a natural appeal, most state-owned companies need strategic partners to become attractive enough to the public. Since liquidity of stocks is also of primary concern for the public, and for the time being no real OTC or other secondary market exists, BSE quotation is likely to gain more significance.

The other main source of capital for Hungarian privatization is international institutional and private investors. For them to be more active on the BSE a more sophisticated and upgraded infrastructure is of prime importance. This lack explains the fact that around 70 percent of trade volume in Hungarian publicly traded stocks is transacted outside Hungary at present.

10

Foreign capital in Hungary's privatization

Tivadár Faur

The shaping of the new structure of ownership in Eastern Europe is inseparably linked to the development of market relations and the re-establishment of enterprises' competitiveness. This process began in Hungary in 1989, and the accelerating course of privatization has stimulated significant foreign interest. New government policies on foreign investment, such as legal and financial regulations protecting property, defining clear business conditions, and providing special incentives for joint ventures, encourage foreign investment. On the macro and micro levels, foreign capital is equally indispensable for the tasks of restructuring, introducing investment resources, modernizing products and technology, and extending markets.

By the end of 1990, total foreign investment in Hungary totalled about 1 billion dollars; this is forecast to double by the end of 1991 (source: SPA). Purchases of state-owned assets account for over half of this investment. In spite of the large number of joint ventures, the incoming capital is essentially tied to only a few dozen investments. With regard to the magnitude of investments, the number of investors, the choice, and the methods of capital associations and purchasers, the characteristics of investment cannot be explained only by local conditions. Often, the impact of changes on the wider international market have been decisive, and the first investments seem to be tantamount to the establishment of bridgeheads.

The nature of the capital market and privatization infrastructure is also a significant influence on foreign activity (for instance the quality of financial and consulting services, state privatization authorities, banks, and property appraisal companies).

This chapter first discusses the importance of foreign participation in the restructuring of Hungary's economy. Next it outlines the legal framework for investors in Hungary as an important factor in investment decisions. Based on a survey of the investment process in Hungary in the last two years, characteristics of the foreign participation are summarized with the aim of discerning the motives and methods of investment. The final section considers some elements of the capital market, one of the most crucial factors but also the most underdeveloped, throughout the East European region.

The roles of foreign capital in Hungary

In the past few decades, as a result of the peculiarities of a series of political-economic arrangements, the economy of Hungary has fallen behind. Technical underdevelopment became widespread and attempts at product and technology adoption from developed countries were unsuccessful. The Hungarian economy survived this period of low production efficiency combined with exaggerated distribution demands only by continually increasing its indebtedness. The restrictive policy that followed led to a reduction in domestic capital formation, which in turn further contributed to the already considerable technical underdevelopment.

Under these circumstances, an influx of direct foreign investment is doubly advantageous, because it simultaneously counterbalances the shortfalls of domestic capital accumulation and narrows the productivity gap by modernizing means of production. In the course of introducing equity capital, the investor becomes interested not only in a passive portfolio investment, but also in actively improving the management and market conditions of an enterprise. Through the introduction of marketable products and by transforming the production and marketing techniques, cooperation with foreign investors can gradually improve the market positions of industrial branches which were previously state enterprises. The separation from developed markets may thus be overcome, and the collapsed internal economic links of Eastern Europe may be reorganized based on new market foundations. Thus, foreign capital can have an indispensable role in accelerating the privatization process and in the development of those market institutions which have a close interrelationship with privatization: management methods, capital mobilization, international market competition, and European integration processes.

Legal and financial regulation and economic policy

In Hungary, the rules which apply to Hungarian citizens are essentially valid for foreigners as well. With only a few exceptions, the object of investment and share ratio can be determined freely. Foreign participation in Hungarian investment does not require specific permission, even if it has 100 percent ownership (except in the banking sector where governmental permission is needed for either staking any shares in existing companies or establishing new ones).

The decisive element in the system of legal regulation is the Company Law, revived in 1988, which in its main characteristics conforms to the systems created and operating in developed market economies. Among the forms of companies, the limited-liability company (partnership) conforms entirely to the norms developed in the West. Compared with the Western form, however, the share (joint-stock) company in Hungary may be slightly less convenient for the foreign investor. Unlike in the West, foreign share ownership must be registered, so that the actual foreign owner is known both to the company and relevant government agencies. Many Hungarian corporations have non-transferable shares that may exist only in registered form, which can impede their circulation.

In addition to general legal guarantees, foreign investment is also protected by a law passed in 1988 just for this purpose: the so-called 'Investment Protection Law'. In the past, bilateral inter-governmental agreements on specific investments had been necessary. The 1988 law guarantees complete protection to every foreign investment without exception (even in the case of nationalization or expropriation), which essentially means an obligation to fully recompense at market value, in hard currency.

Foreign investors may redeem profits (dividends) earned from their enterprise in the currency of the investment and can act according to their own discretion (the possibility of repatriation). The same law applies to invested capital and profits reinvested in the enterprises in the event of liquidation or withdrawal.

Companies can be founded in Hungary not only by foreign legal persons (companies or institutions), as was stipulated in prior restrictions, but also by foreign natural persons (individuals). The foreign monetary contribution must be made in hard currency, but capital in the form of Hungarian forints resulting from dividends from investments in Hungary can be utilized equally. The company can import from this stake (up to the amount of the investment) customs-free, just as the non-cash capital contribution (such as a machine) enjoys customs-free treatment (with a prohibition on its sale for three years).

Joint ventures (companies with foreign participation) qualify as domestic enterprises. They are free to obtain real-estate property, if this is necessary to their operations. Certain state regulations apply to them, concerning the circulation of certain goods, quality control, credit and monetary circulation rules, hard currency rules, and labor law regulations. At present, among these the limitation on direct foreign credit contracts has provoked the most criticism, but case-by-case individual permission can be arranged for financing enterprises in this way, as well.

Domestic investment incentives also apply to joint ventures. Thus, all investments are due a 100 percent return of VAT (value-added tax). Special tax benefits are due economic companies working with foreign participation of at least 30 percent, if they are involved in manufacturing or the hotel industry, and if their founding capital exceeds 50 million forints. (These size and industry stipulations were more liberal until the beginning of 1991.) These enterprises enjoy a 60 percent profit tax discount for the first five years of operation and a 40 percent discount for the second five years. The tax discount is higher, 100 percent and 60 percent respectively, if the enterprise is involved in some particular sectors or activities listed in the Investment Protection Law.

Directors of joint enterprises, if they are foreigners, do not need to obtain special employment permission different from the general regulations; half of their salary can be taken home in hard currency, and they can choose which state's rules on taxation and health insurance they would like to follow.

The government's latest measure to support foreign investment, the founding of the Investment Incentive Fund, supports infrastructural development important to the investment goals of joint ventures. For 1991, the Fund disposes of 600 million forints. It is expected that some larger industrial investment will be supported through additional outlays on the development of local utilities.

Foreign investment in Hungary

Until 1988, foreign direct investment could only rarely be found in Hungary. Until the appearance of the new Company Law and the Investment Protection Law, only a few dozen joint ventures, with insignificant capital investment, operated in the country. In essence, the process accelerated in 1989 with the onset of spontaneous privatization. Until March 1990, there was no central privatization authority; thus, most enterprises operated according to self-management, and enterprise directors started to dispose of state property under the aegis of their enterprises (see Chapter 5 in this volume for a description of this process).

By the end of 1989, 1,200 joint enterprises had been established; most of these, however, were small limited-liability companies and if a state enterprise participated, this involved only an insignificant part of the property. Among the cases involving larger foreign capital participation and fully owned enterprise property, the General Electric-Tungsram purchase and the ÁPISZ (retail sales of stationery) joint venture provoked a greater reaction, because of an alleged injury to state property interests.

In 1990, most cases involving state property took place under the supervision of the State Property Agency (SPA), and 3,814 new joint ventures came into being. Most of these have continued without significant capital participation (the chief motivation was to gain tax benefits described above), but enterprises with a more significant capital base have also been established (see Table 10.1).

The founding fever also continued in 1991, for during the first four

Table 10.1 Share capital of joint ventures established in 1990

Range of share capital (million forints)	Number of companies	Values of shares (million forints)
0.5–1.0	2,165	2,164
1.1–10	1,253	4,000
10.1–50	254	6,353
50–	142	54,490
Total	3,814	70,800

Source: Central Statistical Office

months the number of newly registered joint enterprises was about 2,000, and the total number of joint ventures will have exceeded 10,000 by early 1992.

Surveying the foreign investing partners' composition by country (Table 10.2), it can be established that 40 percent of joint enterprises came into being with Austrian or German participation and that the overwhelming majority of these belong to the above-mentioned mini-enterprise category. The role of American investors is striking in the amount of capital transfer. In spite of the fact that they participate in only 5 percent of enterprises, American companies accounted for close to one-half of the total 1 billion USD in foreign investment by the end of 1990. This was due to the entrance of such international giants as General Motors, Ford, General Electric, Du Pont, United Technologies, Dow Chemical, Rothmans, etc.

Table 10.2 Nationality of foreign investors, end of 1990

Country	Number
Austria	1,000
Germany	1,000
USA	270
Switzerland	230
Italy	180
United Kingdom	150
Sweden	150
The Netherlands	80
Others	1,930
Total	5,000

Source: SPA

Of the large number of joint ventures founded with foreign participation, only a few dozen involve significant capital, that is, a partnership by those considered heavy-weights in the world. By April 1991, combined foreign investment could be valued at an estimated

1.2–1.3 billion USD and two-thirds of this was accounted for by no more than 20 of the biggest investments (see Table 10.3). There were altogether seven cases in which the investment exceeded 50 million USD (not counting some large projects in the automotive industry, still in the planning stages), and altogether these yielded 630 million USD in capital imports. (Of this, four large American investors brought in 400 million USD.) Among the other large investors, Austria still holds a pre-eminent place, with its investment of 200 million USD in the paper, cement, and food industries. Italian investment participation occupies a rather modest position compared with the level of trade ties between the two countries.

Table 10.3 Selected investment in Hungary

Investor	Country	Sector	Foreign contribution
General Electric	USA	Lighting	150
Sanofi	France	Pharmaceutical	75[a]
Guardian Glass	USA	Glass	115
Prinzhorn	Austria	Paper	82
Electrolux	Sweden	Refrigerators	80
General Motors	USA	Vehicles	66
Sara Lee	USA	Food	60
Nestle	Switzerland	Food	38
Agrana	Austria	Food	38
Haidelberger	Austria	Cement	25
Metalgesellschaft	Germany	Steel	24
United Biscuits	UK	Food	20
Tate & Lyle	USA	Sugar	18
Breiten Burger	Austria	Cement	18
Ansaldo	Italy	Electric equipment	18
Merlingerin	France	Electric equipment	13
Total			873

a Half-paid purchase

Source: SPA

Targets of foreign investment

By analyzing the sectoral structure of investment (see Table 10.4), it can be established that Hungary's traditionally developed sectors and those with favorable natural endowments occupy a pre-eminent position. This is true first of all for the food and pharmaceutical industries, which involve more than 40 percent of foreign investment capital value. The most significant of these were the Nestle (Switzerland) investment in Szerencs, the Sara Lee (USA) Compack (coffee, food packaging) and Agrana (Austria) with Szabadegyháza (distilling industry) joint ventures, and Sanofi's (France) entry into the Chinoin Corporation (pharmaceutical industry). Foreign investment likewise has entered some enterprises in the sugar industry.

Table 10.4 Sectoral breakdown of foreign investment, approved by SPA March 1990 to April 1991

Sector	Number of investments	Sum (million USD)
1. Food and agriculture	12	224
2. Mining	3	10
3. Building material	9	74
4. Construction	10	20
5. Metallurgy	2	30
6. Machinery and equipment	9	127
7. Textile and clothing	9	28
8. Paper and printing	4	91
9. Chemical and pharmaceutical	4	85[a]
10. Trade	7	23
11. Transportation	2	7
12. Other services	3	4
Total	74	723

a Not counting the unpaid half-price (75 million USD)

Source: SPA

In the machine industry, the proportion of foreign investment is small compared with its share in the national economy. The Lehel Refrigerator Factory purchase (Electrolux) and the traditional electrical machine-manufacturing enterprise joint ventures (Ganz-Ansaldo, Vertesz-Merlin, ABB-Láng, AEG-VÁV) represent the most significant cases. The General Electric-Tungsram joint venture does not appear in Table 10.4, since it was founded before establishment of the SPA, but in itself it constituted almost the same size investment in the machine industry sector as all the others combined.

Foreign investment represents a surprisingly high proportion of total investment in the building materials and paper industries. Austrian and German capital have targeted both sectors, and signs are that they are aiming for leading (controlling) shares. An important motivation for these investments may be that because of the large amount of environmental pollution in these industry branches, they want to further shift their capacities into East European states that have lower environmental standards. Similar intentions can be surmised in the above-mentioned sugar factories and distilling industry projects.

Up to now, the proportion of the value of foreign investments in retail trade is comparatively insignificant, but in terms of numbers, the majority of joint ventures (which are small firms with small foreign participation) are in this sector. The explanation for this is that the SPA (the state privatization organ) is privatizing the largest enterprises (IBUSZ, hotel chains) in the framework of a centralized program, not in the 'spontaneous' way, and this is somewhat impeding or delaying investment by interested foreign parties.

The most significant foreign investments must be joined with the cases like the already-mentioned Tungsram, which did not take place with the assistance of the SPA (and thus does not appear in Table 10.4). Such are the Guardian Glass (USA–Orosháza) glass industry investment of 115 million USD, and the three automotive industry projects (Ford, GM, Suzuki), of which the already realized investment (altogether, about 90 million USD) is under 20 percent of the entire project's value (statistics from SPA).

Foreign investments through the securities market is a subject requiring separate analysis (see also Chapter 9, this volume). Among these, purchase of shares and convertible bonds (asset-based bonds) mean, in essence (like the above), direct investment. Until now, Hungarian enterprises have not been listed on the stock exchange in significant numbers. The first, and up to now, most significant stock-exchange deal was IBUSZ, which brought an estimated 20 million USD-yielding investment sale. Withdrawal is thus far less likely among foreign investments in Hungary, probably due to the favorable prices of acquisitions. Only one large case has occurred: the Metalgesellschaft–Korf consortium withdrew its stakes in Ozd Steel Works. It had not appreciated well enough the financial and – this is a typical failure – market situation of the company.

International standards are followed for the valuation of state-owned assets and shares. The appraisal of assets and the adjusted book value of companies represent only the first, preliminary approaches to a fair market price. The earnings-based business (commercial) valuation is the underlying method in the formation of final selling prices for acquisitions. Third-party consulting firms provide support to determine these values.

Investment methods

Thus far foreigners' investments have taken place through the following main methods: buying of shares at public offerings or private placement, establishment of a joint venture, and asset purchase or lease.

The fundamental condition for public offering is that the investors have access to dependable and detailed information about the enterprise, which indicates the enterprise's financial stability. In Hungary at present, when the majority of enterprises are compelled to undergo a transformation in technology, management, and finances, an ever smaller number of enterprises can be found that could step into the capital market with a public stock quotation in hopes of success. On the basis of presently existing examples, the enterprises which can put up shares for sale on the stock market are involved in tourism, retail trade, and banking and can show that foreign capital has a serious interest in them (for example, IBUSZ, Skála, Fotex, Danubius Hotels). Several industrial enterprises that have previously established joint ventures with foreign partners are also entering the stock market (for example, Carbon Corporation in the clothing industry, and Pannonplast in plastics processing).

As described above, the foundation of joint ventures, both in number and amount of invested capital, at present constitutes a decisive part of foreign investments in Hungary. In a significant number of cases, the foundation of joint ventures (at least based on the amount of invested capital) involves the participation of state enterprises.

Only in a small number of cases do the foreign partners, for the most part committed investors in the same industrial branch, invest in the enterprise as a whole (see Table 10.5). Of the 28 enterprise transformations (corporatizations) with a foreign investor, many occurred with significant foreign capital participation of over 10 million USD (for example, Lehel, Szerencs–Nestle, Compack, Zalakerámia, GYöri Keksz, several sugar companies, etc.). In these cases, the previous state enterprise becomes a joint venture as a legal successor.

Table 10.5 Privatization with foreign participation (permits approved by SPA until April 1991)

Mode[a]	Number of cases	Foreign stakes (million USD)
1. Transformation of SOEs[b]	28	423
Foreign majority	15	264
equal shares	3	29
minority	10	130
2. Joint ventures with SOE	46	300
Foreign majority	13	91
equal shares	7	36
minority	19	173
Total	74	723
Foreign majority	28	355
equality	10	65
minority	29	303

a Two main methods of privatization: 1. transformation (corporatization) of SOE, then partial or complete divestment of state-owned shares;
2. establishment of new company by an SOE with private stake
b These cases include only those transformations in which foreigners participated, which is about half the total number of transformations

Source: SPA

In addition, foundation of large joint ventures is more frequent when only part of the state enterprise's resources (preferably free of encumbrances) participates in a foreign joint venture. This characteristic of foreigners' investments unequivocally indicates caution and limited risk assumption. The following enterprises brought investment interests into being with larger amounts of foreign capital: Szabadegyházai Distilling Company (distilling manufacture), Ganz Electric (electronic equipment), Paper Industry Company (paper), Pannonplast (plastics processing), Ozd Metallurgical Works (metallurgy), Láng Machine Factory (turbine manufacture), Cement Works (cement).

In the case of private placement (purchasing shares or increasing the share capital directly), the enterprise targeted by the investor is already operating in company form, but its partnership shares cannot be turned over publicly or are not sufficiently mature to turn into tradable stocks. The foreign investor can purchase a business share directly from the owner, or can obtain the offered stocks or business shares through a tender. So-called financial investors usually take advantage of this investment form (for example, Chinoin, Graboplast), because of the capital gain expectation.

According to the most frequently employed privatization practice, the professional or industrial branch investor (strategic partner) plays a determining role (see joint venture) in the foundation of joint companies, and a financial or institutional investor well versed in capital markets can bring about the next stage, a chance for obtaining a public stock quotation. Trade sales (investment by international partner in same industry) are less likely, especially for previously reformed enterprises in operation or those originally in company form. In this case, the investor can significantly increase the business value of the company with the improvement of the enterprise management, and by transferring the technological and commercial knowledge and market contacts of his own branch of business. As a consequence, the strategic investor usually strives to procure the controlling majority of shares or the guarantee for these options (for example, Nestle, Asea Brown Boveri, Ansaldo, General Electric, Sara Lee, etc.).

Foreign investment in a company is possible with fresh capital as well as by purchasing state-owned shares. Investors usually choose the latter because they prefer to assume the highest possible proportion of controlling shares. This also results in higher proceeds from sales. Fresh capital contributions equal to less than a quarter of foreign stakes, are sought mainly in those cases where the need for restructuring of capital is crucial and undelayable.

For a significant number of foreign investments, the purpose is probably not to buy some existing enterprise or to directly found an enterprise with local partners, but to obtain some fixed assets, lasting lease income, or perhaps to prepare a project for later development. Usually the sale of real estate (buildings, land areas) occurs with the goal of further development and later sale, or in order to form a starting basis for a later larger-volume business investment. Experience shows that the greatest foreign interest has been in the purchase of industrial land surrounding large cities and centrally located land suitable for the construction of hotels and office buildings, and in the renovation of hotel buildings. Of these, real estate purchases by Ford, General Motors, and Suzuki in the automotive industry investments are noteworthy. (The entire investment sum in these three already-initiated projects will exceed 500 million USD.)

The controlling majority–minority question in Hungarian joint ventures shows a mixed picture, at least concerning investments taking place in the framework of privatization (see Table 10.5). In the case of partial privatization (detailed in Table 10.5), when the foreign investor can select from among the assets of a state enterprise (and which go into the joint venture without encumbrances), the investor is more inclined to take on the bigger risk associated with a minority stake. In these cases, only 30 percent of investments are made by obtaining a majority share. However, in the case of state enterprises transforming as a whole, foreign investments procure the majority rights in 60 percent of cases.

Note that about one-third of the value of all foreign investment is not purchases of state property. In these investments, at least in bigger cases, the foreign side enjoys a controlling stake.

Infrastructural conditions for foreign investment

Above all, it is necessary to stress the importance of unambiguous and clear-cut investment and privatization legislation. In the interests of decreasing risks, the potential investor endeavors to be as well acquainted with investment conditions as possible. Thus every mistake and misunderstanding has a negative impact on the likelihood of foreign investment.

Experience shows that it was disadvantageous that in Hungary the laws regulating privatization only belatedly and gradually followed practice and have not resulted in an entirely harmonious system.

In contrast to earlier spontaneous privatizations, the appearance of the 'sure owner' in the form of the SPA has meant a positive change. Yet at the same time, the excessive centralization of the process has retarded the implementation of investments. The difficulties experienced with implementing the politically useful First Privatization Program demonstrate the limited practicality of the centralized method. Twenty Hungarian companies were selected for this program which had international bids for privatization advisory posts in September 1990.

Most foreign investment has relied on either trading connections or the use of banks. Through international banking connections, commercial banks have often been the sole foothold for a foreigner 'testing the waters'. In this way, the banks are capable of aiding foreign investments to a significant degree, especially through business information services, negotiation of guarantees, handling of deposits, etc.

Here, too, the results are less encouraging than they could be. Close cooperation between enterprises and banks has become less common since the decentralization of the Hungarian banking system. Furthermore, banks lack sufficient information about the enterprises. The banks' excessively cautious policies, including high interest rates, short terms, and demands for high guarantees, have been disadvantageous for the foreign investors.

The most spectacular development in the infrastructure supporting foreign investment is the growth in the number of consulting businesses. The foreign investment consulting industry has benefited from the appearance of several renowned international consulting firms on the market. Their presence has forced a general acceptance of internationally recognized assessment and marketing methods. The challenge represented by the presence of these foreign consulting firms inspired many entrepreneurs and in this way, several hundred larger or smaller investment and privatization consulting businesses were established. Experience up to now has already created a narrower, better qualified group of consultants, which is capable of realizing the decentralization of privatization.

Index

(*Numerals in bold face indicate a chapter/section devoted to a subject entry. For privatization entries, see privatization under individual countries.*)